ALT DIS

Alternative Discourses and the Academy

Edited by
CHRISTOPHER SCHROEDER
HELEN FOX
PATRICIA BIZZELL

Boynton/Cook
HEINEMANN
PORTSMOUTH, NH

Boynton/Cook Publishers, Inc.
361 Hanover Street
Portsmouth, NH 03801–3912
www.boyntoncook.com

Offices and agents throughout the world

The editors and publisher wish to thank those who have generously given permission to reprint borrowed material:

Page excerpt from "Personal History" by Nicholas Paley and Janice Jipson from *English Education*, Vol. 29, No. 1. Copyright © 1997 by the National Council of Teachers of English. Reprinted with permission.

Library of Congress Cataloging-in-Publication Data
ALT DIS : alternative discourses and the academy / edited by Christopher Schroeder, Helen Fox, Patricia Bizzell.
p. cm.
Includes bibliographical references.
ISBN 0-86709-516-4 (pbk. : acid-free paper)
1. English language—Rhetoric—Study and teaching. 2. Interdisciplinary approach in education. 3. Academic writing—Study and teaching. 4. English language—Variation. 5. Multicultural education. 6. Language and culture. I. Schroeder, Christopher L., 1970– II. Fox, Helen. III. Bizzell, Patricia.

PE1404 .A48 2002
808'.042'071—dc21 2001007472

Editor: Charles I. Schuster
Production coordinator: Lynne Reed
Production service: Colophon
Cover design: Jenny Jensen Greenleaf
Manufacturing: Steve Bernier

Printed in the United States of America on acid-free paper
Docutech RRD 2009

We dedicate this collection to all of the contributors and to everyone who has the courage to experiment with alternatives.

Contents

Preface

In 1974, the Conference on College Composition and Communication passed a resolution entitled "The Students' Right to Their Own Language." Many of us in the profession at that time, I think, viewed the passage of this resolution as a victory for a politically left-liberal, social-justice-oriented agenda in composition studies, but, as subsequent experience has shown, we were never quite clear on what the principles expressed here would mean in practice. The resolution's title implies that students should be able to use whatever language they prefer for their school writing, but, to the best of my knowledge, vanishingly few curricula were ever created to make this degree of choice possible.

Rather, it was taken more or less for granted that students would have to write in English. Moreover, it was generally assumed that they would have to do their formal school writing in the customary Standard-Edited-English dialect of traditional academic discourse. The force of the resolution, then, was to assert that even if these requirements could not be changed, it was still important to recognize that so-called nonstandard dialects of English possessed the full range of meaning-making capabilities present in the more academically acceptable dialect. The Black English Vernacular was the variant dialect most discussed in the resolution, but the general principles applied to any such forms: so-called nonstandard dialects should not be stigmatized in teacher commentary, should not be regarded as retarding anyone's cognitive development, and should even be welcomed in the classroom for use in discussion and in informal writing assignments, such as class journals. Acceptance of so-called nonstandard dialects in these ways would facilitate achievement of the goal to which most writing teachers—including myself—remained committed in those days, namely, mastery of traditional academic discourse by all students. "The Students' Right to Their Own Language," whatever revolutionary sentiments may have animated its framers, turned out to espouse methods to make assimilation to the dominant culture easier, at least in theory, for students from politically marginalized social groups.

Of course, the issues of linguistic diversity that "The Students' Right to Their Own Language" attempted to address have not gone away in the twenty-five years since the resolution's passage. If anything, they have become more complicated and vexed as the school population continues to diversify at a great rate and as no easy method has been found to initiate all comers into traditional academic discourse. Debate has continued over the fundamental assumption that all students need to learn traditional academic discourse. For example, African American educator Lisa Delpit has argued eloquently against denying instruction in Standard-Edited-English and other features of traditional academic discourse to students from social groups who have been denied access to social justice and full participation in the American democracy. Delpit views the traditional discourse as a "language of power" that must be mastered for access to be realized. But, she also urges, it must be taught in a way that respects and makes full use of the linguistic resources students bring to school—in other words, her position is very close to that which "The Students' Right to Their Own Language" has effected. Xin Liu Gale has explored the arguments justifying the teacher's authority to intervene in students' language-using practices in these ways.

In contrast, scholar of Black English Vernacular Geneva Smitherman has promoted BEV as a dialect fully capable of being used for all sorts of academic work, as she has demonstrated by employing it in some of her own published scholarship. Researchers into Latina/o language use Victor Villanueva, Jaime Mejia, and Michelle Hall Kells have likewise questioned whether it is absolutely necessary to eradicate a sort of written "Spanish accent" in the English expository prose of their students. ESL scholar Vivian Zamel has made a similar argument concerning the English writing of international students whose first language is not English.

Indeed, the bibliography of work in basic writing pedagogy ever since Mina Shaughnessy's ground-breaking 1977 study, *Errors and Expectations*, reflects our continued grappling with issues of linguistic diversity. As presented by Shaughnessy and followed by most composition teachers since then, "basic writing" has functioned as a research category to help them cope with the task of initiating all students into traditional academic discourse, to find new pedagogical methods to reach this goal. Writing-across-the-curriculum programs, too, have generally had as one major goal to improve instruction in traditional academic discourse for all students, as it became increasingly clear that mastery could not be achieved in one or two or three semesters of required "first-year" composition. Bruce Herzberg and I once defended this goal for writing across the curriculum against Lil Brannon's and Cy Knoblauch's attacks on it as mere "grammar across the curriculum." Yet our field has not been able to bring all students to mastery of traditional academic discourse in any systematic way to this very day. My own views on whether it is possible or desirable to achieve this goal have shifted under this pressure.

Meanwhile, it seems that the world has moved on. True, many academics, in writing programs and elsewhere, still require students to produce traditional academic discourse and penalize them if they do not. Many writing teachers still agonize over how, or whether, to equip their students to meet this requirement. But meanwhile, many academics and students have been developing new discourse forms that accomplish intellectual work while combining traditional academic discourse traits with traits from other discourse communities. The essays in this book investigate this phenomenon: the emergence of "hybrid," "mixed," "alternative," or "constructed" forms of academic discourse, which many teachers believe that they are increasingly seeing, not only in student writing, but in published professional discourse. The emergence of these kinds of nontraditional academic discourse may soon make the debate over "students' right to their own language" moot. Students, and their professors, are going ahead and developing new ways of writing in the academy that make use of "their own" languages as well as the still-valuable resources of traditional academic discourse.

Some of the essays collected here attempt to describe this phenomenon in more detail, at the same time debating about exactly what it should be called. The label *alternative* is helpful because it gets at what is perhaps the key feature of the discourses we are discussing, namely that they do not follow all the conventions of traditional academic discourse and may therefore provoke disapproval in some academic readers. *Alternative* invokes a sort of counter-cultural image that bespeaks the political resistance to hegemonic discourse that these new forms express—thus we see that the old left-liberal, social-justice-oriented agenda that motivated "The Students' Right to Their Own Language" resolution may be reemerging in a new guise. The term *mixed* helps to convey exactly what makes these discourses "alternative," namely that they exhibit stylistic, cultural, and cognitive elements from different discourse communities. *Hybrid*, although criticized by some contributors here for its biologically essentializing implications, is helpful for a similar reason, suggesting that in the new forms of discourse, traditional academic traits blend with traits from discourses not traditionally accepted in the academy to produce new forms with their own organic integrity. The term *constructed* adds emphasis on the pedagogical methods whereby the nature of the mix in the new forms of discourse is negotiated among teachers and students.

Beyond problems of defining the phenomenon, however, research must address the questions of whether alternative forms of academic discourse actually exist—are writing teachers' perceptions accurate about their emergence?—and if they do, to what extent are they spreading within the academy? Some of the essays included here address these questions, analyzing examples of alternative forms, tracking their emergence empirically across disciplines, or exploring the resources that exist across cultures for legitimating the intellectual work of alternative forms. It is important to note here that scholarly interest in these new discourse forms does not arise only from the hope that the old pedagogical dilemma of basic writing—how are we to teach them all traditional academic discourse?—can at last be set aside, and with it the attendant social justice concerns (is it right to force all students to assimilate to the hegemonic culture? And so on). No doubt this is one motive, as I have suggested in linking the new interest in alternative forms with the political motives of the "Students' Right" resolution, but avoiding this dilemma is by no means the only motive. More important, I think, is the growing awareness that these new discourse forms are developing because they enable kinds of rigorous academic work that simply cannot be done within the traditional discourse. If this is so, then writing teachers need to know about the new forms so that they can help their students deal with the full range of discursive practices they will need to succeed in college and beyond.

Some of the essays in this volume embody evidence that alternative forms are emerging—they employ them. Moreover, these essays provide readers with good test cases for my claim, noted previously and explored further in the opening essay of this collection, that alternative forms enable kinds of intellectual work that cannot be accomplished in traditional academic discourse. At the same time, these essays provide a useful index of some of the many directions in which alternative forms can develop. So-called nonstandard dialects will appear in some of these essays, but it becomes increasingly clear that the phenomenon on which the contributors focus here moves far beyond the issue of whether or not a nonstandard dialect can be employed. The alternatives are far more diverse than that, including different dialects, essay forms, cultural allusions, authorial personae, and more.

If alternative forms are indeed emerging, however, investigation must turn to questions of the implications of this emergence for students of writing. Do students still need to learn traditional academic discourse too? Do teachers now need to learn alternative discourses? Are some alternative discourses more acceptable or useful than others? In what, exactly, does the status "alternative" consist—stylistic features, affect or ethos, political orientation of the writer—or what? Some essays in this collection address these questions. It will be clear that the essays collected here do not urge a unitary view of emerging discourses or present a program for curriculum reform. Rather, we are trying to encourage more writing teachers to acknowledge and explore alternative academic discourses. We are trying to put some provocative questions on the table for discussion, questions that have crucial implications for access to higher education in this country as the college population increasingly diversifies in the twenty-first century. We hope that you will be moved to join the conversation.

Acknowledgments

We'd like to acknowledge each other, as well as Lisa Luedeke and Charles Schuster at Heinemann, for the vision and patience to see this project through to completion.

1

The Intellectual Work of "Mixed" Forms of Academic Discourses

Patricia Bizzell

To identify alternative forms of academic discourse, we need to have some sense of what a "standard" or non-alternative academic discourse, sometimes called traditional academic discourse, might be. A primary way to define academic discourse is to see it as the language of a community—hence the phrase, academic discourse community. I think it is possible to speak of the academic community's language-using practices as conventionalized, that is, there are certain customary ways of doing things. The way one employs these language-using conventions (with familiarity, grace, or tentative bravado, for example) establishes one's place within the community: people of higher status use language (within the shared conventions) differently than do people of lower status. Following these language-using conventions shapes participants' way of looking at the world—their worldview—including notions of what's real, normal, natural, good, and true. The people in the group use the shared language to work together on some shared project in the world—something they are trying to do together.

Because academic discourse is the language of a human community, it can never be absolutely fixed in form. It changes over time, and at any given time multiple versions of it are in use. In this sense, "alternative" forms of academic discourse have always been knocking around the academy. Nevertheless, because academic discourse is the language of a community, at any given time its most standard or widely accepted features reflect the cultural preferences of the most powerful people in the community. Until relatively recently, these people in the academic community have usually been male, European American, and middle or upper class. Hence it is possible to say that traditional academic discourses generally share certain features.

For one thing, such discourses employ a grapholect, the most formal and ultra-correct form of the participants' native language, treating as "errors" usages that would be unproblematic in casual conversation. Also, traditional academic genres shape whole pieces of writing, such as the lab report, the reflective journal, the critical essay, the research paper, and so on. Finally, the ones in power in the traditional academic community create discourses that embody a typical worldview. This worldview speaks through an academic persona who is objective, trying to prevent any emotions or prejudices from influencing the ideas in the writing. The persona is skeptical, responding with doubt and questions to any claim that something is true or good or beautiful. Not surprisingly, the persona is argumentative, favoring debate, believing that if we are going to find out whether something is true or good or beautiful, the only way we will do that is by arguing for opposing views of it, to see who wins. In this view, only debate can produce knowledge. Knowledge is not immediately available to experience, nor is it revealed from transcendent sources. Additionally, the persona is extremely precise, exacting, rigorous—if debate is going to generate knowledge, all participants must use language carefully, demonstrate their knowledge of earlier scholarly work, argue logically and fairly, use sound evidence, and so on.

The academic community is changing, however, and becoming more diverse—more people of color, more women, more people from the lower social classes, more people whose native language is not English or not the so-called Standard English (not all of these groups are mutually exclusive). Gaining access to higher education for these diverse groups has certainly not been easy, of course, and as they brought with them diverse discourses from their various home communities, gaining acceptance for these discourses, too, is an ongoing struggle. Yet, slowly but surely, previously nonacademic discourses are blending with traditional academic discourses to form the new "mixed" forms. These new discourses are still academic, in that they are doing the intellectual work of the academy—rigorous, reflective scholarship. We find these discourses appearing in articles in top-rank academic journals and in books from prestigious academic presses. But they have combined elements of traditional academic discourse with elements of other ways of using language, admitting personal experience as evidence, for example, or employing cultural allusions or language variants that do not match the cultural capital of the dominant white male group. After all, in how many communities is it considered appropriate to critically question everything one's interlocutor says, picking apart the other person's statements and even her or his grammar and word choice, while keeping one's own emotions and investments in the topic carefully hidden?

I want to emphasize that I see these mixed forms not simply as more comfortable or more congenial—they would not be gaining currency if comfort was all they provided, because the powerful people in the academic community are still, to a large extent, middle- and upper-class white men who would have no stake in allowing discourse forms that were alien to them. Rather, I think these new, alternative or mixed discourse forms are gaining ground because they allow their practitioners to do intellectual work in ways they could not if confined to traditional academic discourse. That is why these discourses can be found in so many academic disciplines today. These new discourses enable scholarship to take account of new variables, to explore new methods, and to communicate findings in new venues, including broader reading publics than the academic. I attempted to sketch the contrasts between old and new academic discourses in "Hybrid Academic Discourses: What, Why, How" (Bizzell 1999).

These new forms of academic discourse probably should not be termed *hybrid*, however, a correction I attempted to explain in "Basic Writing and the Issue of Correctness" (Bizzell 2000). For one thing, this concept relies on a reified notion of academic discourse that obscures institutional dynamics of power. Earlier in this chapter I provided a brief taxonomy of the traits of traditional academic discourse in order to conceptualize the hybridization of discourse from two distinct "parents." As I also noted, however, I would not want to suggest that traditional academic discourse was a fixed and unchanging entity until very recently. This is certainly not the case, and one does not need to go back very far to discover that fact.

Moreover, research by Michelle Hall Kells among English-Spanish bilinguals shows why it is dangerous to imply that academic discourse has not changed much over time. Such a presentation tends to give academic discourse an air of superiority that all too readily plays into linguistic minority students' tendency to see the academy's formal language as "more logical" or "purer" than their home dialects—"dialect misconceptions" that lead to "linguistic shame," as Kells describes it, which impedes learning and school success (1999, 137). It might be more accurate to say that what has remained constant is the privileged social position of whatever currently counts as academic discourse.

Furthermore, the term *hybrid* is at once too abstract and too concrete. It is borrowed from postcolonial theory, and the problems with its abstraction are well analyzed in Deepika Bahri's work on applications of postcolonial theory to composition studies. I was attracted to the term *hybrid* because it upsets the dichotomy established in my earlier work between academic discourse and students' home discourses, and thus implies that discursive and cultural boundaries are more blurred and, perhaps because of that blurring, more easily crossed than had been thought in so-called current-traditional, error-hunting writing instruction. But Bahri points out:

> If the concept of hybridity is useful in undoing binaries and approaching the complexities of transnationalism, as many would find in composition studies, I would warn that it also tends to avoid the question of location because it suggests a zone of nowhere-ness, and a people afloat in a weightless ether of ahistoricity. . . . The scores of underclass immigrants in Anglo-America

> and illegal border-crossers not only cannot "make themselves comfortable" with the same ease that other postcolonials have but also know that a border-crossing can be dangerous and potentially fatal. The deeply racial and class segregated nature of our cities, moreover, should also alert us to the intransigent borders within, rather than invoking the more glamorous cultural borders that metropolitan postcolonial celebrities [such as Homi Bhabha and Salmon Rushdie] invoke. (1998, 39)

It would be a mistake to imply that the "mixing" in alternative academic discourses can go on easily, naturally, or without political opposition from the powers that be.

At the same time as the concept of hybrid gets in trouble for being too abstract, however, it can also be critiqued for being too concrete. Hybrid, after all, is a biological metaphor, as in such statements as, the mule is a hybrid of the donkey and the horse. Using a biological metaphor for discourse risks essentializing people's language use. Thus, for example, while Black English Vernacular is deeply significant to many people of African descent, deeply rooted in their sense of their individual and collective identities, its linguistic features are not genetically determined, and people of African descent may well be able to use and to enjoy using other dialects of English. There is a larger problem here, as well, and that is the nature of the variant forms that are coming into academic discourse. The biological metaphor of hybridity implies that what mixes in the new forms, as I noted earlier, are two distinct "parents," that is, distinct, well-defined, and culturally independent linguistic and discursive practices. It is not at all clear that this is the case, however.

In short, we must not ignore the profound cultural mixing that has already occurred in the United States. Even students who are the first members of their families or their communities to attend college come with already mixed linguistic and discursive resources, as Scott Lyons explains in discussing the narratives of American Indian students:

> To my mixedblood mind, the stories of Indian students are clearly *heteroglossic*—produced against, within, and in tandem with the grand narratives of contemporary American life and culture . . . . There is a European in every Indian and an Indian in every "white"—each relationship positioned differently—and the two are not together by choice. It is this kind of *contact heteroglossia* that has been repressed by educators and theorists for centuries, and that Indian students not only know, but also use daily—we can all learn from them in this respect. (1998, 88–89, emphasis in original)

Lyons argues forcefully for the need for Indian students to use Indian discursive resources in their college writing, but at the same time, he shows how very difficult it would be to tease out the Indian strands in academic writing that nevertheless may be clearly recognized as "non-traditional," variant, or new.

Moreover, Lyons points in passing to another important aspect of mixing that many of us have experienced in our classrooms today, and that is the "contact heteroglossia," to use his term, that can be seen in the writing of European American students. Basic writing teachers know that it is a mistake to expect something like traditional academic discourse from all the students who appear racially white or who self-identify as white. Experimentation with new discourse forms certainly cannot be attributed to any essentialized linguistic heritage in the case of these students. Yes, increased access has happened, and a wide range of published scholarship employs new forms of academic discourse, as I have noted, but it is misleading to imply that new forms have emerged simply to make new students and scholars feel more comfortable. The new forms are being used by everyone, not only by students and scholars from underrepresented social groups, and the reason is not far to seek: as noted previously, they make possible new forms of intellectual work.

The best evidence I can present for the compelling nature of this new intellectual work is to find examples of powerful white male scholars who are employing alternative discourses, possibly at some risk to themselves, because they cannot do what they want to do in their scholarship any other way. Especially persuasive might be examples drawn from elsewhere than English studies, a field that has been experimenting with alternative discourses for some time, particularly in the work of feminist theorists and scholars in composition and rhetoric. Accordingly, I offer an example from *The Journal of American History,* the official scholarly publication of the Organization of American Historians.

A long meditation by Joel Williamson, a very senior and eminent scholar, leads off the March 1997 issue. Williamson attempts to explore how his own personal background has affected his scholarship, and thus to make a point about historiography in general. Williamson is interested in trying to understand why he, a southerner "born and bred" (1228) as he describes himself, took so long to realize that lynching and other racially motivated forms of violence were important factors in black-white relations in the South. His meditation is triggered by the Clarence Thomas confirmation hearings, in which Thomas clinched his own defense by accusing his critics of perpetrating a "high-tech lynching." Thomas' use of this metaphor spurs Williamson to examine how knowledge of lynching and understanding of its cultural significance are variably distributed according to race. Williamson argues not only that white people are ignorant on the subject of racial violence, but that they are willfully so—that there is a deliberate forgetting or erasure going on, and that it has affected even the practice of research in American history, even the research done by scholars such as himself, whose focus has been race relations. Williamson has published an important book on lynching and racial violence, and yet, in this essay, he indicts himself for the unconscionably slow growth of his own awareness of the importance of this topic and for the blind spots that he knows exist in his vision even today. He concludes by noting that a major blind spot has to do with the sexual politics of lynching, and he calls for a new vision of southern history that deals more frankly with gender as well as with race.

Scholars in composition and rhetoric may find nothing surprising in Williamson's meditations other than that 1997 seems rather late for the discipline of history to be examining the personal roots of its scholarly agendas, compared to what has gone on in our field, in the work of Helen Fox, Keith Gilyard, Mike Rose, and Victor Villanueva, to name a few examples. But David Thelen, editor of the journal when Williamson's essay appeared, finds Williamson's experiment so challenging that he takes the very unusual course of printing Williamson's essay as he submitted it, along with six referees' reports as they submitted them—nothing edited for publication. Evidently Thelen is so anxious about publishing the Williamson piece that he must invite the journal readers to scrutinize the evidence on which he made the decision to print. Ongoing anxiety is evinced, too, in Thelen's decision to commission a seventh response to Williamson's piece from a woman who is a scholar of women's history, once he noticed that Williamson's six referees, all male, were none of them scholars of women's history. She is the only one of the reviewers who knew she was writing for publication.

What interests me about this now rather notorious fracas is that the reviewers, all but one, clearly address themselves to the issue of whether the historiographical insights provided by Williamson's essay are worth struggling with his alternative discourse form. Five end up voting in the affirmative, though there is ample evidence that the form disturbs them. A principal concern seems to be the nonlinear structure of the essay, familiar to writing teachers from what we call the personal essay, but not the traditional structure of academic argument. Williamson's reviewers react to this structure by finding it hard to connect the themes he broaches. Steven M. Stowe notes "two strands" of thought in the essay that "do not always adhere": "the author plays with one and then the other, then both, but shifting and spinning them in ways that/are not always clear" (1264–65). David Levering Lewis finds "three themes" in the essay that "are insufficiently explored, and their putative interconnectedness is either strained or fallacious" (1261). David W. Blight condemns "a cacophony of themes and subthemes, plots and subplots" in Williamson's essay—he counts no less than eight (1255).

The reviewers also notice the personal style of Williamson's essay, his use of autobiographical examples and his willingness to reveal his emotions. Lewis, the most negative of the seven reviewers, is repulsed by this style; he says, "the tone of the piece borders on self-promotion written in mighty florid prose" and he finds some passages "embarrassing" (1261). The majority of the reviewers, however, seem to react more like Edward L. Ayers, who, although "embarrassed to admit how much I like this essay," feels that it is "revealing without being self-indulgent," and he is "pulled along by this essay's momentum, by its revelations and emotional power" (1254). Stowe characterizes the essay as "a kind of heart of darkness journey" that "seeks out something horrible at the center of things" (1264; a perhaps unintentionally ironic reference, given the well-known controversy in literary studies over the racism of Conrad's story—does Stowe enact with this reference another sort of the willful blindness Williamson condemns?). Stowe asserts that "the most powerful parts of this paper are when the author speaks most personally about his struggle to understand" (1266). George M. Frederickson states the dilemma for the male readers most clearly:

> It is a highly personal, partially autobiographical statement that lacks the objective tone and scholarly apparatus of the normal *JAH* article. It is, *however*, intelligent, incisive, and full of interest for anyone concerned with southern history. . . . Should the *JAH* publish this kind of piece? It would be a new departure, I think . . . but my view is that essays of this kind, if they possess the authority and quality found here, deserve/a place in the *Journal*. . . . The personalized, confessional mode does not seem to me objectionable when used in historiographic essays that involve the author's own work. In fact, a good argument could be made that such disclosure is not only appropriate but highly desirable. (1257–58, emphasis added)

It is interesting that Jacquelyn Dowd Hall, the woman invited to compose a seventh response to Williamson's piece, does not seem to be bothered in the slightest by the mode of discourse the male reviewers found so complicated, although she takes exception to Williamson's preference for military metaphors. Perhaps as a feminist historian, she has encountered alternative discourse forms often enough—unlike the male reviewers—to be comfortable with them.

In spite of some reviewers' struggles with Williamson's alternative discourse, most found much to value in the intellectual work he accomplishes, as Frederickson hints when he notes that "such disclosure is not only appropriate but highly desirable" (1258). Here is how some of the other reviewers articulate what they find of value in Williamson's piece:

> Hall praises the analysis Williamson provides, however unconventionally, of what she calls the "symbiosis between cultural amnesia and historiographical neglect" and its impact on southern history (1268).
>
> Blight calls Williamson a "wise provocateur" who "has much to say about the cycles of historiographical discovery and decline"; Blight finds "stimulating" Williamson's call at the end of the piece for "a fuller embrace of gender—a new men's and a new women's history of the South" (1256; is there a pun intended here?).
>
> Stowe provides perhaps the most detail about what Williamson contributes.

> He notes that Williamson illuminates the ways that "the historiography of southern race relations in the past thirty to forty years divides into three overlapping vistas," dealing with slavery, segregation, and lynching, and that Williamson helpfully points out "how dim and limited the last one is" and asks "Why do we not know how to write about lynching?" (1265) Stowe believes that Williamson's valuable answer to this question is that historians need to do more self-searching work of the kind Williamson does in this essay. In other words, Stowe sees the essay as exemplifying a new kind of history writing that addresses the critical problems to which it calls attention, or as Stowe puts it, "the author suggests that historians look, not just in a different direction, but to a different dimension of experience for the next step in the history of the races" (1266).

It would seem, then, that for five of Williamson's seven readers, the alternative mode of discourse enables valuable, even uniquely valuable, intellectual work.

Two of the original six referees, however, recommended against publication, and most vehemently. But their objections do not seem to focus primarily on the use of an alternative discourse. Before I discuss them, however, I want to mention that Williamson's essay, and all seven responses, were accompanied by photos of the authors. No other articles in this issue of the *Journal of American History* are accompanied by photos of the authors, so evidently it is not this journal's usual practice. Are these photos included to let us know that the two negative reviewers, David Levering Lewis and Robin D. G. Kelley, are African American, without having to tell us? Racial identity is not always evident from photographs, but I wonder.

Although Lewis, as noted previously, makes clear that he does not like Williamson's alternative discourse, he condemns Williamson's entire body of work in southern history. Lewis's review is by far the longest of the seven and ranges over many issues only tangential to the Williamson essay he is reviewing. Not knowing the field of American history, I can only guess that in this review, a long-standing scholarly rivalry reemerges. Certainly Williamson's discursive experiment did nothing to win over an old adversary. I have to wonder, though, whether, since Lewis is African American, his rancor was motivated at least in part by some of the objections Kelley raises.

Kelley does not seem to be bothered by Williamson's alternative mode of discourse, either. At any rate, he does not say anything about it. His chief objection is that Williamson talks about his own problems of what Hall calls "cultural amnesia and historiographical neglect" as if they beset American historians universally. Kelley does not say in so many words that black historians have no problem with amnesia where lynching is concerned, but he devotes much of his review to citing works on racial violence that Williamson has neglected to mention, at least some of them, I know, by African American historians. Kelley argues forcefully that Williamson's portrait of a forgetful profession can only hold through the use of a prejudicially defined "we" that neglects, most ironically, the work of historians who clearly have not suffered from Williamson's own debilities.

Yet, I don't think Kelley's strictures destroy my point about Williamson's essay doing valuable intellectual work. Rather, Kelley prompts me to ask, valuable intellectual work for whom? In this case, it seems that Williamson's willingness to dig deep within himself and reveal the emotional underpinnings of his work is most valuable for other white male historians. Their reviews answer the emotion in his piece, bespeaking their embarrassment, explicitly in Ayers, and at the same time, expressing gratitude for Williamson's intensity, most notably in Stowe. Perhaps the white male readers are assisted in identifying with Williamson because, as Hall notes, he tends to couch his emotional disclosures in military metaphors—scholars rush to combat, hold the high ground, look over the battlefield, etc. Perhaps Kelley and Lewis, on the other hand, are left cold by this essay, and Hall tempers her enthusiasm, because historians of color and white women historians do not need so much assistance in exploring the emotional roots of their scholarly agendas.

I want to make clear that I do not mean to devalue Williamson's contribution by suggesting that his alternative intellectual work is not equally valuable for everyone. On the contrary, Kelley helps me make the point that a diversity of intellectual approaches is exactly what we need. That is why, as I have argued, alternative forms of academic discourse are emerging. The academy collectively has finally grasped the point of the old fable about the blind men and the elephant. One gets a hold of the elephant's ear and says, "The elephant, I find, is very like a fan!" Another gets a hold of the elephant's trunk and says, "No, the elephant is very like a snake!" A third grabs the leg and says, "No! Very like a tree!" And so on. If we want to see the whole beast, we should be welcoming, not resisting, the advent of diverse forms of academic discourse, and encouraging our students to bring all their discursive resources to bear on the intellectual challenges of the academic disciplines.

Works Cited

Bahri, Deepika. 1998. "Terms of Engagement: Postcolonialism, Transnationalism, and Composition Studies." *JAC: A Journal of Composition Theory* 18 (1):29–44.

Bizzell, Patricia. 1999. "Hybrid Academic Discourses: What, Why, How." *Composition Studies* 27 (Fall):7–21.

______. 2000. "Basic Writing and the Issue of Correctness, or, What to Do with 'Mixed' Forms of Academic Discourse." *Journal of Basic Writing* 19 (spring):4–12.

Kells, Michelle Hall. 1999. "Leveling the Linguistic Playing Field in First-Year Composition." In *Attending to the Margins: Writing, Researching, and Teaching on the Front Lines*, edited by Michelle Hall Kells and Valerie Balester. Portsmouth, NH: Heinemann-Boynton/Cook.

Lyons, Scott. 1998. "A Captivity Narrative: Indians, Mixedbloods, and 'White' Academe." In *Outbursts in Academe: Multiculturalism and Other Sources of Conflict,* edited by Kathleen Dixon, 87–108. Portsmouth, NH: Heinemann-Boynton/Cook.

Williamson, Joel. 1997. "Wounds Not Scars: Lynching, the National Conscience, and the American Historian." *The Journal of American History* 83 (March): 1221–53; preceded by David Thelen, "What We See and Can't See in the Past: An Introduction," 1217–20, and followed by referees' reports by Edward L. Ayers, David W. Blight, George M. Frederickson, Robin D. G. Kelley, David Levering Lewis, and Steven M. Stowe, with "A Later Comment" by Jacquelyn Dowd Hall, 1254–72.

2

Listening to ghosts: an alternative (non)argument

Malea Powell

> Do you remember when you twisted the wax from your ears and shouted to me, 'You finally speak!' because now you could finally hear? . . . and from the pain of forgetting we almost agreed.
>
> —Wendy Rose, "For the Scholar Who Wrote a Book About an American Indian Literary Renaissance"

This is a story.

Hueston Woods (Oxford, Ohio), 1997
The sun rises above the heartbeat blue of this man-made lake and illumines the beach with the stark-sharp shadows that only a midwestern morning can withstand. This is the spot where, blanket and book in hand, I held theory-communion with a deer. She'd come to investigate my readings of Kaja Silverman; I'd come to hear the voices of my ancestors, their songs woven into the wind burning my cheeks as I tried to discern "the subject of semiotics." We drew breath together, the deer and I, and the first shadow of this writing rose from the long grass at the water's edge as I stood on that beach, all my relations peering over my shoulder, creeping into text.

From the Conference on College Composition and Communication (CCCC) 2001 "Composing Community" program, page 27, "Topic Index to Concurrent Sessions," Alternative Discourses: C.14, C.16, D.15, E.20, E.29, F.29, H.9, H.33, I.28, J.15, K.24, K.30, K.33, M.11, M.14, M.28, N.2, N.20. . . . A quantum array, coded in conference shorthand, "which K-session did you go to?"

Good papers, funny, poignant, well-performed. Rap, local culture, other histories, composing ourselves, ESL, hugely attended featured speaker sessions, students' rights to their own language, assessment, rhetorical sovereignty, affirmative action, language reclamation, multiple identities, curriculum design, bridging, voice, language communities. I laughed. I cried. I applauded. I cursed. I wrote furious notes in/on my program. Language, language, language, language— what's right? what's wrong? what's allowable? assessable? what about justice? and creation of the self? and play? All important questions, provocative answers at every turn. I left with questions still: what **about** alternative discourse? whose/who's discourse? whose/who's alternative? and, "for whom are we doing what we are doing?" (Christian 1987, 54).

This is a well-ordered essay.
This is a ghost story.

I think a lot about ghosts. No, not white-sheeted apparitions, but the ghosts who appear in the stories we tell each other here in the academy. Not only those arisen from the mess of blood and bones upon which "America" is literally built, but also those rooted in other knowledges, other ways of knowing, other ways of being and becoming that frequently go unheard and unsaid in much scholarly work: For me, ghost stories are **both** the stories of material colonization **and** the webs and wisps of narrative that are woven around, under, beneath, behind, inside, and against the dominant narratives of "scholarly discourse." I think a lot about what ghost stories can teach us, how in telling them I might **both** honor the knowledge that isn't honored in universities **and** do so in a way that interweaves these stories with more recognizable academic "theorizing" as well. For me, this is the most exciting component of "alternative discourses"—telling a story that mixes worlds and ways, one that listens and speaks, one that participates in Lyotard's language games as both a rule-governed subject and a paralogic trickster, a **use**, as deCerteau would have it, that is more tactical than strategic, a pose that uses historical knowledge as a heuristic in creating a written, writing self (Royster 2001b).

Much of how I came to know myself as an academic has been predicated on what Janice Gould has called the fundamental relationship of Indians to the academy; that is, "there is not a university in this country that is not built on what was once native land" (1992, 81–82). The histories of Native peoples on this continent are shadows, present only in their absence from the promises of Manifest Destiny and New Age spirituality: these shadows, the "names and nicknames" of ancestors are stories (Vizenor 1994, 14). These are troublesome stories, rife with blood and anger, conciliation, assimilation, blood quantum, enrollment, removal, resistance. My writing has always been an attempt to live in the shadows of presence. To insist upon an existence, a voice. To write myself and my body into comprehensible space. But human existence is haunted by leavings, by disappearance. In disappearing, the writing moved from paper to flesh.

I got my first tattoo the summer I wrote my master's thesis.

It is a circle of spirals on my left wrist. I used to wear a watch on my left wrist. I don't anymore. Lots of people would be happy if I said something about "Indian time" here. If I claimed that my tattoo was a way to step away from the clock-watching of the Western world. But it's not. The spirals roughly mimic similar drawings on the cliffs at Puye—a petroglyph site in northern New Mexico where some of the oldest inscriptions on the continent of North America wait for us to read them. The spiral describes the path we take through life—recursive, fluid, maze-like. Both the visible line and the space it denotes have meaning here, one an erasure of the other—the line an erasure of space, the space an affirmation of the line. The spiral also represents the sun, another set of meanings delineated by dis- and re-appearance.

When I enter a classroom, in my students' eyes I enter as a teacher who is "also" an Indian. When I speak at a department meeting. In many of my colleagues' eyes, I speak as a faculty member who is "also" an Indian. In that "also" is the reiteration of the very rhetoric of empire that enabled Euroamericans to found and build their universities on lands that belonged to tribal nations. During the fall of 1999 I attended a "Native American Literature" conference in Puerta Vallarta, Mexico. The cost and location of the conference prevented many Native scholars from attending, so we ended up with an interesting assortment of Native scholars who had managed to scavenge for funding from their home institutions and non-Native scholars and hobbyists, many who were excited about the promise of sun, sea, surf, and free drinks disguised as a conference. Knowledge hit hard in Puerta Vallarta. I now know exactly how many Indians it takes to start an intellectual revolution, and how many white-ladies-who-love-Indians it takes to remind me of why we need what Robert Allen Warrior has called "intellectual sovereignty" (1995, xxiii). For Warrior, such sovereignty is "a cultural criticism that is grounded in American Indian experiences but which can draw on the insights and experiences of others who have faced similar struggles" (1995, xxiii).

One thing I know for sure. My own scholarly practices are firmly rooted at the crossroads between what Gerald Vizenor calls "trickster hermeneutics" ("the uncertain humor and shimmer of survivance") and "narrative chance" ("the counter causes in language games") (1994, 15; 66). This crossroads offers points of entry into discourses, language games, meant to discipline me and those like me. A signpost reads "look for other ways of being here." Roads run in every direction. One road takes me to the standard story of my own scholarly work: American Indian public intellectuals . . . negotiations of dominant notions of Indian-ness . . . tactical authenticity . . . rhetorics of survivance . . . pow-wow observations and postcolonial theory . . . expands the discipline of rhetoric and composition . . . aggressive anti-imperial pedagogies . . . and so on, and so on. *It's not that I don't believe in that story. It's not that I'm not committed to that story. It's that there's so much more involved in being able to have this story than the telling of it can hold. The having spills over, the seemingly unutterable excess of the story.* Another road reminds me that I do this "alternative" work to save my own life, to give sense and meaning to my existence as a human, that the simple possibility of what I have elsewhere called "mixed-blood rhetoric" is at the center of my having a story to tell at all, and that I am haunted by that *having*. Another road haunts me differently. This is the road of remembrance, one traveled by those who have walked this earth before me, literally and figuratively. Native people like Sarah Winnemucca Hopkins and Charles Eastman and Gertrude Bonnin and Susan La Flesche, Tecumseh and Tenskwatawa and Little Turtle—those who encountered Euroamerican culture, learned the language of the colonizers, and negotiated the demands of "civilized" life as they critiqued, resisted, and survived its impositions.

CCCC2001, Session K.30, "Resistant Communities: Indians Writing (and Speaking) as Indians":

Joyce Rain Anderson and Janice Gould talk about tribal language traditions, both oral and written, and both talk about language reclamation work within their tribal communities, Wampanoag and Koyangk'auwi Maidu, respectively. I look around the room as we all ponder the weight of language loss, and thus the miracle of recent language revivals, among the indigenous tribal nations of North America. What does it mean to speak as an Indian*? to have "the words to carry a friend from her death to the stars correctly"? (Harjo 1994, 3).*

> *Because of relocation, loss of land base and the dispersment of tribal members, Miami language quickly deteriorated until the last of the fluent speakers had passed on by the mid 1900's. What has survived into modern times are several prayers, songs, Miami naming practices and several elders who remember the language spoken. . . . [Miamis] are actively pursuing revitalization efforts and have active language programs. . . . (The Miami Language 2001)*

Iilaataweeyankwi. We speak such a language.

More than once during these forty minutes the listeners in this room have been moved to tears. We are crying in a conference room in a multinationally owned Denver hotel. The simple knowledge of Native people speaking our languages *again makes us weep with joy and with sorrow. We wonder aloud if the other folks who attend this conference would be interested in language reclamation. We ponder the organizational commitment to Students' Rights to Their Own*

Language and question if that includes Native students and their rights to reclaim *their own languages.*

So what does Lyotard have to do with language reclamation? What does de Certeau have to do with intellectual sovereignty? In drawing on the "insights and experiences of others" who at least have faced similar projects of alter/nativity, why might I turn to French theory? Can I do so without worshiping at the alter of the wisdom of the Theorist, without committing that act of cultural homage that so angered Barbara Christian in "The Race for Theory?" Good question. Christian frames her 1987 essay by claiming that "there has been a takeover in the literary world by Western philosophers from the old literary elite" who have separated the "author" from the text and thrown "meaning" out the window (51). This, she says, they have done for their own purposes, and because the literature of the West "has become pallid," leaving critics less concerned with literature than "with other critics' texts" (51). Further, because these critics have the power "to be published, and thereby to determine the ideas that are deemed valuable," they have turned this Theory into a commodity in a continuing race for "academic hegemony" (52–53). Christian does not see this turn to Theory as innocent. Even as it lays claims to ideas that Christian claims "her folk" (African American women) have long understood—imagining text as "the hieroglyph, a written figure that is both sensual and abstract" and "dynamic and fixed—this theory still wants to imagine itself as "major" in relation to the rest of the world, still "tries to convince the rest of the world that it *is* major" (52, 54). For Christian, "they" are out to silence "us" with Theory.

The inevitable parallel arises here—"alternative discourse"—what discourse is this Other discourse alternative to? Academic discourse, after all, isn't at the center of the lives of most of the humans on the globe. As Jackie Royster recently remarked: "academic discourse is an invention, not a natural phenomenon" (2001, Academic). And why am I even interested in alternatives at all when we already have so many categories for describing what we do here in the academy—American Indian Studies, English Studies, Composition Studies, Rhetoric Studies, Literary Studies—that we have lost sight of the simple fact that the only difference between a history, a theory, a poem, an essay, is the one that we have ourselves imposed. We have cut the wholeness of knowledge into little bits, scattered them to the four winds and now begin to reorganize them into categories invented to enable empire by bringing order to chaos and civilization to the savage. So, is this turn to alternatives just another ploy to convince ourselves that the academy *is* the center, that we are *major*? Or is this a genuine turn to a embrace "alternative assumptions about discourse" (Royster 2001a)?

The ghosts raised by Christian's configuration rise before me. As resonant as I find her objections to Theory, I also find her separation of "literature" and "theory" into distinct and antagonistic categories troubling in the face of her claims that women of color *are* theorizing "in narrative forms, in the stories we create, in riddles and proverbs, in the play with language"—in other words, in "literature" (1987, 52). Of course "we" theorize in literature, but what about her "them," those white-guy-philosopher-types? Don't they also theorize in literature, in stories and riddles and proverbs? Yes, yes, her point is about "kinds" of theory, "kinds" of writing, and the kinds of values assigned to those theories and writings, but assigning value—and allowing assigned values to intimidate and silence us—is also what troubles me here. I am unwilling to cede to what Christian calls "literary critical theory" the place of Theory that towers over and intimidates story/stories. To do so is to participate in a project of internal colonialism whereby the colonized believe in and accede to the terms and hierarchies of the colonizers. What Christian marks out as white-guy-philosopher-type Theory (and what we call Academic Discourse) *is* stories and riddles and proverbs which we've been taught are "special" and central to the survival of "civilization" and Western culture because, in fact, they *are* the stories that create the rhetoric of civilization, the riddles that inaugurate Western culture, proverbs which make us believe that the earth is made of folks either "savage" or "civilized."

The Penn State Conference on Rhetoric & Composition, July 1995, Session E3, "The Rhetorical and Literate Strategies of Marginalized Peoples":

I am sitting in a cement-blocked classroom where this presentation is taking place. Ellen Cushman begins her talk with an explanation about the connections between her and the subjects of her research, welfare recipients from an upstate New York community. As she invokes those days when she and her mother were also welfare recipients, she begins to weep. Some of us weep with her. When she is finished, Jackie Royster (one of the featured speakers for this conference) offers advice to us, a collection of mostly grad-student scholars. She says something like "your work should move you." I thought about this for a long time. Several years later I am sitting in the living room of an old Craftsmen home in Lincoln, NE. A young Chicana scholar is reading a paper for "the minority lit group"—a friendly collection of local scholars who listen and respond to one another's work. She is about halfway through the paper, recounting the death of an important Chicano writer and activist, when she begins to weep. She apologizes and says, "I'll never be able to read this paper at a conference. At conferences you have to pretend not to care about your work." When she is finished reading I tell her what Jackie said in Pennsylvania—"your work should move you." She agrees. But we both know that crying at conferences is generally not allowed, is not interpreted as "scholarly" or "professional" behavior. And I wonder anew at a discipline that asks its participants to dedicate their lives to its expansion, but that requires a kind of imperial objectivity, a gaze that sees but rarely feels. And I wonder why it is that I so often **do** *cry during conferences. And I hear Janice Gould in my head:* "Now I see how we must decide, how we must make a choice. We think we are limited, but forms are tricky things" *(1996, 17).*

"This is a book about a belief" (xvii). Thus begins Roy Harvey Pearce's now-classic *Savagism and Civilization: A Study of the Indian and the American Mind* (1988), in which he makes the now commonplace claim that both "savagism" and "civilization" are simply beliefs, ideas (constructions, discourses, imaginings) imposed by Europeans and Euroamericans as a way to make sense out of the seeming chaos of this "New World" (1988, 3). Pearce writes:

> *The colonial concern with the savage Indian was a product of the tradition of Anglo-French primitivistic thinking—an attempt to see the savage, the ignoble savage, as a European manqué. When, by the 1770's, the attempt had obviously failed, Americans were coming to understand the Indian as one* radically different *from their proper selves . . . [they] worked out a theory of the savage which depended on an* idea of a new order *in which the Indian could have no part. (1988, 4 emphasis mine)*

Pearce links this new "theory" about Indians to a burgeoning nationalism, and emphasizes that this new "American" came "to know who and what he was and where he was going," to know [his] past and [his] future" most effectively through comparison with "the Indian who, as a savage, had all past and no future" (1988, 135). Richard Slotkin's *Regeneration Through Violence: The Mythology of the American Frontier, 1600–1860* (1973) offers a slew of companion stories to Pearce's book about "belief." Slotkin's "Americans" are created in relation to and at the expense of indigenous peoples. Newly arrived European colonists, according to Slotkin, brought their own "myths" about the order of the universe; their continuous contact with what they saw as "primitive" cultures "ensured that the colonists would be preoccupied with defining, for themselves and for others" the nature of their relationship with this "other" (1973, 16). This process of defining ultimately resulted in the violence through which Slotkin claims "America" was constructed as a utopian space, able to offer European settlers the opportunity to "regenerate their fortunes, their spirits . . . their church and nation" by removing the one obstacle in their way—the Indian (1973, 5). In Richard Drinnon's *Facing West: The Metaphysics of Indian Hating and Empire Building* (1990), the project of imagining "America" is seen as primarily a project of destroying memory—"they sought to cut off the Remembrance of them from the Earth," writes Captain John Mason of the colonial intent during the Pequot War of 1637 (quoted in Drinnon 1990, xii). The thread of "belief" which runs through the analyses of these three white-guy-American-Studies-scholar-types is that "the Indian" was (is) a figure against which "the American" can be rendered from the raw materials of "the Euro-colonist," and rendered most effectively by making "the Indian" a thing of the past.

My troubling with Christian's story is not to say that hegemony doesn't "exist" and that these discourses that have come to be dominant don't have power over material bodies. Clearly, as Pearce, Slotkin, and Drinnon have all argued in detail, discourses matter. Dominant discourses are not "merely imaginative"; they are an "integral part of European *material* civilization and culture" (Said 1993, 87). I just want to suggest that one way to change the manner in which they matter is, quite simply, to divest them of their initial capitals—Theory to theory, Discourse to discourse—and hear them as what they are: stories that explain how the world works. If dominant narratives only attain dominance through imagining themselves whole in contrast to other/Other narratives, then we must imagine those narratives differently, imagine ourselves in a different relationship to them. The challenge, then, is to imagine an alternative, not an Alternative, one that confronts difference and race, racism and empire, in the very discourses that bind us. This imagining "must penetrate to our very bones" (Okawa 1999, 141). It "require[s] stamina and perseverance, a preparedness to incur risk, often a willingness to absorb the consequences of revolt, whether overt or covert" (Churchill 1996, 286). Remember Pearce—"this is a book about a belief"—and believe differently. Better yet, remember Captain John Mason—"to cut off Remembrance of them from the Earth"—and remember differently.

Tattooing is a way of disappearing, of rewriting trails across the signifying space of my body, reimagining the stories that can be heard in the text that is my flesh, inscribing an accumulation of histories alongside the history told by the privilege of my skin color, the seeming surety of my biology. A needle slipping into skin, marking, inscribing, erasing. A pen marking paper, ink injected into wood fiber, soaking through. Binding layer upon layer of accumulated blood, skin, paper, ink. Binding. Leaving a space to mark the presence of absence—a story tying me to this land of indigenous bones and blood. Ghosts. University buildings sunk deep into my skin, alleyways where young gay men are beaten and bloodied, classrooms where young middle-class white students imagine themselves oppressed. All this anchored in the land, my skin.

A new French and Indian War, part one: Lyotard offers a flexible, if imperfect, concept of participation in the world as a language game. Language is a game in which we occupy stations/positions through which narration moves. What we can say to each other is governed by "rules"—we play by those rules in order to be heard. There are ways, however, to say "that which cannot be said" but to do so runs the risk of encountering terror (the coercions that keep us from breaking the rules) and of not being heard. Consensus keeps the rules in place, keeps us in place, and remember, this consensus is held together through terror, not justice (Lyotard 1984). "But there are language games in which the important thing is to listen, in which the rule deals with audition.

Such is the game of the just. And in this game, one speaks only insomuch as one listens, that is, one speaks as a listener, not as an author" (Lyotard and Thebaud 1985, 71–72). Listening becomes a way to justice **in another game**, the other game, the alternative discourse. Participation in both of these games is parallel and contiguous, simultaneous. Joy Harjo writes: "We gather up these strands from the web of life. They shiver with our love, as we call them the names of our relatives and carry them to our home" (1994, xvi). A metaphor, then, for a kind of scholarly work that listens, and speaks, doubly. We gather up the strands from our multiple participations + we love them, name them as relatives and take them home = alternatives to academic discourses = listening to ghosts.

In the early 1990s the Miami Nations of Oklahoma and Indiana began holding language workshops. This was made possible through the work of Daryl Baldwin Jr., an Indian Miami descendant of Little Turtle, who took the time to get a master's degree in linguistics in order to be able to understand the scholarly work of linguists who study our language so that he could then develop a series of course materials—booklets, cassette tapes and an interactive CD-ROM—to bring the language back to the people.

Lafayette, IN, July 2000: I am in the great room of a lodge overlooking Waapaashiki (the Wabash River) watching an impromptu puppet show performed by a few Miami children. The storyline is imperfect but as we watch these kids huddle behind their makeshift puppet-theatre table and struggle to keep their story afloat, many of us begin to cry. We are watching Miami children speak the language of our ancestors. We are hearing a new generation of Native children create themselves as Native people, as Miamis, in the language that named this land long before Europeans made the scene. I order the first packet of instructional materials immediately. I devour the words and phrases: alénia *(man),* mitémhsa *(woman),* pyaayaáni *(I come),* iiyaayaáni *(I go),* eeyiihkwiaáni *(I am hungry),* weehs'iniaani *(I eat).*

A new French and Indian War, part two: In *The Practice of Everyday Life*, Michel de Certeau argues for the importance of studying the **use** to which groups and individuals put the representations and behaviors of the society in which they live. This **use**, or making, is "a production, a poiesis," hidden and "scattered over areas defined and occupied by systems of 'production'" and imposed upon by "a dominant economic order" to such an extent that the methods of possible consumption, the ways of **using** are themselves controlled, limited (1984, xii–xiii). For de Certeau, there are two basic practices of **use** possible in relation to this dominant order—strategies and tactics. Strategies are "circumscribed as *proper*," they postulate "a place that can be delimited," and they "serve as a base from which relations with an *exteriority* composed of targets or threats [to the dominant order] can be managed" (1984, xix, 36). Strategies are, then, actions that are delimited by the propriety of the system. They are connected to the power of the dominant order, sustained by it. Tactics, contrarily, are not proper; they have no sense of "a borderline distinguishing the other as a visible totality" (1984, xix). They don't recognize the propriety of the system as binding. Tactics are "calculated action[s] determined by the absence of a proper locus" (1984, 37), a production of knowledge determined by its absence, not its presence, in discourses of power, which are "bound by [their] very visibility" (37). The place of the tactic, then, is "the space of the other," able to insinuate itself into systems of dominance (37). De Certeau's example of tactical **use** is that made by *los indios* (the indigenous inhabitants of Central and South America) of the products of Spanish colonization: "the Indians often used the laws, practices, and representations that were imposed on them by force or by fascination to ends other than those of their conquerors; they made something else out of them; they subverted them from within" (1984, 32). It is the ability of indigenous peoples to consume and not be consumed, "to remain other within the system" that has seemingly assimilated us, which maintains our "difference in the very space that the occupier was already organizing" (32). This is survivance.

Native scholars Joy Harjo (Muskogee) and Gloria Bird (Spokane), in the introduction to their edited collection *Reinventing the Enemy's Language: Contemporary Native Women's Writings of North America*, argue that

> We are coming out of one or two centuries of war, a war that hasn't ended. Many of us at the end of the century are using the "enemy language" with which to tell our truths, to sing, to remember ourselves during these troubled times. . . . But to speak, at whatever the cost, is to become empowered rather than victimized by destruction. . . . These colonizers' languages, which often usurped our own tribal languages or diminished them, now hand back emblems of our cultures, our own designs: beadwork, quills if you will. We've transformed these enemy languages. (1997, 21–22)

To reinvent ourselves in English is, then, for many of us already alternative. We are all already alternative. What many of us are faced with now is the possibility of reinventing ourselves again, in the indigenous languages that named this continent. Muskogee scholar Craig Womack envisions a tribally based scholarly intervention, one that "emphasizes Native resistance movements against colonialism, confronts racism, discusses sovereignty and Native nationalism, seeks connections between literature [broadly conceived] and liberation struggles," a kind of scholarly performance that is rooted in "land and culture" (1999, 11). Imagine that. Imagine an American scholarly practice that both confronts racism and roots itself in land and culture. A practice that challenges "the nature of what we have inherited in the discipline" (Womack 1999, 303). What will our models be? our standards for tenure and promotion? our guidelines for assessment? our affirmative actions? How can, how could, this be? An American scholarly practice that is local, particular, unremittingly honest about privilege and power and money and language? Imagine. We are, after all, as Momaday says "what we imagine"—the who, the what, the "that" we are (1975, 103).

I end this story, then, with an invitation, an invocation for all of us to listen, listen, listen to the whispers of those continental ghosts. To feel their shadows skim along the surface of our skin. To write our bodies into text and reinvent our writings in another voice, another language. To use history and family to remember the land upon which we play. To play these language games lovingly, tenderly, remembering that "all acts of kindness are lights in the war for justice" (Harjo 1994, xv), all acts of scholarship are battles in a war of words, and of worlds.

Works Cited

Christian, Barbara. 1987. "The Race for Theory." *Cultural Critique* 6:51–63.

Churchill, Ward. 1996. "White Studies: The Intellectual Imperialism of U.S. Higher Education." In *From a Native Son: Selected Essays on Indigenism, 1985–1995.* Boston: South End, 271–93.

de Certeau, Michel. 1984. *The Practice of Everyday Life*, translated by Steven Rendall. Berkeley: Univ. of California Press.

Drinnon, Richard. 1990. *Facing West: the Metaphysics of Indian Hating and Empire Building.* New York: Schocken.

Gould, Janice. 1992. "The Problem of Being 'Indian': One Mixed-Blood's Dilemma." In *Decolonizing the Subject: The Politics of Gender in Women's Autobiography*, edited by Sedonie Smith and Julia Watson, 81–87. Minneapolis: Univ. of Minnesota Press.

Gould, Janice. 1996. "This Energy in Which We Exist." *Earthquake Weather.* Tucson: Univ. of Arizona Press, 16–17.

Harjo, Joy. 1994. *The Woman Who Fell from the Sky.* New York: W. W. Norton.

Harjo, Joy, and Gloria Bird, eds. 1997. *Reinventing the Enemy's Language: Contemporary Native Women's Writings of North America.* New York: W. W. Norton.

Lyotard, Jean-François. 1984. *The Postmodern Condition*, translated by Brian Massumi. Minneapolis: Univ. of Minnesota Press.

Lyotard, Jean François, and Jean Loup Thebaud. 1985. *Just Gaming*, translated by Wlad Godzich. Minneapolis: Univ. of Minnesota Press.

Miami Nations. 2001. "Miami Language." Miami Nations Web Site. [Online] Available: <http://www.geocities.com/RainForest/7156/language.html>

Momaday, N. Scott. 1975. "The Man Made of Words." *Literature of the American Indians: Views and Interpretations*, edited by Abraham Chapman, 96–110. New York: Meridian.

Okawa, Gail Y. 1999. "Removing Masks: Confronting Graceful Evasion and Bad

Habits in a Graduate English Class." *Race, Rhetoric and Composition.* Portsmouth, NH: Boynton/Cook, 124–43.

Pearce, Roy Harvey. 1988. *Savagism and Civilization: A Study of the Indian and the American Mind.* Berkeley: Univ. of California Press. Revised edition of *The Savages of America* (Baltimore, MD: Johns Hopkins Univ. Press 1953).

Rose, Wendy. 1993. "For the Scholar Who Wrote a Book About an American Indian Literary Renaissance." In *Going to War with All My Relations.* Flagstaff, AZ: Entrada, 53–54.

Royster, Jacqueline Jones. 2001a. "Academic Discourses, or Small Boats on a Big Sea." Paper presented at the Conference on College Composition and Communication, March 16, Denver, CO.

——. 2001b. "Using History to Invent a Speaking Self." Paper presented at the Conference on College Composition and Communication, March 14, Denver, CO.

Said, Edward. 1993. *Culture and Imperialism.* New York: Knopf.

Slotkin, Richard. 1973. *Regeneration Through Violence: The Mythology of the American Frontier; 1600–1860.* Middletown: Wesleyan Univ. Press.

Vizenor, Gerald. 1994. *Manifest Manners: Postindian Warriors of Survivance.* Hanover, NH: Wesleyan Univ. Press.

Warrior, Robert Allen. 1995. *Tribal Secrets: Recovering American Indian Intellectual Traditions.* Minneapolis: Univ. of Minnesota Press.

Womack, Craig S. 1999. *Red on Red: American Indian Literary Separatism.* Minneapolis: Univ. of Minnesota Press.

3

Academic Discourses or Small Boats on a Big Sea

Jacqueline Jones Royster

In recent years, discussions of academic discourse in rhetoric and composition have raised provocative issues about the nature and processes of language use in the specialized territory of academe, but particularly the use of written language. A most distinctive dimension of these discussions has drawn contrasts between language in the academy versus language outside of it. By 1983 when Shirley Brice Heath published *Ways with Words: Language, Life, and Work in Communities and Classrooms* and 1985 when Odell and Goswami published *Writing in Nonacademic Settings*, we were becoming increasingly aware of how thoroughly we had been ignoring in both research and practice the fact that writing (and literacy as the broader concept) occurs in many places using many forms and that there are quite likely intersections and resonances between academic and nonacademic settings that might be instructive to our work inside the academy.

Shortly after Heath and Odell and Goswami came the work of Harvey J. Graff (*The Legacies of Literacy: Continuities and Contradictions in Western Culture and Society*, 1987), Linda Brodkey (*Academic Writing as Social Practice*, 1987), Paolo Freire (*Pedagogy of the Oppressed*, 1988), and Deborah Brandt (*Literacy as Involvement: The Acts of Writers, Readers, and Texts*, 1990). By 1994 when Beverly Moss published *Literacy across Communities* and 1995 when Brian Street published *Social Literacies: Critical Approaches to Literacy in Development, Ethnography and Education*, we were well on our way to understanding the cultural, social, political, and economic implications and consequences of literacy. Simultaneously, however, a second dimension of the discussions was also gaining momentum. In this case, the focus was on the subtle and not so subtle distinctions among disciplinary communities, and we became more consciously aware of disciplinary values and expectations as they are enacted through various language practices. This research (e.g., Young and Fulwiler 1986; Russell 1991; Herrington and Moran 1992) energized the writing across the curriculum movement, creating successive waves of understanding, as illustrated most recently by scholars such as Zamel and Spack (1998), Duszak (1997), and Hyland (2000) who are encouraging us to raise different questions about how we might build language knowledge and enhance language abilities. Moreover, amid these concerns have been lingering issues of identity, gender, race, class, and culture, as evidenced recently by Gadsden and Wagner (1995), Shepard, McMillan, and Tate (1998) and Gilyard (1999) to name just three of an ever-growing set of volumes.

While the general conversation has indeed been varied and rich, when we place the focal point more directly on the teaching of writing in academic arenas or communities, we tend, nevertheless, to encapsulate this broader discussion of language use and to speak more reductively. Certainly, we acknowledge academic arenas or communities and disciplinary discourses, but, more often than not, we articulate our theories and pedagogies using images that inscribe a more monolithic viewpoint. Our use of such terms as academic language and academic discourse do not convey a sense of a collectivity of uses. These terms come through instead in quite untextured and singular ways. There is *the* language, *the* discourse of academe and there are *other* languages and discourses that are not academic. We distill the variations that we otherwise specify and use general terms in ways that suggest sameness, tacit understanding, and static, non-contentious representations, not just of language or discourse but also of *goodness*. Despite our occasional intent to suggest otherwise, such habits of distillation have engendered in our field hierarchies of power, privilege, and value, and they have continually reified notions of insider/outsider, center/margin, us/other, and also notions of good/suspect.

While these oppositional categories have, to some extent, actually helped us to see, display, and interrogate features of academic language use more dynamically, over time these binaries have also engendered a sense of primacy. Whether by intent or default, we have centralized in our conversations a default view of what can be sanctioned as good writing (as enacted often through a traditional view of the freshman essay), a view that has functioned ultimately to tether, rather than enable an evolving discussion. My purpose, then, with this short essay is to pose a shift in our thinking that begins by acknowledging the inconsistency with which we have accepted what we know about the nature of language and the formation and operations of language communities on one hand and marginalized and ignored this knowledge on another.

As evidenced by the body of research to which I refer earlier in this chapter, generally we have come to the following insights:

1. Academic discourse, like all language use, is an invention of a particular social milieu, not a natural phenomenon.
2. Academic discourse is not now, and quite likely never has been, an *it*. We recognize now that discourse in academic arenas is, indeed, plurally formed, not singularly formed, within the contexts of varying disciplinary communities as these arenas have been sites of social and intellectual engagement and as they have developed and changed over the histories of these engagements.
3. Academic discourses, even plurally formed, should *still* not be perceived as existing apart, above, or beyond the varieties of discourse around them.

These three points form the basis upon which I assert that academic discourses are small boats on a big sea. In placing this idea on the table in *bold* relief, instead of just in passing, I am suggesting that paying direct attention to these three basic points sets different parameters for a discussion of the future of literacy instruction.

Let's start with insight #1. As a concept, *academic discourse* exists within a social milieu. In academe, as in other arenas of language use, we form communicative/interpretive communities based on sets of values, expectations, protocols, and practices. Thus, a central insight to keep fully present in our thinking, rather than on the periphery, is the necessity of resisting a tendency to view discourse (language in particular use) as a disembodied force within which we are inevitably, inescapably, innocently swept along. Quite demonstrably, as evidenced by the body of research cited earlier, discourse is *embodied* and it is *endowed.* It is, in fact, quite a *people-centered* enterprise, and it is the *fact* of its *people-centeredness* that endows it so insidiously with the workings of social, political, and cultural processes. By such processes, we contend with the imposition of values, beliefs, and expectations through language; with the deployment of systems of power, control, privilege, entitlement, and authority through language; with the engendering of habits, protocols, systems of value through language—all processes with which we are now all too familiar.

The point is, if we can acknowledge overtly that discourses operate at the hands and the will of a *people*, rather than as instruments or forces of nature, or as systems formed by an innate cloud of right-ness and good that floats around in the air somewhere just waiting to unleash its power, *then* we have already shifted the possibilities of literacy instruction. We shift because we start, quite simply, from a very different place in the scheme of things. In particular, we do not start instruction by assuming that our *boats* are gifts from nature, all duly constructed and already afloat, or that we are all in the same one. We start from a different point of view, from a different set of assumptions, assumptions that make clearer that there are many vessels in addition to our own on the sea around us and they are all sailing interestingly along, and that we—as the historically mandated champions of righteousness and good in our own boat, academic writing—are not really being invaded at all. In fact, the enterprise is not about war or invasions; it's about sailing.

If we can shift assumptions overtly and explicitly so that we start with the question of how discourses are embodied and endowed, then the *alternative* in a conversation about alternative discourses is, quite simply, not really about alternative discourses at all, but about alternative *assumptions* about discourses. The process of interrogating discourses via the *people* who shape the discourses, use them, monitor them, and enforce their values helps to dismantle the mythology of *rightful stronghold* and *invading hordes* that has been so militaristically rendered in our field. The stronghold is not so *rightful*; the hordes are students, teachers, and other constituents on a variable and real sociocultural terrain; the invasion is the infusion of new understandings of the nature, ways, and means of knowledge-making processes as these processes operate in academic and nonacademic arenas. Debunking the myth, then, shifts our positions away from the limitations of such a myth in the interest of finding a view that is more generative and offers better interpretive possibilities for instruction. With a better and more enabling image, we have the capacity to think again about literacy instruction and to re-envision what and how we teach and learn. The opportunity is an opportunity to enhance our vision, as well as an opportunity to increase the capacity to see, interpret, and address problems with better effects for larger numbers of students.

To restate the point in different terms, what we have traditionally done is to set our assumptions in ways that prohibit a more fully textured sense of an analytical matrix that is keyed by contextual factors from operating with vitality and consequence. Typically, we have naturalized the academy as an exclusive space with predetermined, preset values and operations that should reign supreme and that can do so without such reflection or negotiation. Current research is compelling us, however, to move interpretively to alter these protections and to critically engage, raising questions about exclusions, about what is endemic, what is socially, politically, and culturally assignable, about what can be questioned and negotiated. The basic advantage of opening up our critical perspectives in such ways is that more discourses (inside of the academy and outside of it) can have room for inclusion in this general arena and, more importantly, room to operate there with greater visibility and consequence. In other words, there is considerable potential to create new possibilities for enabling both rhetoric and action. I note in particular the following:

1. Viewing literacy instruction as a people-driven enterprise dictates that we pay attention to who the people are in the arena, to their personal, social, institutional, and public locations; to students as *subjects* in the classroom, not objects; quite similarly, to teachers, the institutional keepers of rules and rites, as *subjects* too, and not just instruments. We notice discourse as an embodied experience with endowments that are often differently perceived by classroom *subjects*, i.e., often understood differently by students and teachers.

2. We recognize, as writing textbooks have been moving toward in recent years, the importance of meeting students wherever they are in their knowledge, experiences, and thinking, and finding ways to expand their horizons, and to enhance their abilities. The shift has been away from an absorption of knowledge by those in varying states of ignorance to a recognition of prior knowledge, the constructing of knowledge pathways, and an understanding of what it means to participate in knowledge making as an ongoing, rather than a static, enterprise. We envision the work of classrooms as dynamic, multidirectional engagement with the expectation of dynamic rewards, rather than as places where the goal is mainly to match the norms and to replicate ordinary outcomes (e.g., to produce a grammatically flawless text that answers the questions asked).
3. Provocative questions arise about rhetorical decision making and the use of various resources in definable arenas of engagement. In other words, the language of the academy becomes an analytical moment for both the academy itself, as well as for a variety of communicative opportunities within the academic world. Such notions also raise, perhaps even more provocatively, questions about the personal as an appropriate site for learning, intellectual engagement, and writing, and they raise as well the more intimidating specter of the ethical complexity of understanding where *privacy* begins. How do we set values for communicative/expressive success in arenas that we are seeing now, interpreting, and understanding in more open and fluid terms than ever before? Where do we start our intellectual work? How do we direct our reflections and inquiries? How do we encompass personal, social, institutional, and public imperatives while simultaneously respecting the often competing mandates for both privacy and well-deliberated public engagement?

Using this last point as a springboard, my experience as a teacher and researcher suggests that the search for ways to talk about the differences between the personal, the social, the institutional, the public, the private is just not enough. In the least, I see the need to talk with students directly about the truths and consequences of disclosure, about ethos (see Crowley 1994 and Royster 2000) as a situated identity and an invented or negotiated identity, about the importance of assessing, not just using, personal knowledge and experience in making good decisions about what is private, what is social, what is public, what should be written or said, while recognizing in explicit ways that classrooms are not private spaces. They are public spaces and require of students tremendous leaps of faith, especially when their sociopolitical locations situate them as intruders, or at best visitors who must/should be tolerated, or perhaps from a more liberal view, as outsiders who should be graciously accommodated—alternate though they are quite likely to be positioned still. In other words, when we anchor instruction as a people-centered enterprise, what becomes visible is more than the interplay between anointed and alternate/other discourses. What becomes visible is that writing and learning in a socially and politically contentious nation is for many students and teachers alike—who embody variously those contentious—a high-risk act, especially when we define the academy (i.e., the context of their engagement) in passive, disembodied ways.

Finally, in focusing more on one of the pedagogical mandates that arise from this type of paradigmatic shift, when we position literacy instruction as helping students to understand and to participate flexibly in multiple discourses, and especially multiple academic discourses, then part of the pedagogical mandate is a question of identifying, negotiating, and reconfiguring certain communicative gaps. Again, we start with *who* is bridging the gaps in which contexts with what range of prior experiences, for what range of purposes across what range of available rhetorical options and genres. Given the mounds of recent research and scholarship that we have already generated in the field, we, of course, acknowledge the resources that students bring to the communicative enterprise, regardless of where they begin. We are also beginning to acknowledge the extent to which more open communicative enterprises ultimately function to question and reshape what constitutes a bridge, an architecture, a connective artery, a mechanism, and thereby to reconfigure the possibility that knowledge and experience is capable of having significant impact, regardless of the source from which it comes.

If a critical goal in literacy instruction, especially in higher education, is to help students to forge connections between what they already know as language users and the more that is available to be known, we, along with our students, can explore how to strike good balances across various gaps so that affirmation, empowerment, and ultimately learning are possible. The mandate is to search for ways to connect, for ways to engage masterfully. The mandate is to search for classroom practices that use, build upon, and enhance experiences and that permit the re-definition and reconfiguration of acceptable forms of expression, representation, and presentation—a mandate, of course, that explodes the primacy of the academic essay. By contrast, the mandate is not focused so much on the effort to conform to the already tried and prescribed or on having work anointed only by traditionally valorized beliefs, expectations, and habits.

The bottom line here is that new assumptions, new paradigms, and fewer imperial exclusions in academic arenas should give rise to new forms of expression and to unanticipated values added, and that, I believe, is exactly what we are seeing in progress across composition programs around the nation and, indeed, around the world. This thought brings me full circle to where I began. In academic arenas we find ourselves traveling in small boats on a big sea that we have virtually ignored as a sea because we could. Typically in the presence of our students who are testing our commitments to just staying where we are, some of us are being pushed to notice that life in the world of composition could occupy a different space. If we really think about it, we might not even want to limit ourselves to traveling in boats anymore. We might want to experience the sea of discourse in a different way. In other words, if we set our minds to it, the world of composition could actually turn on different assumptions. Change is possible. At this point, however, in determining whether our possibilities will have consequence, the question that remains is whether we will seize the opportunity to chart new, and, possibly, different theoretical, methodological, and pedagogical pathways where the openness and fluidity that we know exist have the capacity to flourish.

Works Cited

Brandt, Deborah. 1990. *Literacy as Involvement: The Acts of Writers, Readers, and Texts*. Carbondale: Southern Illinois Univ. Press.

Brodkey, Linda. 1987. *Academic Writing as Social Practice*. Philadelphia: Temple Univ. Press.

Crowley, Sharon. 1994. *Ancient Rhetorics for Contemporary Students*. New York: Macmillan.

Duszak, Anna, ed. 1997. *Culture and Styles of Academic Discourse*. Hawthorne, NY: Mouton de Gruyter.

Freire, Paulo. 1988. *Pedagogy of the Oppressed*. New York: Continuum.

Gadsden, Vivian L., and Daniel A. Wagner, eds. 1995. *Literacy Among African-American Youth: Issues in Learning, Teaching, and Schooling*. Cresskill, NJ: Hampton.

Gilyard, Keith, ed. 1999. *Race, Rhetoric, and Composition*. Portsmouth, NH: Boynton/Cook.

Graff, Harvey J. 1987. *The Legacies of Literacy: Continuities and Contradictions in Western Culture and Society*. Bloomington, IN: Indiana Univ. Press.

Heath, Shirley B. 1983. *Ways with Words: Language, Life, and Work in Communities and Classrooms*. New York: Cambridge Univ. Press.

Herrington, Anne, and Charles Moran, eds. 1992. *Writing, Teaching, and Learning in the Disciplines*. New York: MLA.

Hyland, Ken. 2000. *Disciplinary Discourses: Social Interactions in Academic Writing*. New York: Longman.

Moss, Beverly J., ed. 1994. *Literacy across Communities*. Cresskill, NJ: Hampton.

Odell, Lee, and Dixie Goswami, eds. 1985. *Writing in Nonacademic Settings*. New York: Guilford.

Royster, Jacqueline J. 2000. *Traces of a Stream: Literacy and Social Change among African American Women*. Pittsburgh: Univ. of Pittsburgh Press.

Russell, David R. 1991. *Writing in the Academic Disciplines, 1870–1990: A Curricular History*. Carbondale: Southern Illinois Univ. Press.

Shepard, Alan, John McMillan, and Gary Tate, eds. 1998. *Coming to Class: Pedagogy and the Social Class of Teachers*. Portsmouth, NH: Boynton/Cook.

Street, Brian V. 1995. *Social Literacies: Critical Approaches to Literacy in Development, Ethnography and Education*. London: Longman.

Young, Art, and Toby Fulwiler, eds. 1986. *Writing Across the Disciplines: Research into Practice*. Portsmouth, NH: Boynton/Cook.

Zamel, Vivian, and Ruth Spack, eds. 1998. *Negotiating Academic Literacies: Teaching and Learning Across Languages and Cultures*. Mahwah, NJ: Lawrence Erlbaum Associates.

4

"New Life in This Dormant Creature"

Notes on Social Consciousness, Language, and Learning in a College Classroom

carmen kynard

I. Understanding Jim Crow Inventions: Opening Notes on Writing and Teaching This Piece

It was my first day at my urban, four-year college in Bronx, New York. I was waiting for the previous class to leave so that I could go in, set up chairs in a circle, and write an agenda on the board. As all the students filed out of their classrooms, an explosion of sound, seemingly antithetical to the voices of bellowing professors ten minutes before, rang through the hallways: the rapid swirls of Spanish that sometimes, and sometimes not, moved through fusions of Spanglish; urban, African American English twisted around the words from my radio when tuned into HOT 97's Blazin Hip Hop and R&B; the swift, yet sometimes punctuated nuances that West African languages seem to dance through; varied versions of Patois which seem to meld together these urban Ebonics and nuances of West African language systems yet add on something else; and then Frenchified sounds spun onto African cadences from Haitian and Francophone African students. On that first day, however, these were mostly the sounds of the hallway and not the sounds of the classrooms.

Before my classes start, I like to take a look around and see how students present themselves to the world—like the big baggy pants that the boys especially like to wear. While the looseness may seem lax, I know from watching the flop-over process of the leg bottoms that it takes quite a bit of tinkering to achieve that perfect number of layers on both pant legs. The young women mostly wear bellbottomed pants also with a carefully manipulated, new foldover at the bottom. There are thick-soled boots in black or the latest blond and red leathers that make their walking more like thumping across the ground. Sneakers and casual boots ironically have these thick heels also, but these are made instead according to Michael Jordanian concepts of flight with colorful air pockets laid into the sides. The fellas' well-tapered sides take on adult significance when replacing their baseball caps (which have brims folded just right in the middle to form a perfect arc over their round faces), or their wool caps topped off in the shape of a banana, or the doo-rags that snuggle the roundness of their heads. The young women have their hair pulled back very tightly to showcase an explosion of curls at the nape of their neck or long cornrows lining the contours of their heads. Most seem to experiment with dark-lipsticked lips outlined with an even darker, outer edge.

My description of these images is not meant to serve as a mere backdrop for an academicized, ethnographic story. These images represent a specific lens through which I look to construct the contours of the landscape of my classroom. The episodes I recreate here marked a semester begun with a mandatory brunch-type affair for freshman instructors where an administrator, one of the few people of color in the room who was not a peer tutor, offered an ominous warning. He explained that these students required a different kind of education. These students, he argued, wear doo-rags to class and traverse the campus and hallways wearing walkmen. As such, they are unlike his own Latino son, who had gone to the best private schools and was currently attending an ivy league school. His son was ready for intellectual work (based solely on his not having a walkman and doo-rag) in a way that "our students" simply were not. This administrator's utterance was greeted with attentive nods by the petit bourgeois in the room disguised as educated/educators. I would argue that this administrator's system of logic comprises the everyday discursive and ideological apparatuses that operate underneath curriculum and instruction for working-class students of color, which also includes: "these students" belong in remedial courses only, cannot write and speak except in "street language," do not know how to think, have no work ethic (i.e., do not come to class, turn in work late, etc.). Graduate Ph.D. students, who often seem to take Incompletes, do not align the constraints imposed on their intellectual work by the exploitation of their part-time labor with the similar constraints imposed on the time of working, single mothers in their classrooms. Adjunct instructors who are also M.A. students at this very city college, students who themselves have taken five years to complete a two-year program, also claim not to understand what is wrong with "these students." What lies at the root of what I am calling here *everyday discursive practices* is a fundamental belief that the language, literacy, and cognitive functioning of working-class students of color are simply inferior. This then shapes my purposes for writing and teaching at the university, from here on referred to as *my story*: to unravel the tangled knots of the rhetorical and institutional practices endemic to the racist, class-based, hierarchical functioning of higher education that chokes out the intellectual, human capabilities and revolutions of poor and working-class students of color.

This writing is about one group of students and focuses specifically on one young woman (who, remember, was introduced aggregately as not being ready for intellectual work). Within this I attempt to place my story in dynamic dialogue with the narratives of my students to disrupt the smoothness of the way the business of higher education is done. This writing is also an attempt at what Mary Louise Pratt (1991) defines as an autoethnographic text, a text in which I describe myself and my students in ways that dialogue with representations others have made of us. Instead of simple self-representation, a collaboration of idioms of the dominant order merge with what I will call my own indigenous idioms to intervene in dominant modes of understanding. Thus, as Pratt suggests, such a text addresses one's own community as well as a dominant system as a point of entry into those circuits (184).

It is also necessary to delineate here what is not contained in this writing. After all, what is not included in a story is always already part of its ideological makeup. I make no attempt to determine my and my students' "transgressions" of academic conventions for the sake of aggregating, labeling, cataloging, and packaging their formalistic properties in a newly sorted census of marginal, hybrid discourses and rainbow-coalitioned, identity positions. I am not interested in vesting students' literacy and language practices with technical sophistication and canonical authority so that they appear sanitized and acceptable in the elitist world of higher education. I am not interested in proving my and my students' literacy and intelligence but in examining the political dynamics that deny it. As Adolph Reed reminds us, such a project is closely connected to "the definitive role of the black public intellectual [as] interpreting the opaquely black heart of darkness for whites." (2000, 77) I have a simple belief that questioning and understanding how we operate inside of literacy, language, and the social world along the axes of race and class can and will shape consciousness and action. What I hope to achieve in my teaching and writing is a strategizing that will transform institutions and the social relations that they render, where language and the university system are simply cogs in a larger machine.

I am also not speaking for my students as a teacher of color from a working-class background. I am not interested in providing Booker T. Washingtonian formulas for moving students *Up from Slavery*. This belongs to the historical process of choosing a black middle-class elite (chosen by whites) as the Race Leaders. These leaders direct their aims toward white supremacy and dummy-talk conservative agendas while pimping a discourse of race upliftment (you can only lift someone up when you prop yourself along the superior upper ranks). I am also not interested in a middle-class self-help ideology of taking responsibility for improving the lives of the people in my community. As Reed also reminds us, this notion is located in capitalist privatization schemes. This is not a social critique or demand. I am also not interested in providing formulas for grammarizing/skills-traditionalizing *Other People's Children because they need the explicit, direct, tough instruction* (which sounds like slavery to me). I refuse to be a chocolate or honey-dipped Miranda of Shakespeare's *The Tempest* who will give students, as the embodiment of the savage Caliban, THE language of the university. Whether or not I speak THE language remains questionable and if I do so without a social critique or demand for social change, then I was better off mute.

As Sylvia Wynter argues, teachers are mainstream-initiating and mainstream-bearing. Most of us are not the site of social revolution or consciousness. We liberal-humanize our doo-rag wearing, walkman-rap-chanting students so that we can marvel at our new de-nigger-fied and de-spic-afied products. We replicate all of the existing, repressive conditions of the social order more than question or transform them. We teach the "standard" with missionary zeal in the belief that it will save the youth. Historically, there have been legalized rules against blacks learning to read and write, de facto segregated schools, a 101st Airborne Division escorting black kids to school in a place called Little Rock, de facto integration with de facto segregated zoning. Yet today all students of color in America need do is simply speak and write in the "standard" and material success, economic mobility, and equity will come shining through. Now if that ain't a lie, I don't know what is.

Let me break it down like this:

writing is the property that we stand at the door of. here's what students gotta do before we let them come in: wipe the bottom of your shoes—dress up real nice—bring a nice gift from a really nice store—cologne yourself up—stand up straight—don't talk too loud—brush your teeth—feet side by side—polish your shoes—clean your nails—hands at your sides—press your suit and your hair . . . and then you can come in. this ain't about writing, communication, language, literacy. this is about entrance requirements . . . and keepin some folks out. yeah, we do the "real work" of the university, don't we?

if we teachers allow students to hybridize on the page (which isn't really the problem. It's just that some folks hybrid is too hybrid), we gotta control it. We gotta be able to understand one another (thereby making colonization and management easier). so we ask:

> is this hybrid too hybridized? is it too trendy (and now how is my African American English trendy? we BIN doin it.) would a different form be better?

We enforce these neo-formalist rules. we align ourselves up with that. our talk about giving students access to academic discourse is our secret LIE. this is just the postmodern description for college grammar skill-drills and instruction in the formal, surface aspects of writing. we never ask the questions: what the hell students writin? for whom? and for what? there is no interrogation here of social consciousness and change, just form over substance. seem like only a fool would see this lie as radical or revolutionary when it really just the same ole, same ole.

and here's another of our lies: the notion of w(h)id(t)er communication. as if the discourse of my first seven paragraphs, as opposed to this mini-section here, is gonna impact and transform the white liberal, progressive, petit bourgeoisie who nodded their heads at the public pronouncements of my doo-ragged students as intellectually incapable. this is a dangerous thing. it uses this notion of w(h)id(t)er communication to direct students to write for a white, middle-class, consuming audience. if they succeed, they win the prize of being the one good, moral voice who intervenes in the humanity of whites . . . while preparing and serving their dinner like the black maid (Old Delie) in William Faulkner's *The Sound and The Fury*. again, this is not about social transformation but about accepting a prescribed, subordinate role.

real world preparation for me & my students why u makin us marketable again? I've been to the market before a slave auction and ain't tryin to go there no more is this the real world? slick me down and shine me up? and profit offa my back?

GRE, canon, SAT, MCAT, GMAT, LSAT, ETS, ACT, speech classes, formal properties of poetry, state standardized/regents tests, "new" standards, college entrance exams, standard written edited american english, academic discourse, bell curve. Ain't nuthin but Jim Crow Laws i know when I'm bein lynched for the inventions which others use to imagine themselves

. . . so I imagine my classroom, writing, and consciousness as achieving something else.

II. "New Life in This Dormant Creature"

Introduction to Humanities 101 is required of all freshmen in their first year. It meets for one semester and is designed to introduce students to art, music, literature, philosophy, and drama through the required course coverage of Michelangelo's Sistine Chapel, Beethoven's Fifth Symphony, Plato, Shakespeare, and Toni Morrison. The class meets three days a week for an hour and is part of a freshman core block design. This means all students in this section are full-time freshmen who take all classes together in their first semester in an attempt to acclimate them to college (since that they will not have a dorm experience). Students in this block also take required courses in speech, first semester college writing, and Introduction to the Modern Age. In the spring semester of 2000, however, it was my hope that my students and myself would read, write, listen, and feel the arts to help us to make sense of the world in which we live. To this end, I asked students to bring in words (music, poetry, excerpt of a story, etc.) to share with the class at various points in the semester as another way of contextualizing their own worlds. Students were required to distribute copies of the piece, introduce it, direct fifteen minutes of writing on the piece (which I collect as part of their weekly journal responses to the week's assigned readings), and direct a discussion of the piece based on what and how their classmates responded. There were also intermittent, formal (nonjournal) writing requirements asking students to synthesize and reflect on the texts of the course. Students wrote letters, plays, narratives. One student, Rakim, even created a curriculum packet for youth in his community organization. Many wrote poetry or entire poetry anthologies indicating their stops and turns in the course's readings and discussions.

I look back at this particular semester and know that at least for some students, reading and writing at the site of their own sociopolitical realities instead of from a hyper-Westernized, bourgeois, literary imposition (the de facto curriculum of freshman core courses) meant something for them and allowed them to get in touch with something inside of themselves that they did not know they had. I also know that for some students, I failed. When there is a huge disconnection between my class and the rest of the courses my students must take, I sometimes cannot help them carve out a middle ground.

Do I even have a choice as to whether or not students/me need to engage an alternative pedagogy and classroom structure when for some it's a life and death matter? I'm still training myself to get the chatter of this oppressive system outta my head. sometimes i hear voices that are not my own. sometimes i read my students' poems and the first thing that comes to mind . . . is this rigorous enuf? did they do enuf work? WORK! yes that was my language!

enuf, enuf, enuf, enuf, enuf . . . ENUF of me thinking this!

enuf of my schizophrenia.

enuf of these ventriloquist routines where i put the words in my students' mouths with the joke being that it looks like it comes from them. where a dominant elite puts the words in my mouth with the joke being that i act like it is good to just MAKE EM MO BETTA, MO BETTA WORKERS! I'm henry ford's dummy.

April, take me outta here with the opening stanza to one of your poems:

my eyes have been opened
To a new picture
I found new life
In this dormant creature.

She laid asleep
I had to wake her up
Reality check
was like a hit from a truck.

Yeah girl, I'm finally waking up now too. This dormant creature gon find her some new pictures too.

III. Settin It Off

April is the young woman who showed me the power of students' intellectual needs and commitments. I sat in on a partner discussion with her and Arnetha in the first week of class before we read a piece about the racialized, historical origins of Tango in the African-Argentine communities of the late 1800s. In introduction to this piece, we wrote about a time when we noticed racial, class, or gender stratifications. It seemed April's pen could not move fast enough to capture all of what she had to say: questions like when people get killed in her community, why is that not televised while a white woman who says that a black man killed her children gets national attention (even though she killed the kids herself)?

While the fire in her soul was already quite apparent, I would never have imagined what April would share with us next. As the first to present a piece of music that impacted her, she chose "Zion" by Lauryn Hill, who she described as "a strong woman who . . . doesn't use simpleton rhymes in her raps. She tells a story or sends a message and she doesn't focus only on love and money. She also writes about life." Hill's song is dedicated to her young son and reminisces about her fear and lack of support during her pregnancy. As we listened to the music, April passed around photos of a child without introduction or explanation, just letting the lyrics tell us that this little boy was her son, her "manchild" as Lauryn Hill would say.

April then told us what the song had meant to her when she was pregnant in her last year of Catholic high school. Once when she had a picture taken with some friends when her belly was beginning to show, the nuns quickly confiscated the film so as not to tarnish the image of the school. From that point on, April was not allowed to interact with the rest of the school population. She was only allowed to come to school twice a week where she had to take her classes in a custodian's room in the basement where the nuns gave her missed assignments. She had to complete these assignments there in the basement so that she could be kept away from the rest of the students as well as from the teachers, thus receiving no direct instruction or interaction with faculty.

The class gasped as April told the story of her pregnancy and some of the students began to get a charge from imagining suing this school for violating April's civil rights. Arnetha remarked that her only connection to these experiences was the time that she thought she was pregnant and attempted to throw herself down the stairs to get rid of the baby. An argument ensued when three women declared they were against abortion. The men got into it too, one telling how he matured when his girlfriend miscarried, another expressing confusion about why women would have sex if they couldn't afford a child. I marveled that this was only the second week and they were takin it there. And I marveled at what April had survived. In my note in her journal that week, I told her that she had the same power to blaze forth an intellectual and emotional path for young people as Lauryn Hill had done for her.

While April's former school had explicitly and literally locked her down at the bottom, I knew that the normative curriculum and instruction that stitched together the fabric of the university system did the same thing. Somehow we would have to make central to our semester a careful examination of how society is made. Writing would be the scene to question social reality, of which the university's practices and privileges would be only one aspect. That this writing would represent many mixed forms and languages seemed only a natural path to rupture the interferences higher education makes in students' thinking by eradicating and rendering inferior any discourse and language that is nonwhite, non–middle class, non-masculinist.

The students themselves offered many opportunities for this questioning. Though Mary and Katrina were the two quietest women in the course (and I often worried about the source of their almost muteness, feeling completely inept about mentioning it to them), somehow they decided to give a joint presentation of "Love Is Blind" by the female MC (rapper) Eve. Their choice shocked me not only because I had never seen Mary and Katrina so much as acknowledge each other in class, but also because of their chosen theme of domestic violence and murder. Katrina introduced the song by saying that domestic violence is not construed as violence—not like manslaughter or any real charges of battery—because the offense is perpetrated against women. Right when she was on a roll, she stopped herself and apologized for being nervous and not making sense. We were on the edge of our seats as she broke it down for us, and we reassured her that she made all the sense in the world. Mary then picked up where Katrina left off, passing out a handout that she had retrieved from the Internet with quotes from abused women. Because I was familiar with the rap, I asked the ladies privately if they wouldn't mind playing the skit before the song, which depicts a woman being beaten by her boyfriend with his friend cheering him on since she was dressed too scantily for the streets at that time of night. They said they'd wanted to show it, but they weren't sure how I'd react. "Play that shit," I told them, it's an important factor in the song.

After the video, the classroom was a very quiet place, and an open discussion didn't seem to match the vibe of the room, so Mary and Katrina asked people to respond in a go-around. Many gave personal examples of how domestic violence affected the families of their "friends." April, however, did not offer the example of a "friend." She began by saying that she had lived the words in the song because her mother . . . and then she stopped short. The tension rose as some of the men questioned why women in these relationships didn't just leave. What marked a soon very, very heated exchange in the classroom was the absence of one female player, April. Still fighting back the tears, she had picked up her pen and was writing furiously while the rest of the women talked and argued as if they were trying to fill the class with her energy for her. Finally, one of the men said that perhaps they needed to take the issue of domestic violence seriously, because if not, women would all become lesbians. Now why did he go and say that for? Katrina (and mind you, this was the "quiet" one) steered the women into direct questioning of each man in the room, asking why they were so inept at being critical, going back and forth between the song lyrics, the literary texts from the course, and their own experiences.

Afterward, Katrina asked April if she was okay, and April shook her head, not a yes or no, just moved her head like maybe she wasn't sure. And with this, the women gathered around to talk with her and to hold their own class session after class had officially ended. When they left, April handed me a piece of paper, saying, "This is what I couldn't say earlier. It'll explain everything." She was right. It did explain everything. In a way, I think the women in the course all sensed these explanations, which is why they had no choice but to fill in with her story that day.

This is what April wrote:

See now this is the fuckin
shit I be talkin about in
class . . .
My mother was abused.
Almost every fucking boyfriend
(including my punk ass
father)
beat her. I seen the shit
go down. I had to jump in
while my stepfather strangled her
I hit him over the head with the
telephone . . .
Yo Carmen I did
everything for him. I thought
it was real. No matter what he said or did I made
excuses for his sorry ass. when I
was pregnant I was
still waitin on his ass hand and
foot. Why did I stay?
shit I wish I had the sense to
figure it out. It's not easy. I came from
a fucking broken home
Abusive in all ways. I was kicked out
at 16 . . .

This is why my mother stabbed my pops. she got fed up with the cheating and the abuse.

She was abused as a child then got with men who abused her
She abused her children and now her children are with men
who abuse them.
I am breaking the cycle
My son will not abuse women or anyone
He will respect his mother and wife and children.

And this is what I wrote back:

April, I'm not even sure where to start.
Your letter/poetry takes me back to all those places. i feel you. i know what it means to have to pull a man offa your momma.
a different kinda lesson in our womanhood and motherhood, huh?
and then hafta turn around and be stuck somewhere, someday
wondering how and if this is what is shaping the way you interact w/men . . .
realizing that of course it is.
it was a long time before i could talk about
and write about and locate this politically
but i did   finally   still am
but at first it wasn't with the strength and dignity that i see in you.
you already on your way, girl! shit, you already there . . .

and yeah i see where you coming from about that cycle spinning around and around   and around   and around
just pullin you right in
but you and your son, yall will break that shit down
cuz you already have!

V. The Miseducation of April Melendez: Palante!

April had written extensively in her journals about the way the attitudes of the Black children in Morrison's *The Bluest Eye* were still typical today. She wrote about how she had learned to believe not only that white was better, but that black and Hispanic were ugly. "I had it set in my mind that anyone with a Spanish accent was unintelligent. I had a firm belief that Hispanic men beat their wives and children and were horny pigs who always cheated." Sharing this writing seemed to open the way for other students to admit the same. I offered my own example of having once felt the same way. That such attitudes could happen so lawlikely and so consistently, whether it be 1970 or 2000, suggested to me, and I hoped to the students in the room, that this issue was part of something much larger than just our individual selves.

April's light-skinned-ness would also become a central issue for her. What accompanied her realization of her anti-Hispanic sentiments was a questioning of her Puerto Rican identity: "Today I regret not knowing Spanish and I wish I looked more Puerto Rican (darker skin and kinky hair) so I could identify myself better as Hispanic." This was something I warned her against: seeing herself as not Puerto Rican enough would be just as alienating, torturous, and self-hating as being ashamed of being Puerto Rican (I'd been there before is what I told her). My colleagues sometimes criticize these kinds of interactions as "therapy" and "social work," and object to these topics as too personal and private (a departmental observer once reported that my classroom offered no examples of academic writing and discussion). But I had no intention of asking students to be merely objective about their own racialized self-hatred when the sociopolitical imposition of a Dick-and-Jane world was formulating their everyday lives—who they thought was worth listening to, looking at, being with, and speaking to.

I can't help but think back on the way my colleagues viewed April's questions around her light-skinned status as merely an individual issue of depression. That skin color is a historical, social phenomenon was not a thought these instructors were willing to entertain. To me, all of this smacked of the way light-skinned children on slave plantations were shunned by their slaveowner fathers and other whites in their families. April's issue of skin color is no individual thing, nor is it an historical accident. As if her light-skinned-ness isn't part of everyone's story! To not conceptualize April and her peers grappling with skin color erases an entire body of literature and thought central to the Americas in the works of people like Nella Larsen, Zora Neale Hurston, Charles Chesnutt, James Weldon Johnson, Langston Hughes, Dorothy West, Piri Thomas, Ramon Betances, Nicolas Guillen . . . the list is endless. I shudder at the way I have not even begun to articulate the historical and contemporary complexities of this system enveloping April that go all the way back to (1) how the Spanish Crown was flooded with letters from settlers in places like Cuba and Hispaniola, requesting that rules be made against the liaisons between Spanish men and Mulatto women on the islands; (2) the laws in Hispaniola where Mulatto women were forced to look to the ground and dismount their horses when they passed a woman from Spain, lest they think that their light skin and good hair made them as worthy of human and civil rights. To see April locating the politics of her own light-skinned-ness as merely an individual, psychological disorder is a ploy to wipe out all of this . . . to continue to wipe out *her*.

> So are we, at the university, nothing more than the new slavemasters?
> locking April out of the family again
> (this time by noting her deficiencies as a lack of
> academic discourse, distance, and objectivity
> vs. last time by noting her deficiencies as
> a lack of pure white/European blood)
> because examining her sociohistorical experience may unravel the
> very world in which we have constructed ourselves as master?

I wanted this course to connect to students' lives and to provide a space for questioning social reality. I refused to summon up literature and the arts as a warm and nurturing world that redeems our humanity in what Reed castigates as "imposing ideological order on a messy world" (2000, 16). I would not train students to bow before the secularized God of Bourgeois Liberal Humanism. Yet I also was failing April, her classmates, and our combined political and intellectual commitments. Yes we had set it off. We were on our way to questioning and criticizing social reality. But we were not talking about how to change all of that and we were not organizing together to reach a new vision. Our discussions always spilled past the allotted class hour. But our work needed to extend even further outside of the classroom.

To match my students' intellectual stirrings with new texts, I gave them a choice of readings by and about former members of AIM, MECHA, the Young Lords Party, The Combahee River Collective, Little Rock Nine, the Brown Berets, and the Black Panther Party (none of which the students were familiar with, although two had heard of Little Rock Nine). April chose to explore the Young Lords Party, a revolutionary group of young Puerto Ricans in the 1970s. Although she spoke only briefly about the impact of the Young Lords on her thinking in my humanities class, I heard from her friends that everyone in her speech class knew and understood the revolutionary and historical power of young Puerto Rican people that semester! This was the first time April had been aware of Puerto Ricans who were proud of where they had come from and who changed the way things were for her people. The Young Lords seemed to open up a whole new role for April and spur her to work out a new political ideology and movement for herself. When a classmate did his presentation on "Redemption Song" by Bob Marley, April responded with the following comments:

> This song means a lot to me now after watching the video about the Young Lords. I never realized that my people struggled so hard to make a change. My god some were even like me. Light skinned with straight hair and guess what? A lot of them didn't speak Spanish!! I was so happy to hear that I am just as Puerto Rican as them. I don't have to be ashamed for not speaking the language. . . . They stood up and fought for our rights and changed the people's way of looking at themselves. Not only for Puerto Ricans but for all oppressed cultures! Palante![1]

With those final words, tears began to form in her eyes. We had already gone over our time limit and it seemed that everyone was looking at me as if I was supposed to bring closure to the session. I asked if anyone in the room wanted to close the day for us. No one said anything for quite some time. Then one of the men said "I got it," and put on Bob Marley. Yeah, let Bob take us outta here. And with that, everyone packed their things and quietly left.

> Dear April,
>
> Well, I guess this is it, huh? The end.
>
> I sit here and I can't help but think that you set all this off with "Zion"

from an album entitled, "The Miseducation of Lauryn Hill" . . . this issue of our miseducation has been so heavy on my mind all semester.

Let me hit you up with some Carter G. Woodson from his book The Miseducation of the Negro from way back in 1933 . . . him (and Sonny Carson) are where Lauryn took the title and theme of her first album . . . and, thus, your opening presentation! Deep! So let me drop some of his words:

> No systemic effort toward change has been possible, for, taught the same economics, history, philosophy, literature and religion which have established the present code of morals, the Negro's mind has been brought under the control of his oppressor. . . .

I leave you those words because you WILL sit in classrooms where instructors will suggest or make clear with their pedagogy that there is no use in your cussin out/spittin on/throwin out capitalism, the welfare system, university elitism, racism, homophobia, sexism. Do not heed them. You ain't gotta take nuthin you don't want to. Ever.

And whatever happens, keep experimenting with what you want to say and how you want to say it. I see you, now at the end of the semester, MAD OPEN on a spoken word kinda vibe. Do not accept any notions that academic writing can't be that. We got other models. So do your thing, girl. Keep writing and if they don't like it, too bad. We know what they really scared of. They will try to disguise this by suggesting a lie to you: that your "dialect" is inappropriate for academic work because it is merely a stepping stone as you move UP to the sophistication of academic discourse. Puhlllease! Your spoken word style is NOT about what you can't do, but what you CAN! There may be times when you have to cakewalk in university coon shows. But never make the mistake of thinking and writing exactly what some seem to want us to do. Remember the music and complexity you invoke in the language and content of your discourse . . . and then the lie becomes quite apparent.

I started out writing this letter to you as almost a way for me to prepare you for what lies ahead. But now as I close, what I realize is that you are already more than ready . . . you always were. What you have done is prepare me for what lies ahead . . . for the kind of classroom and world I must always strive to create alongside you so that people like us will be able to make up our own minds and change what is in front of us. I will carry you in my heart and head always. I won't say good-bye . . . just Palante!

carmen

Notes

1. Palante-Forward/the name of the Young Lords Party newsletter.

Works Cited

Morrison, Toni. 1970. *The Bluest Eye*. New York: Washington Square.

Pratt, Mary Louise. 1991. "Arts of the Contact Zone." In *Profession 91*. New York: MLA, 33–40.

Reed, Adolph Jr. 2000. *Class Notes: Posing as Politics and Other Thoughts on the American Scene*. New York: New Press.

Woodson, Carter G. 1933. *The Miseducation of the Negro*. Wahington, DC: Associated Publishers.

Wynter, Sylvia. 1990. *Do Not Call Us Negroes: How Multicultural Textbooks Perpetuate Racism*. San Francisco: Aspire Books.

5

A Problem with Writing (about) "Alternative" Discourse

Sidney I. Dobrin

One of the fascinating things regarding recent discussions of "alternative," "hybrid," or "mixed" discourses is that all are discussed as alternatives or melding of academic discourse or Standard Written English. For instance, Patricia Bizzell points out in her article, "Hybrid Academic Discourses: What, Why, How," that "in many, many academic disciplines today, traditional academic discourse must share the field with new forms of discourse that are clearly doing serious intellectual work and are received and evaluated as such, even as they violate many of the conventions of traditional academic discourse" (Bizzell 1999, 8). Bizzell's article is very much a starting point for discussions of hybrid discourses as it introduces the term *hybrid* to discourse studies, and later in her article "Basic Writing and the Issue of Correctness, or, What to do with 'Mixed' Forms of Academic Discourse " as Bizzell rethinks the use of the term, she instead introduces the concept of "mixed" discourse. Yet, in both instances, *hybrid*, *mixed*, and even *alternative* all refer to forms of and reactions to academic discourse—note both of Bizzell's titles. Yet, for users of discourses that are being grafted to academic discourse to create hybrids, the original—or "parent" language (Bizzell notes the difficulty in use of this term, and I agree, but use it here for effect)—discourses are not "alternative"; they *are* discourse. Academic discourse is the alternative. To discuss hybrid discourses is to enact a meta-discourse that is wholly academic and functions to label, identify, and codify "alternative" discourses not as equivalent to academic discourse, but as alternative to that accepted discourse. Think, for instance, about how the phrase "alternative lifestyles" is perceived, the notion not only of difference, but often of inferiority, deviance, as well. To discuss alternative discourse as discourse of difference (albeit Bizzell and others move to show why such alternative discourses are being and should be accepted), as discourse different from academic discourse, in some ways does both disservice to and violence to the nonacademic portions of the hybrid. In fact, as I will explain, academic discourse more often than not appropriates the nonacademic portions of the hybrid. Hence, for many who we ascribe (or encourage) the use of hybrid discourses, we may be enacting a kind of silencing, enacting a move toward hegemony through hybridization rather than an opportunity for empowerment.

In addition, we must understand that all discourse is hybrid, mixed, even "alternative" and that labeling and discussing any particular discourse as somehow a hybrid unlike other discourse or an alternative form of discourse suggests that there are somehow identifiable, codifiable, recognizable discourses that we can clearly identify and study. That is, my argument here is twofold: first, as an underwritten and risky position (with many questions and few answers), that talking about particular discourses as hybrid discourses risks nullifying or neutralizing home discourses. Second, I posit that actually all discourses are mixed or hybrids. Thus, in my title I have placed the term *alternative* in quotes to first identify that no discourse is alternative in that all discourse is both parent or home discourse *and* that all discourse is alternative and mixed.

Hybridization and Neutrality

Discourse itself is a discursive construction. To refer to a particular kind of discourse as "academic" or "parent" or "alternative" is to construct a parameter of what that discourse can and should be, what it can and should say; it is mapped within a particular discursive identity. Discourse itself is a manner in which to construct a narrative, a grammar, a rhetoric. That is to say, like all categories, artifacts, labels that we now recognize as socially constructed—gender, race, class, culture, environment, ideology, etc.—discourse, too, is a construction, a label attributed for the sake of convenience, to provide a vocabulary through which we (think we) can discuss and study discourse. And, of course, it is an academic construction. All discourse, labeled academic or any of the many other terms we use to delineate difference from academic discourse, such as "home discourse," "parent discourse," or "personal discourse," all identify discourses as nonacademic discourse, as other, and do so only in the language of academic discourse. In other words, to invoke a discourse about hybrid discourse, alternative discourse, mixed discourse, is to invoke academic discourse as the language through which, by which, and in which other discourses are codified. The very notion of hybrid discourse serves to fold all other "parent" discourses into the hegemony and master narrative of academic discourse.

In "Writing against Writing: The Predicaments of *Ecriture Féminine* in Composition Studies," Lynn Worsham (1991) makes the poignant point that one of the primary risks in bringing a discourse as radical as *écriture féminine* into contact with academic discussions, as Hélène Cixous offered might be possible in her 1981 essay "The Laugh of the Medusa," would ultimately be the neutralization of the radical edge of the outside discourse and the possibility that it would be subsumed into the master narrative of academic discourse. In a moment, I will explore Cixous' notion of *feminine writing* and its potentially powerful agenda as an alternative discourse and, in turn, both how her notion of *feminine writing* was brought into composition studies and how Worsham then identifies the neutralizing effect of bringing radical French feminism and Cixous' *feminine writing* into contact with academic discourse. In the mean time, it is critically important that we consider this potential of neutralization in our discussions of mixed or alternative discourses. As I understand it, one of the goals of identifying and encouraging the use of mixed discourses is to better equip students (and faculty or other users of discourse as well) to function—more accurately, to survive—in academic settings by encouraging (read: permitting) them to create discourses that blend home or parent discourses—discourses with which they are familiar, comfortable—with academic discourse, and that those new discourses be accepted within the standards set by that academic discourse, that the new discourse not be devalued because it is not academic discourse. The problem is that the relationship that is set up between the two discourses assures academic discourse a position of dominance, and ultimately allows that academic discourse to envelop the mixed discourse—or more specifically the nonacademic portion of that mixed discourse—in such a way that renders it silenced.

Recently, Christian R. Weisser and I completed a book called *Natural Discourse: Toward Ecocomposition* (2002) in which we examine and extend Marilyn Cooper's metaphor of the web to describe one way of thinking/talking about writing and discourse. As we explain it, all writers must enter into the web in order for their writing to reach an audience. Sometimes, that writing may shake the web, disturb it, resist it. However, the further away from the disturbance one is on the web, the less of an impact one feels from that disturbance. Ultimately, the web absorbs shock and maintains its structure. Similarly, as academic discourse allows for—in fact, invites ("come sit beside me," said the spider to the fly)—other "parent" languages to enter into the web, it will absorb those discourses into what is and can be called academic discourse. In doing so, those parent discourses become lost in the web, no longer identifiable as having originated outside of the web; they are merely a part of what the web has become. The web maintains operational integrity. Whether those parent discourses retain any of their original characteristics is dependent upon the power with which they enter the web. They may certainly contribute some new characteristic to the web, but are, nonetheless, rendered part of the web, not outside of the web. This effect, then, serves to silence those parent discourses, robbing them of any disruptive power, robbing them, in fact, of any of the "home-ness," "parent-ness," or even "alternative-ness" they may have had. The web of academic discourse serves to enslave those discourses so that their users must learn to identify academic discourse as the one true parent discourse. Resistence is futile; home discourses will be assimilated.

I think at this point it might be of use to make a slight distinction between the three terms that have been used in conjunction with these conversations:

hybrid, *mixed*, and *alternative*. It seems to me that the first two terms are closely related and have entered this conversation through Bizzell's two important articles. In her first article on the subject, Bizzell suggests that new forms of academic discourses that "violate many of the conventions of traditional academic discourse," but that are accepted on par with traditional academic discourse are a form of hybrid discourse. The metaphor of hybridization, borrowed from the genetic sciences, and in turn, as Bizzell notes is borrowed from postcolonial studies, is wrought with problems, ranging from problems of parentage to problems of offspring infertility. Bizzell, of course, recognized many of the problems with this metaphor, and in her follow-up article she identifies several of these problems.

I want to note specifically Bizzell's critique of the use of the term *hybrid* and her shift to the idea of "mixed" discourses. There is, as Bizzell acknowledges, a difficulty in adopting the term *hybrid*. The term *mixed* is more ambiguous, leaving room for interpretation and maneuvering, and the term is not loaded with the scientific and postcolonial baggage that *hybrid* carries with it. Her move to shift her use of the term is savvy, and (one of the reasons I've always loved Bizzell's work) she's willing to say publically, "perhaps I was wrong. Let me rethink that" (see for instance *Academic Discourse and Critical Consciousness,* 1992). However, what I particularly want to note here is that both the term *hybrid* and the term *mixed* refer to discourses that combine some element of an outside discourse and elements (usually dominant elements) of academic discourse. They are forms of academic discourse. On the other hand, the term *alternative* may also be used to suggest a similar kind of "mixed" discourse, but also has the potential to refer to a discourse that serves as an alternative to academic discourse, that manifests little if any characteristics of academic discourses, that even has the potential (and promise) to disrupt the traditions of academic discourse. This is an important distinction in that while I argue that ultimately bringing any home or parent or even completely alternative discourse in contact with academic discourse—an institutional power of great force—will render the outside discourse neutralized, we do need to see that some alternative discourses are not in any way mixed versions of academic discourses.

In perhaps what has been one of the most important discussions of alternative discourse to date, Hélène Cixous forwards in her essay "The Laugh of the Medusa," an idea of a truly alternative discourse. Cixous proposes that women break with phallocentric discourses and produce a feminine writing unlike any male-centered writing, a kind of writing that disrupts the historical notion of what writing is. Cixous' notion of feminine writing seeks to unbound the discourse of male-centeredness, of history. She proclaims that

> It is by writing, from and toward women, and by taking up the challenge of speech which has been governed by the phallus, that women will confirm women in a place other than that which is reserved in and by the symbolic,

> that is, in a place other than silence. Women should break out of the snare of silence. They shouldn't be conned into accepting a domain which is the margin or the harem. (Cixous 1981, 251)

Yet of this new *feminine writing* for which she calls, she notes that

> It is impossible to *define* a feminine practice of writing, and this is an impossibility that will remain, for this practice can never be theorized, enclosed, coded—which doesn't mean that it doesn't exist. But it will always surpass the discourse that regulates the phallocentric system; it does and will take place in areas other than those subordinated to philosophico-theoretical domination. It will be conceived of only by subjects who are breakers of automatism, by peripheral figures that no authority can ever subjugate. (Cixous 1981, 253)

In other words (though I dare not/would not put words nor interpretation in Cixous' mouth), *feminine writing* cannot be identified by, theorized by, codified by, and ultimately possessed by academic discourse, a phallocentric discourse. It cannot, that is, exist as an alternative to academic discourse because it cannot be represented in relationship with or to academic discourse, yet at the same time, it serves as an example of a truly alternative discourse because it resists and refuses such a relationship with academic discourse, though our discourse of academic discourse knows no other vocabulary by which, through which, in which to address its potential. It is so alternative that it is no longer alternative. And as academic discourse tries to find a position from which to address a discourse as radically beyond alternative as *écriture féminine,* it does so in order to find a place within academic discourse for *écriture féminine* to fit, a place in the web for it to become part of the conversation, not apart from the conversation.

I have quoted Cixous directly here, because to paraphrase her work is to render it powerless. In fact, I might/should argue that to quote her, translated in English for our benefit, is also to neutralize her power. Yet, this article of mine—male-authored for publication (read the historical/ideological significance of that word, too) in academic venue—must assimilate the alternative discourse in order to survive. Yet, I cite her here to show that some alternative discourses are more alternative than others, that some discourses resist entirely becoming parent to a hybrid offspring (to think what Cixous would do with such a concept, particularly tethered to her notion of *feminine writing*, patricide? Infanticide?). And that an alternative discourse may not be in any way mixed. Yet, even the most alternative of discourses risks neutralization when introduced to academic discourse. If academic discourse seeks to absorb a discourse such as *écriture féminine* in any way, even in discussions such as the one I've just provided, it does so as an act of colonizing that discourse for its own purposes and for the sake of constructing a vocabulary about which to discuss that discourse in direct relationship to academic discourse. In essence, my discussion here of Cixous' *feminine writing* does an academic-discursive injustice to the described discourse in the act of describing it. If Cixous' *feminine writing* is truly an alternative discourse, then academic discourse cannot address it or any form of it without subsuming part of it and turning it into academic discourse or some hybrid form of academic discourse.

In her 1988 article, "Writing (with) Cixous," Clara Junker seeks to create an alliance between Cixous' *écriture féminine* and composition studies noting that its radical edge and "the smell of menstrual blood and mothers milk surrounding *l'écriture féminine* has scared off many a potential ally" (Junker 1988, 424). She contends, though, that melding—or "mixing" in the current discourse—*l'écriture féminine* with composition holds some promising possibilities. What Junker suggests is that by borrowing from French feminism and *l'écriture féminine* and bringing them into contact with composition studies that

> what we can do as teachers of composition, then, is to allow for multiple kinds of writing, to invite our students into the non-encore-là and back again so as to encourage them to exist simultaneously in the realms of "reason and folly" (Conley, "Misstery" 75). Whether we consider the long-limbed athletes or the bright-eyed sorority pledges of freshman comp, our students are writing from a "feminine position," as from the margins they seek entry into the symbolic order of the university. By dislocating this order, we might enable student writers to (re)invent themselves and to inscribe différance in(side) academia. (Junker 1988, 434)

In fact, what Junker is calling for is a hybrid discourse that provides students with new accesses to academic discourse. Yet, Junker's hope that these "multiple kinds of writing" will allow students to (re)invent themselves in the university is, perhaps, too wishful, in that it does not take into account the power that academic discourse has over (and on) new, multiple kinds of writing. This danger in bringing discourses such as *l'écriture féminine* in contact with academic discourse has not gone unnoticed.

In her remarkable essay "Writing against Writing: The Predicaments of *Ecriture Féminine* in Composition Studies," Lynn Worsham discusses the awkward, if not aggressive, reaction between the meeting of *écriture féminine* and composition studies (a decidedly academic discourse). "On the one hand," she writes, "we have a discipline that defines itself largely as a discourse community whose positive task is to teach academic discourse(s); on the other, we have a language 'event' that, in its more accessible moments, unleashes a damning critique and denunciation of academic discourse as the instrument par excellence of phallocentricism" (Worsham 1991, 82). What will surely ensue when these two discourses meet, she claims, is that they "will lock in mortal combat—a battle royal—over the issue of academic language" (Worsham 1991, 83). She goes on to theorize how the work of French feminist thinkers such as Cixous, Luce Irigaray, and Julia Kristeva enter into such a battle. Ultimately what Worsham contends is that these two discourses cannot be freely bound together, or in the discourse of this collection, a mixed discourse cannot occur. She explains:

> If composition studies were to make any sustained contact with *écriture féminine*, one of two things would happen. Either composition would neutralize the radical potential of *écriture féminine* in an effort to appropriate it to serve the current aims of the profession and, beyond this, the university, or *écriture féminine* would cast such a suspicion on the whole enterprise of composition studies as an accomplice of phallocentricism that composition would be transformed beyond recognition. (Worsham 1991, 93–94)

In either case, Worsham's prediction as to what happens when discourses mix with academic discourse seems quite accurate: either academic discourse neutralizes the outside discourse or the outside discourse neutralizes academic discourse. But, let's face it, in terms of the kinds of mixed or hybrid discourse, even in terms of the alternative discourse that Bizzell and others allude to growing into academic discourse, it is more plausible that the first of these predictions would occur. As Worsham quotes Julia Kristeva in her epigraph:

> Academic Discourse, and perhaps American University discourse in particular, possesses an extraordinary ability to absorb, digest, and neutralize all of the key, radical, or dramatic moments of thought, particularly, a fortiori, of contemporary thought. (Quoted in Worsham 1991, 82)

This is precisely why hybridization risks neutralizing, silencing, appropriating, even eliminating home discourses that attempt to mix with the institutionally and powerfully entrenched academic discourse.

Now, of course, *écriture féminine* is an extreme example, a discourse defined with an agenda of alternativeness, with a potential for a wholesale battle royal with academic discourse, but what of parent discourses with little or no active motivation to resist academic discourse? How easily can they be subsumed? Identified as other than academic discourse, and whose users are told that this otherness is a flaw, an inferiority, a retardation, few home or parent discourses stand the chance of casting "such a suspicion on the whole enterprise of composition studies as an accomplice" to any one of countless acts of silencing beyond phallocentricism alone. There is a danger in discussing hybrid, mixed, and alternative discourses as a means to invite other discourses into alliance with academic discourse, one of assimilation, of silencing, of neutralization.

Hybridization and Non-codifiable Discourse

It is now clear that within composition studies, the move post-process has taken strong root. In fact, the discussions of hybrid, alternative, and mixed discourses are explicitly part of the post-process era as they address issues not of individual writing processes, but of larger systems of discourse and the political, ideological, and historical environments in which discourse is produced.

These are important conversations, and as I have argued elsewhere, post-process composition is the place from which most of the important conversations in composition emanate. Included among the work being forwarded in post-process theory is the exciting theoretical work of Thomas Kent in the area of paralogic rhetoric. I won't rehash all of Kent's ideas here regarding paralogic rhetoric, as I have addressed that subject in detail in both my book *Constructing Knowledges: The Politics of Theory-Building and Pedagogy in Composition* and in my contribution to Kent's book *Post-Process Theory: Beyond the Writing Process Paradigm*; however, based on the post-process notion of paralogic rhetoric, I want to make my second point in this argument: that all discourses are hybrids, mixed, alternative, and none are codifiable in any way that allow us to identify any as parent or hybrid. That is to say, while I have just discussed alternative discourses in ways that allow for discussion, there is some serious question as to whether such discussions can even be had as all discourses (be they academic discourses, public discourses, personal discourses) are never stagnant long enough to codify, study, identify characteristics, label in ways that allow us to identify parent discourses or mixed variants.

What I am arguing here is that, ultimately, we must identify all discourses as hybrids. As Bizzell notes in "Basic Writing and the Issue of Correctness, or, What to Do with 'Mixed' Forms of Academic Discourse," "In order to conceptualize the hybridization of discourses from two distinct 'parents,' I have provided a taxonomy of the traits of traditional academic discourse. Doing so, however, seems to suggest that traditional academic discourse was a fixed and unchanging entity until very recently" (Bizzell 2000, 6). That is to say (not wanting to put words/interpretations in Bizzell's mouth either), discourses such as academic discourse are not mono-discursive entities; they exist as amalgams, anomalies, hybrids in a continual state of flux, (re)invention, (re)inscription. Paralogic rhetoric (quite simply—or overly simplified) posits that all moments of discursive interactions, each communicative act, is unique unto itself, and that in each of these unique moments, communicators rely on series of past theories developed through past communicative experiences in order to create a passing theory—a theory of how to engage the current communicative/discursive scenario. All passing theories become prior theories, and communicators, users of discourse, continually develop their prior theories to become more efficient users of discourse. However, because no two discursive scenarios are identical, discourse itself is/becomes a perpetually shifting set of phenomena. And, as Kent argues in his 1991 article "On the Very Idea of a Discourse Community," there may be no accurate way to label any singular discursive act as being a part of a discourse community or even being able to label discourse communities. That is, if we are to accept the paralogic rhetorical understanding of discourse, there can actually be no codifiable "academic discourse" and talking about any particular discourse as an identifiable entity is to engage in an act of charity for the sake of convenience. So, Bizzell is exactly right in suggesting that academic discourse is not a fixed entity.

To turn back to Worsham for a moment, I think it is important to note that she is clear that

> When French feminists say that *écriture féminine* is a new language, epistemologists in several disciplines quite predictably set to work trying to identify and isolate its distinctive features and the source of its coherence as a system of discourse. They expect to find, if not a theory, then a loosely related group of theories or propositions about language, "woman," "the feminine," or "female experience," including the nature of feminine textual practice. They assume an interpretive stance toward *écriture féminine* as an object of knowledge and a repository of truth. (Worsham 1991, 84)

Of course, what Worsham is saying is that (certain) discourse theorists seek to codify, identify, label what is *écriture féminine* and what is not. Yet Worsham, like Cixous and Junker, is clear that *écriture féminine* resists such cartographic attempts:

> Submitted to the discursive obligations of political interpretation, however, *écriture féminine* is typically found lacking, fraught with contradictions, riddled with (theoretical) inconsistencies, and short on concrete strategies for changing the material conditions of everyday women's lives. (Worsham 1991, 84)

Though many would argue that discourses in general have provided access to changing everyday folk's lives, I argue that what Worsham has to say about *écriture féminine* is true of all discourse, that all discourse is wrought with contradictions, does not hold still long enough for (theoretical) stability, and is, ultimately, in a perpetual state of hybridization, metamorphoses, anomalies, inconsistencies.

This being the case, all discourse, then, is a perpetual mix of individual prior theories developing passing theories. Passing theories are developed not solely in one kind of discursive scenario—academic discourse, for instance—but in an array of discursive encounters every day. Over periods of time, then, individual users of discourse mix discourses to develop their own passing theories in ways that leave no one discourse free of influence from other prior theories. What we then label as "discourse communities" are merely convenient ways to label what we see as similar conventions of discourse, though paralogic rhetoric identifies that these codifications are false, mere matters of convenience and not actually identifiable. If, then, each user of discourse is internally creating hybrids with each moment of discursive interaction—each moment of triangulation—and we then attempt to identify individual discourses through conveniently labeled like-conventions, these moments of similarity are ultimately hybrids developed from a milieu of hybrids. Mixing is perpetual, ongoing, never-ending. Each instance of discursive interaction, each discourse that we (think we can) label are always already (said under erasure) hybrid and are always in process of creating new mixes, alternatives. Academic discourse is in a fluctuating act of hybridization everyday in every classroom; no matter what any student does, says, writes, they are contributing to that mix, materially changing academic discourse. Granted that web will absorb those changes, assimilate them, make them silent in the larger power of academic discourse, but that is a function of any discourse as institutionally powerful as one such as academic discourse, to steer the hybridization for its benefit. Parent discourses come to academic discourse, they create hybrids, and they are silenced. The very nature (if there is such a thing) of discourse—that which we construct—is a nature of hybridization. All discourse is hybrid; all discourse is academic.

Conclusion

My conclusion should, at this point, seem fairly straightforward: we may be risking silencing and neutralizing a good number of discourses when they interact with academic discourse. To make a push to include more forms of hybrid or mixed discourses is certainly important, and I encourage any work that promotes change, shift, alteration in the entrenchment of academic discourse. However, I think it is crucial that we carefully examine the total ramifications of such work. Also, I am concerned that we overlook the more encompassing notion of discourse as a perpetual hybrid as we try to establish boundaries for what is and can be hybrid academic discourse.

To be blunt about it, I'm not sure I agree with discussions of alternative discourses, hybrid discourses. If all discourses are hybrid and discourse itself is not codifiable in any way that can lend to identifying what is alternative and what isn't, I'm concerned with the agenda for creating such a conversation because of the potentially silencing outcome for parent discourses. Also, we need to understand that in our conversations about hybrid discourses, alternative discourses, mixed discourses, our agendas may be honorable in hoping to provide more access to our students, to open spaces for their home discourses, to encourage critique and change of academic discourse, but we must be conscious of the fact that what we risk in trying to change academic discourse versus what our students risk is a very different thing, with very different material ramifications. What we risk in saying that it is good to bring parent discourse to academic discourses, in saying that the creation of hybrid discourses is of use, results in an exclusively different response than if a student presents a text to an instructor, making use of home or parent discourses and—whether intentionally or not, whether efficiently or not—fractures the boundaries of academic discourses and creates a form of hybrid, mixed, alternative discourse. We must not presume our conversations as having the same material consequences. For instance, let us consider a minor infraction of academic discourse convention and ask as to what if I had submitted this piece with the Works Cited page on the first page, which I was tempted to do both for the visual effect and because when I served as coeditor of *A Journal of Composition Theory* and was reading large numbers of submitted articles, the first thing

I would read was the Works Cited page to see what the author was working with—an alternative way of reading. In fact, whenever I pick up a new article or book, I always look first at the Works Cited page and make some judgment about the value of the work, and I'm willing to bet this is a common way for academics to read, a common way for many of us to assess worth before we read the body of the text. I would even argue that it is a better way of reading scholarship. It may not be very alternative in the ways that *écriture féminine* is alternative. It may not even be a hybrid discourse as it involves no second parent (asexual reproduction of a hybrid?), yet it questions academic conventions in a flagrant—if not overly simplistic—manner. And if I had made such a maneuver? Chances are that most editors would simply "correct" my mistake and re-insert the Works Cited page where it "belonged." If, in this collection, I had explained my textual adjustment, it may have been left as is as an example of "alternative," as a trite, token example. But how many readers would wonder if this new printing was a publisher's error. And, what if I submitted articles in this format to other forums? Certainly such a disruption would not be tolerated, even if I explained that my format was designed as an aid to readers. Or, if it was tolerated, how soon would it become a fixture for some writers to use this form? Even if no other article ever appeared in this format, the simple fact that it was published identifies it as acceptable (if not trivial) academic discourse. Certainly, my position as professor, published writer, compositionist allows me to take such chances. But what if a student had used a similar strategy, even explained it? Chances are the reactions would be less accepting. Chances are, this thing we've called academic discourse would swallow up, silence the student's parent discourse, her voice, her power.

My fear here, of course, is that discussions of hybrid discourses, when set up as discourses in relation to academic discourse, will overlook the issue of how powerful academic discourse can be. As we've seen, institutionally entrenched discourses like academic discourse appropriate nonacademic portions of the hybrids with little effort because of the material weight academic discourse carries and the fact that it serves a gatekeeping function to upper-middle class, phallocentric values. What I am ultimately cautious of here is that in discussions of hybrid, mixed, or alternative discourse, that we not overlook the assimilative powers of academic discourse when it enters into a hybrid relationship with a nonacademic discourse. I also wonder, in conjunction with this fear, whether or not some nonacademic discourses are better off not having contact with academic discourse, because where as in instances of genetic hybridization also necessitate moments of genetic displacement (the opposite of hybridization) in order to maintain diversity. Briefly, according to evolutionary biology, when two species converge and exchange genes (the act of hybridization) the resulting hybrid is ultimately a move toward similarity. That is, some of the original content is lost. However, in displacement, when two species engage, they move apart, maintaining genetic difference, adding to diversity. Of course, in considering this notion of displacement, it is necessary to consider that discourse and genetics are not equivalent. That is, for compositionists, it is important to note that it is impossible for two discourses or cultures to converge and then move apart while maintaining some unchanged, authentic, original form (or self). But then the question arises, how can we discuss nonacademic discourses and afford the power of those discourses to their users in academic settings without risking assimilation? I don't believe that we can. And second, because of this perpetual assimilative structure of academic discourse and because of the non-codifiable nature of academic discourse and all discourse, perhaps the notion of mixed or hybrid discourses is itself a mislabeling. That is a problem for discussing and enacting mixed and hybrid discourses.

Works Cited

Bizzell, Patricia. 1992. *Academic Discourse and Critical Consciousness*. Pittsburgh: Univ. of Pittsburgh Press.

———.1999. "Hybrid Academic Discourses: What, Why, How." *Composition Studies* 27:7–21.

———. 2000. "Basic Writing and the Issue of Correctness, or, What to Do with 'Mixed' Forms of Academic Discourse." *Journal of Basic Writing* 19:4–12.

Cixous, Hélène. 1981. "The Laugh of the Medusa." *New French Feminisms*, edited by Elaine Marks and Isabelle de Courtivion, 245–64. Brighton, MA: Harvester.

Conley, Verena A. 1984. *Hélène Cixous:Writing The Feminine*. Lincoln: Univ. of Nebraska Press.

Cooper, Marilyn. 1986. "The Ecology of Writing." *College English* 48:364–75.

Dobrin Sidney. 1997. *Constructing Knowledges: The Politics of Theory-Building and Pedagogy in Composition*. New York: State Univ. of New York Press.

———. 1999. "Paralogic Hermeneutic Theories, Power, and the Possibility for Liberating Pedagogies." *Post-process Theory: Beyond the Writing Process Paradigm*, edited by Thomas Kent, 132–148. Carbondale: Southern Illinois Univ. Press.

Dobrin, Sidney I., and Christian R. Weisser. 2002. *Natural Discourse: Toward Ecocomposition*. Albany: State Univ. of New York Press, forthcoming.

Junker, Clara. 1988. "Writing (with) Cixous." *College English* 50:424–36.

Kent, Thomas. 1991. "On the Very Idea of a Discourse Community." *College Composition & Communication* 42:425–45.

———, ed. 1999. *Post-Process Theory: Beyond the Writing Process Paradigm*. Carbondale: Southern Illinois Univ. Press.

Worsham, Lynn. 1991. "Writing against Writing: The Predicaments of *Ecriture Féminine* in Composition Studies." *Contending with Words: Composition and Rhetoric in a Postmodern Age*, edited by Patricia Harkin and John Schilb, 82–104. New York: MLA.

6

Being an Ally

Helen Fox

Here is my dilemma. I have been put in charge of a program at my university that will expand our services to graduate students who have trouble with writing. In fact, I proposed this project. The precipitating incident was an African American student who came to me for help because she was about to fail out of her Ph.D. program. Her papers were unfocused, her professors told her. She rambled. She introduced all sorts of irrelevant ideas. Did she really understand the reading? That, too, had been questioned. Maybe she had never learned to read and write properly. Maybe she wasn't up to graduate level work. She was crying as she told me what her professors had intimated, but she was angry, too, and I considered that a good sign.

She had come back to school after working for years in the corporate world. Oh yes, writing had been part of her job. No one *there* had suggested she didn't know how to write. So I asked her if she could write an executive summary of one of her rambling research papers. She'd try that, she said. It came back in near-perfect form: a crisp, focused, one-page report. None of her professors had suggested any link between writing for business and writing for graduate school. I doubt if they knew she had written high-level documents as part of her job. After I assured her—no, guaranteed her—that she would not fail her comprehensive examinations if she came in regularly, we started through her papers. I would be the interested listener and she would translate, sentence by sentence, from her tangled phrases into no-nonsense business prose, with frequent asides to fill me in on details she had left out. "Write that down!" I would say. "*That's* interesting. Why didn't you put *that* in?"

It's not that graduate students like these have "trouble with writing," I realized. Here they are in a high-stress situation where they are faced with new intellectual demands, new social relationships with professors and advisers, and extremely high expectations of themselves. And compounding this, very few of their professors give them a clear idea of the forms and structures their new audiences expect, or provide practice in building up from shorter, low-stakes papers to the kinds of writing they need to do for their examinations and longer projects. So when their writing falls apart, their worst fears about themselves are confirmed, and this only reinforces societal notions of incompetence about people of color, about women, about second language writers, about people from working-class backgrounds, about people who were raised speaking a language or dialect or regional or class or cultural variation of the language of power—that is, just about everybody who has been "invited" into the university in the past hundred years.

Anyway, at the end of the semester, after her committee was satisfied with her "new" writing skills, this student sent me a friend who was in even more trouble than she was. The friend had been doing doctoral research for years in South Africa, and she, too, was about to fail because her writing had become confused and stilted as she struggled with the forms and language of academic discourse. But as she described the complexity of her project with the passion and insight of our best professors, I could just see it—another great mind missing from the academy because nobody had the time or interest or faith in her as an intellectual to help her work her material into academic prose. So I got mad, too, and I proposed this graduate writing project, and by now we've started all kinds of initiatives: more one-on-one tutoring; a workshop series, a summer dissertation laboratory for writers whose progress has been slow, a website with links to writing resources all over the nation.

But the more I work on this project, the more nervous I get. Because what I'm finding, as if it were news to me, is that what graduate students need to learn is the language and values of the academy, its styles and structures, its vocabularies and uses of voice, its relationships with authorities, its attitudes toward evidence, its beliefs about what is worthy of being discussed and what is not. And that is exactly what this book has been questioning. What passes for "good academic writing" is socially and culturally constructed by scholars who are both narrow in their vision and exclusionary about their club. And the terms of membership in this club are, of course, those of acculturation; to join, one must discard perfectly reasonable ways of thinking and communicating and, in the process, learn to disparage those ways, and pity those who cling to them. As Chris Schroeder says, academic discourses are "the sanctioned versions of literacy—not only certain ways of writing and reading but also, through these practices, versions of who to be and how to see the world" (2001, 6). So why am I spending my time helping students gain access to a profession that, to put it mildly, does not have their best interests at heart?

Second part of my dilemma: the obvious. Students want access, even if it isn't in their best interests or defined in their terms. So what kind of an ally would I be if I declined to help them achieve their academic and professional goals? After all, *I* have a place in the academy—a place, by the way, where I can choose to write in the "alternative," personal, storytelling way I prefer at least some of the time. I can also write a dry, "objective," grant that has a good chance of being funded. I can write an oped piece critiquing the educational priorities at my school. I can even write a book proposal that convinces an editor that alternative discourses make sense. Should I give up the responsibility of teaching my students the rules because I don't approve of the game—a game I can play just fine?

Even more disturbing—I actually enjoy writing in Strunk and White style. I memorized that book years ago when I had aspirations to write for the newspapers. And to be frank, I have noticed in myself a compulsion to indoctrinate others in its rules for good writing. "Prefer the specific to the general, the definite to the vague, the concrete to the abstract." "Vigorous writing is concise." "Different *from*—not different than." My peer tutors will tell you that I send back their papers again and again, ungraded, save for the dreaded "RW"—rewrite—if they say something halfhearted, or imprecise, or only vaguely intellectual. I want my students to care about the sounds and meanings of words. I want them to notice the beat of a sentence, its power on a reader's attention. I want them to learn the fears and prejudices of their readers and speak to them, manipulate them, pander to them. I want them to become sorcerers, with occult knowledge of all the taboos, charms, and ritual combinations, the exquisite poisons and their antidotes: *these* words transform the reader's mental landscape, while *these* cannot. As witchcraft, writing is high art. And as a witch, I am bound to teach the spells to those who show promise. Though mastering the spells of one sort does not preclude learning of those that work their magic on readers in other contexts, other countries, other time periods, other languages . . .

Which brings me to a third complication. Learning to write for readers who hold different cultural assumptions and expectations can be broadening, even transformative, but it is not an easy thing, as international students will tell us. Cultural ways of knowing and communicating are so basic to our conception of ourselves, learned so early and internalized so thoroughly that we hardly consider them cultural at all, but rather "smart thinking," "effective communication," "good writing," or just—"normal." Being told that your writing is "not analytical enough" or "too descriptive," or "hard to read" by professors who take Strunk and White maxims for good writing as universal, can be confusing and disheartening. So the answer is, teach the teachers, right? That's what this book is about. Let's all learn those different communication styles and incorporate them into our classroom assignments, and eventually, into a more truly global curriculum. Ha. Easier said than done.

To explain this part of my dilemma, I'd like to go back to my book, *Listening to the World* (1994), where I categorize (in a nice, academically analytical way) three fundamental differences in the ways east and west approach oral and written communication and the thinking that lies behind them. First, a preference for indirect forms of discourse versus a preference for straightforwardness and specificity; second, promoting the goals of the group versus those of the individual; and third, valuing ancient knowledge and wisdom versus valuing novelty and the peculiar kind of creativity that comes from the idea of an independent mind, a mind that is its own agent, its own authority. In fact, I argue that these differences characterize not only the east-west dichotomy so dear to Kipling (and so problematic to postmodernists), but also, the split between those touched most strongly by the western tradition (whatever country, or class or subculture they live in) and those who make up the rest of the world—the "world majority."

The easiest of these differences to recognize is a preference, on the part of the world majority, for subtle or discursive communication that puts the responsibility for interpretation and understanding on the audience, rather than on the speaker or writer. Many composition teachers and ESL instructors have noticed the results of these cultural values in writing of students from other countries and language backgrounds: the senior from Brazil, effortlessly bilingual, who writes elegantly about issues that seem totally extraneous to her problem statement; the Japanese freshman who starts each paragraph with abstract, general comments that lead gradually up to her point, with the expectation that the reader will not mind waiting patiently for the meaning to come into focus, and then beginning again, slowly, with other general abstractions before getting to the gist of the next paragraph, and so on. Or the Chinese American sophomore, writing about his father's profession as a traditional healer, who tries to convince us of the credibility of eastern medicine not by giving reasons, but by simply listing the names and categories and functions of various herbs, letting us come to the conclusion that such a pharmacology must have a history as distinguished and complex as the western and thus, have similar value and effectiveness. These are not writing styles per se, but tendencies to display learning and intelligence in a way that is sophisticated and interesting and sensitive to particular audience expectations. For regardless of what they have learned about English language and style in their ESL classes, students brought up to value subtlety or to give sensitive and thorough attention to context feel it is only natural to spare the reader the boredom of a plodding text with its step-by-step logic, its frequent and obvious signposting, its words chosen more for their precision than for their power of suggestion.

Now if this tendency toward indirectness were the extent of the cultural differences, we might not have too much trouble imagining that the U.S. university could eventually move out of its narrow idea of good writing and good thinking if pressed to do so by the likes of the authors in this volume. Building on the kinds of indirection the university has long considered "normal"—poetry and fiction, for example, and perhaps incorporating some of the abstractness and discursiveness of other western cultural styles such as those of, say, French philosophy, and perhaps encouraging the more unapologetically fragmented postmodern argument that is now becoming visible, even mainstream, in the writing of English and American Culture and Women's Studies faculty, we might be able to enlarge the academy's vision and make students who value indirection feel more at home—at least in some university departments, some of the time.

But traditions of indirection are based on deeper assumptions about how society should work that seem directly at odds with those of many U.S. university instructors, especially the most progressive among us. And that makes introducing these alternative forms in the U.S. university a little more tricky. For if we wanted to transcend the boundary between western and world majority communication and thinking styles, we would have to agree—or more than agree, I think—we'd have to be *convinced* that maintaining group solidarity or harmony is more important than being yourself, that tradition is more meaningful than history, that aesthetic or spiritual order, created out of an unspoken, or perhaps "felt" dialogue between subject and object, is more valuable than rational order that provides a framework for objective analysis; and that the students' role is to thoroughly internalize what others have done rather than to critically question their own assumptions or the words of their teachers and texts.[1]

Let's look at some of these styles and the values that lie behind them. If you come from a society that in general, promotes group solidarity or harmony over self-expression or self-actualization, you have learned very early to pay close attention to others' unexpressed thoughts and feelings. Because you "know" what others are experiencing, you don't need to put everything into words. And because you expect others to pay attention to your own unexpressed thoughts and feelings, you assign more responsibility for miscommunication to the reader or listener.[2] In a group-oriented society, questions about personal identity — who you really are or what you are becoming, what your true voice sounds like or whether you can make your mark on the world before you retire—all of these are less important than your feelings of belonging and connectedness and agreement with what everyone in your group thinks, and does, and aspires to.[3] Thus when you write, you are not so concerned about whose ideas are whose. Intellectual property isn't much of an issue to you. The idea of plagiarism may seem curiously illogical. Your goal in communication is expressing what "we" think, rather than what you as an individual might really think. But your primary goal isn't what many U.S. educators would call "effective communication" at all, but rather effective listening and interpretation. Sometimes you are listening to nature. Sometimes you are listening to a painting, or an arrangement of stones, or an elder, a teacher, a public figure. Often, just as in any culture, you are listening to people tell their stories. These narratives might be incredibly rich and complex, but they also might leave out details that in the U.S. university context are considered essential. You are supposed to hint and imply, and your audience is supposed to "get it." And in your culture, they *can* get it, both because they have been brought up to attend to the unspoken, and because they have agreed to agree with you.

In most of the world's cultures, tradition is a more meaningful interpretive context than history. In a fascinating, difficult book called *Thinking Through Confucius* (1987), David Hall and Roger Ames attempt to interpret central problems in western philosophy by using Confucian categories of experience.

These categories, the authors claim, have been misinterpreted in the past because of translation difficulties, not only in finding English words that describe the Chinese experience, but also in understanding that experience well enough to communicate it at all. The authors' idea that tradition, rather than history is the interpretive context for both Chinese philosophy and Chinese cultural experience can be applied more widely, I believe, to any culture that sees itself as more rooted in "traditional" than "enlightenment" values (although those terms are problematic in so many maddening, yet interesting ways).

Hall and Ames remind us that the central concept of history is the idea of agency. Historical figures act, and historians and philosophers interpret their acts by determining causes and meanings of events. Their task, and the task of the student of history, is to break down the stream of life into pieces, assign value to each of these pieces, shuffle them around, and fit them into an analytical grid or framework that will help make meaning of the chaos of events. In contrast, societies where tradition is more central are not as concerned with what caused this or that event in the past, or who invented this or that custom or came up with a particular idea. Even Confucius himself, the authors suggest, may not be an historical figure at all, but a composite, a "'corporate' person who is continually being seen in a new way by virtue of the participation of later thinkers in the ongoing transmission of cultural values" (Hall and Ames 1987, 24). Since the purpose of tradition is to "maintain institutional and cultural continuity with a minimum of conscious intervention," (22) the task of the student is to "become aware," (44) to appropriate and embody one's cultural tradition, to memorize, and internalize, and finally, when one becomes a scholar, to elaborate and refine and articulate human values in order to preserve them, to transmit them to the next generation.

Thus, when students who come from world majority cultures are perplexed or frustrated at the insistence of U.S. instructors that they dissect their personal experience and make explicit meaning of it, that they come up with their own thesis to analyze a piece of literature, or that they apply a psychological theory or historical framework to particular events, we can understand, perhaps, how uncomfortable our progressive teaching can make them feel. But if, in an attempt to introduce alternative discourses into the U.S. university, we would say, "All right, let's value the inherent feeling of rightness of ritual rather than being so concerned about causes; let's internalize group norms and stop making such a fuss about being individuals; let's get away from this cult of creative problem solving, and get into feeling and sensing the rightness of our cultural heritage. . . ." Well, here we would be deep in the layers of a logical dilemma, unless we were really ready to go out on a limb and put aside strict logic, and say that things can be understood or valued in seemingly opposite ways simultaneously, which, I learned was possible—even "normal"—in India, where I myself became perplexed and frustrated as a young science teacher, many years ago, not yet having examined my own cultural assumptions.

Of course assumptions can be stronger or weaker, and they can change, gradually, as one begins to understand a new cultural context. Since universities and even high schools abroad are based to some extent on western models, world majority students come with a general idea of the assumptions and expectations of U.S. professors. But because assumptions about knowledge and communication style are so deeply embedded in human ways of thinking, major difficulties still arise.

A Thai student once came to me for help on his statement of purpose for a Ph.D. program in architecture. He wanted to research contemporary Thai architectural theory, which, he told me, has never been written down, nor is it mentioned in lectures or professional conversations. But it is there, he believes, inherent in the buildings themselves, and in the minds of architects whom he planned to interview about how they conceptualized and designed their particular work. Their thinking has been influenced by architectural "theory" of the past—similarly unwritten and unspoken, but possibly referred to obliquely in ancient documents, which he planned to research.

I love this idea, that theory can be embedded in buildings, that it can be deduced from indirect references in ancient texts and in the subtle, discursive, or highly contextualized speech of interview subjects, and that one might use these hints and essences as "evidence" that the theory is there. But because U.S. academic assumptions are individualist, because they assume the rightness of explicit communication, solid evidence, and theory that is based on principles, or general laws, I was quite sure this student would have trouble with his dissertation committee. For the process he had in mind was holistic, empathetic, and appreciative, requiring much skill in creative interpretation. And the knowledge to be gained would not be entirely separate from the texts or the buildings or the people who designed them, and thus would be resistant to demands for clarity and critical analysis.

It's not that there are no examples in western culture of such ways of thinking and communicating. Quakers (invoking my own religious affiliation here) have a way of determining "the sense of the Meeting" that resonates with the process the Thai architecture student wanted to employ in his Ph.D. research. In a Quaker Meeting for Business (which is called "Meeting for Worship for Business"), Friends have a chance to speak their feelings and ideas about a matter to be decided with no interruptions, no requirements to follow the previous point or stick exactly to the subject. After everyone has had the opportunity to speak their mind—though no one is required to do so—the Clerk determines, for the record, what the group as a whole has decided, that is, "the sense of the Meeting," not by tallying yeas and nays, as in Robert's Rules of Order, and not exactly by consensus, either, but by a felt sense of how the body as a whole is responding to the question at hand. It takes practice, concentration, empathy, attention, and something more, perhaps, something English has no adequate vocabulary to describe, to feel the sense of the "corporate body" made up of the many opinionated and highly individualistic people Quakers are known to be. Even with its individualistic overlay, finding the sense of the Meeting is a collectivist process; it's more of a back and forth sensing, a felt dialogue, than it is a tallying or an analysis. It is a beautiful, meaningful interaction. But if you or I were to become expert in this practice and then try to introduce it into the university as a new variety of data collection, if we were to claim that we "know" how people think without asking them explicitly, or without having something we could call clear evidence, we would have trouble with the sociology department and the political science department, not to mention the economics people and the geologists, and the biostatisticians, and so on. Like it or not, the U.S. university is still based on a powerful, but at the same time, extremely narrow conception of thinking and communicating that has made possible all sorts of scientific explorations and ideas and inventions. But imagine its potential to understand and value and dignify all of human experience if it were only aware of the cultural assumptions, the rigid rules of logic, the dismissal of the spiritual, and the fear of the unfamiliar, the unacknowledged uses of power that limit its imagination . . .

* * *

Well, okay, that's all very nice. But if I want to be an ally I have to be more than wistful. I have to figure out what I'm going to do with my dilemma. If I want to be an ally, I do have to teach my craft rigorously, both because students want to learn it, and because like all cultural forms, it is powerful and pleasing if practiced well. Strunk and White style (and its cousins, the academic discourse family) can be useful, even beautiful, to those who have been trained to appreciate its logic, its spare use of words, its almost mathematical precision. The problem is that its proponents tend to ignore or disparage almost everything else. Evidence. Ways of being and knowing the world. Logical, reasonable, expectations of readers and listeners: slow down, listen, work harder at deciphering the meaning. Or wait until you are more sophisticated, more learned, and the meaning will come to you. Listen to the emotion, to the story, without objecting that what happened to the author's grandmother may not be generalizeable—for isn't it possible that Grandmother is not a person at all, but a metaphor?

I need to teach students these things. All students. It's not enough to teach second language students, under-prepared students, graduate students who have been abandoned by their dissertation committees. I also need to teach mainstream students, English majors, future English teachers who have never imagined that they, too, speak with an accent, or that their idea of good writing is influenced by their culture (since they believe they have no culture), or that African American Vernacular English is a rule-governed dialect or even a language in its own right. I need to seek out students at our "world class" university who have never met an international student on campus, or who try to avoid Asian-looking instructors, believing that their speech will be unintelligible. I need to recruit students to my classes who have interacted with the rest of the world only from the deck of a cruise ship, or through the purchase of cocaine on a certain forbidden city street, or who wear the colorful artifacts of native cultures and a hip, ethnic haircut guaranteed to shock their mom, all the while declaring themselves world citizens, color-blind. And I've got to remember to stop putting these students down, because they need me as an ally too, maybe more than anyone.

I've got to continue to question myself, shake up my own certainties. Believing as I do that cultural differences are real and significant, I need to pay more attention to the ways that those boundaries are blurred and changing. I need to remind myself and my students of the ways that cultural learning is complicated by gender, religion, education, family, class, life experiences, personality—not to mention global capitalism, world trade agreements, transnational border crossings, the explosion of information on the Internet. I need to remember, as Native American author Carl Urion says, that "(a)ny global generalization about the separate traditions of (discourse) has to be formulated cautiously, because both traditions are complex. Apparent appositions, maybe even contradictions, are inherent in both traditions. . . . (B)road characterizations can be either instructive and explanatory, or they can be reductionist and simplistic" (1999, 7). I need to preface my discussions of cultural difference with the reminder that there are many ways to be black, many ways to be Chinese, or Israeli, or Mexican American.

I need to listen for intriguing questions to bring into my classrooms. Here are some from Shondel Nero, a native of Guyana, Montreal, and New York, and a professor of TESOL who specializes in teaching Caribbean Creole English speakers: "What do we mean by a 'native speaker' of English? Is nativeness linguistic or political? On what basis do we determine nativeness, and who gets to make that determination? Furthermore, what do we mean by English? Given the globalization of English, can any one country or culture claim exclusive ownership of the language?"[4]

These should be the questions for discussion in graduate seminars, faculty development sessions, and undergraduate writing classes, alongside and equal to the standard discussions of voice, style, authority, teaching strategies, assignments, evaluation of standard academic discourse and writing across the curriculum. Here is another quote for discussion from linguist Rosina Lippi-Green (1997, 63–64):

> We do not, cannot under our laws, ask people to change the color of their skin, their religion, their gender, but we regularly demand of people that they suppress or deny the most effective way they have of situating themselves socially in the world. "You may have dark skin,'" we tell them, "but you must not sound Black." "You can wear a yarmulke if it is important to you as a Jew, but lose the accent." "Maybe you come from the Ukraine, but can't

> you speak real English?" "If you didn't sound so corn-pone, people would take you seriously." "You're the best salesperson we've got, but must you sound gay on the phone?"

And throw into the mix thoughts from activist-academic Frances Aparicio (1998). Celebrating multiculturalism is problematic, she asserts, when white privilege is unquestioned. At the same time bilingual education programs for families whose native language is Spanish are being dismantled by well-financed media campaigns, middle-class Anglos increasingly send their children to Spanish immersion programs in order to add to their educational experiences and "foster positive self-esteem, heightened social status, professional enhancement, and economic gain" (10). Meanwhile, native Spanish speakers "are silenced for speaking Spanish, for not speaking English, for speaking only English, for mixing both, for not owning either lengua" (16). Latino college students who want to learn or improve their Spanish are derided by other students as taking "easy classes," and are humiliated in class when their Spanish is not "pure"—in other words, mixed with English. " . . . Latino/as who carry a Hispanic last name yet need to be taught basic Spanish, usually by non-native speakers, experience contradictory feelings about their cultural identity and authority. While they may feel empowered reclaiming the "lost" language of their heritage and of their past identity—*a language that was once who I was*—feelings of infantilization, cultural betrayal, inauthenticity, and public humiliation surface during the process of learning" (16).

I need to look at the assumptions behind the questions I ask, the comments I make, the advice I give. And I need to ask you to do the same:

> "Should we teach them . . .?" *(Paternalism stands tall and kindly behind this question. Or maternalism, reflective, deeply concerned: Should we teach them academic discourse at all? Should we teach them in their own dialects? Should we allow both? Should we? Should we?)*
>
> "How should we teach them . . .?" *(the inevitability of acculturation lurking behind this ordinary, everyday question)*
>
> "Their ways of knowing are different and wonderful." *(So it is reported on the travel channel.)*
>
> "Which is better, our way or their way?" *(Dualism is bad, remember? Complexity is good.)*
>
> The simple truth—or is it simplemindedness?—in the mantra: "Western = direct; Eastern = indirect."
>
> "They may have trouble with western forms of analysis." *(True, but can't you hear the history of racism and colonialism reverberate in that statement?)*

Why do we have to choose between individualism and collectivism, critical thinking and harmony, direction and indirection? Why not both-and, or sometimes one and sometimes another? *(Why not create a cafeteria of cultural values?)*

The color-blind, power-blind, culture-blind assumptions in: "We're all humans with the same abilities, dreams, and desires, and thus the same interests in expressing ourselves clearly and concisely, with correct citations and in Standard English."

The power play masked in intellectualism: "There are no cultural boundaries in this postmodern world since all cultures are so fluid and dynamic, boundaries so permeable—so can we really talk about culture anymore at all? *("the postmodern fascination with the exchange of cultural property and with completely deracinated identity can seem for many people of color less like emancipation and more like intensified alienation"* [Fusco, 1995, 27]).

Notes

1. See Chapter 7 for Haixia Lan's thorough and knowledgeable explanation of the differences between Chinese and U.S. cultural assumptions.

2. See work on individualism and collectivism such as Singelis, Theodore M. and William J. Brown. 1995. "Culture, Self, and Collectivist Communication." *Human Communication Research* 21 (3):354–89; Triandis, Harry C., Robert Bontempo, Marcelo J. Villareal, 1988. "Individualism and Collectivism: Cross-Cultural Perspectives on Self-Ingroup Relations." *Journal of Personality and Social Psychology.* 54 (2):323–38.

3. See, for example, Hord, Fred Lee, and Jonathan Scott Lee, eds. 1995. *I Am Because We Are: Readings in Black Philosophy.* Amherst: Univ. of Massachusetts Press.

4. Personal communication.

Works Cited

Aparicio, Francis. 1998. "Whose Spanish, Whose Language, Whose Power?" *Indiana Journal of Hispanic Literatures* 12 (Spring):5–25.

Fox, Helen. 1994. *Listening to the World.* Urbana, IL: National Council of Teachers of English.

Fusco, Coco. 1995. *English Is Broken Here.* New York: New Press.

Hall, David L., Ames, Roger T. 1987. *Thinking Through Confucius.* Albany: State Univ. of New York Press.

Lippi-Green, Rosina. 1997. *English with an Accent.* New York: Routledge.

Schroeder, Christopher. 2001. *ReInventing the University.* Logan: Utah State Univ. Press.

Urion, Carl. 1999. "Changing Academic Discourse About Native Education: Using Two Pairs of Eyes." *Canadian Journal of Native Education* 23:1.

7

Contrastive Rhetoric
A Must in Cross-Cultural Inquiries

Haixia Lan

To say that contrastive rhetoric is necessary in cross-cultural inquiries is to take for granted a twofold premise: diversity is both inevitable and healthy. The focus of this chapter is to support this premise. First, I will discuss the nature of discursive difference. I will show that discursive practices are intertwined with the culture that gives rise to such practices and that these cultural/discursive differences, although often subtle, are a given, thus the fundamental *need* for contrastive rhetoric. Once established, the need, in turn, obliges us to foster and to cultivate a legitimate and favorable *space* for contrastive rhetoric, where alternative discourses are examined in contrast, as well as in comparison, with each other and with mainstream American academic discourse. Obviously, more variables than one are indispensable to the existence of this space, but one of the most challenging is our commitment to preserving and studying alternative discourses as they are, or on their own terms. In the second part of this chapter, then, I will explore the nature and characteristics of this space. What is it like in the curriculum and classroom? Do we have such a space yet? And, what still needs to be done?

The Need

To prove the need for contrastive rhetoric, I shall illustrate how cultural/discursive differences are a given. However, before turning to the nature of cultural/discursive differences, I should clarify the kind of differences that are under discussion. Cross-cultural differences are not absolute; rather, they are a matter of emphasis. In other words, to identify a discursive difference in a certain culture, for instance the practice of a more individualistic orientation, does not imply that this certain culture necessarily has had no communal thinking. Instead, a discursive difference is indicative of a predominant cultural tradition and/or a present cultural trend, which interacts with all of its undercurrents and its peripheral developments.

Even though discursive differences are not absolute, they are nonetheless real, significant, and rooted deeply in each culture's heritage. This means, among other things, that, ultimately, our understanding of discursive differences is inseparable from our understanding of the cultures where discursive practices are embedded. Further, this means that investigating cultural/discursive differences is a multidisciplinary undertaking. To explain some of these complex and real differences and their implications, I shall use the comparison and contrast between the Chinese and the Western cultures as the main example of illustration.

Philosophically speaking, for example, the West has a more essentialistic and individualistic orientation and the Chinese a more communal and relational tendency. Culturally and discursively, therefore, the West believes that light has transcending power over darkness, thereby dichotomizing the two, while the Chinese see darkness as the indispensable and not-absolutely-inferior complement to light, and vice versa. This difference is noticeable in rhetorical invention, the process in which writers come to propositions or theses. For instance, according to the third edition of Professor Martha Kolln's *Rhetorical Grammar: Grammatical Choices, Rhetorical Effects*,

> "linking-*be*" sentences are called "Categorical Propositions" (CPs) by logicians and rhetoricians. The CP makes an assertion—it states a proposition—about a particular subject. (1999, 21)

Indeed, not all propositions in the West are categorical propositions. Overall, however, and in Western discourse, as seen in the enduring power of Shakespeare's famous line "to be or not to be," the tendency of either to be or not to be is distinct. In Chinese discourse, however, the impulse to choose between the two is minimal. Students of the Chinese language could testify that the verb *be* is conspicuously missing in many cases, and this lack of attention to the essence, or the ontological state of things, is not accidental. Instead, other linguistic evidence systematically bears this out as well. As sinologists/philosophers Roger Ames and Henry Rosemont Jr. point out, "classical Chinese has no definite articles" (1998, 21). As a result, the Western concept of the one and only, the eternal and absolute is a more complicated concept to convey in the Chinese language. One cultural and discursive effect of this philosophical difference is that Chinese propositions sometimes frustrate Western readers because these propositions are often not either to be or not to be. I've heard my colleagues comment a few times: "Which side is she on?" To be sure, there are many reasons for this confusion, but one has to be the philosophical/cultural/discursive difference. For meaning in Chinese, to quote the Russian linguist M. M. Bakhtin, "only reveals its depths once it has encountered and come into contact with another, foreign meaning" (1986, 7). Light, in other words, cannot have any real meaning unless it engages another meaning, including that of its opposite, darkness. The "side" that "she" is on, in other words, is complicated; her proposition is neither to be nor not to be and yet is both.

Let me use a more concrete and extended example to explain. My own understanding of some of these differences started gradually coming into focus in the summer of 1998 when I attended an National Endowment for the Humanities' Summer Institute titled Philosophy and Religion in China. In class one day during the institute, Roger Ames in his characteristically quiet and friendly way invited my expertise by asking me to translate the English word *thing* into Chinese for the class. Without thinking, I heard myself say in Chinese *dong-xi* / "east-west." That moment, however, has become a significant turning point in my own understanding and teaching of the complex cultural/discursive similarities and differences between China and the West.

The basic difference between the word for *thing* in both cultures is not hard to explain. A rather long Western tradition, Platonic, views truth as permanent and absolute, while an equally long Chinese tradition, both Confucian and Daoist, views it as co-relational and ever changing. On the one hand and according to this Western more essentialist tradition, permanence and eternity are characteristics of a thing's essence, which is superior to the various forms that the essence assumes. The word *table*, for instance, is steps away from the essential and true Form of table, which, in the worldly reality, can be approximated but cannot be achieved. On the other hand and according to that Chinese tradition, such certainty is fleeting and such permanence, rare. For a thing is not defined in and by itself; its definition is contingent upon its relations to other things and is relational to time and space as well. In other words, the only certainty is uncertainty according to this Chinese tradition, thus Ames' point that the very concept of *thingness* in Chinese is sustained by the mere correlation between east and west, two rather mundane, concrete, and changing worldly concepts. In contrast with the Western tradition that maintains that existence derives its meaning from the ideal unchanging Form above and beyond the human realm, the Chinese tradition views the meaning of thing as derived from its relationships with every thing that it comes in contact with in the human realm.

An example can be the identity of a person. To the philosophical question of identity, the Western tradition may send the inquiry in the direction of the soul, that is more or less a predetermined and whose wings, if lost, according to the "Decree of Destiny," take about ten thousand years of time to regenerate (Plato 1987, 31–32). For the most part, therefore, the essence of each individual self is not determined by the changing and transcient now and here. Henry Rosemont, however, answers this question according to the Chinese tradition, defining his identity "I" as his father's son, his daughter's father, his wife's husband, and his students' teacher, and so forth (Rosemont, 2001). In other words, unlike Plato, Confucius defines the entire person-hood as shaped by what's now and here.

This different cultural orientation entails important differences in discursive practices. From invention/thesis, to lines of reasoning/development, to organization, and to style, almost every important aspect of the rhetoric of writing is affected by this philosophically different view of the world. Take the issue of creativity, an issue of rhetorical invention, as an example. According to the Confucian tradition, a sage is a consummate communicator. The character *sage* in Chinese consists of the graphs for ear, mouth, and king. To Confucius, these consummate communicators are cultural ideals, are gifted, but nevertheless have to work on improving their communication abilities to realize their sage-hood. Meanwhile, most of us, among whom Confucius includes himself, were born rather similar in nature, but learning makes a difference in our endeavor to achieve the cultural ideal that sages set for us (1980, 181). The process of learning, therefore, becomes critical, the learning process that, to Confucius, is eminently social. By observing, mimicking, reflecting upon ritualistic communication behaviors, we gradually become more and more fully participating members of our cultural/discursive communities. As cultural ideals, which embody the Tao, become natural to us, we interpret these cultural norms for each given situation, thus becoming creative ourselves.

Certainly, none of these is absolutely unheard of in the American academic discourse. In fact, social constructionists, for instance, have been advocating a very similar view for the past few decades. Kenneth Bruffee, for instance, and other social constructionists characterize knowledge as a social artifact (Bruffee 1996, 91b) that is constructed and reconstructed through time, thus problematizing the permanent essence, or being, of knowledge. Nevertheless, the idea that creativity is letting out that innate, quintessential, original *I* is so ingrained in many of our students that the idea that creativity, epistemologically, comes from lifelong efforts of observing, respecting, absorbing, as well as negotiating with traditions and conventions is not only shocking but also offensive.

Even more sensitive yet is the concept of hierarchy that's inherent in the relational concept of community. Indeed, it doesn't take much discussion at all for students to realize that their daily activities depend on not only benign but also indispensable and invaluable hierarchies. Nevertheless, not having had to wrestle with the complexity involved in some fundamental contradictions in their deep-seated convictions, many students take for granted absolute equality as this culture's ideal. This can be traced back to one widely held belief in the West, the belief that human beings directly relate to God as autonomous and equal beings to each other. As a result of this thinking, mimicking and modeling our fellow human beings who are better writers are often uncritically dismissed as harmful to a writer's creativity. Further, borrowing of any kind without compensating the ideas' originators is indiscriminately and simplistically viewed as the absolute equivalent of stealing that which is uniquely the originator's. From the Confucian point of view, this mentality is puzzling because an idea's sole owner is not traceable, for knowledge is constructed communally.

Obviously, a host of issues are involved here, from ethics to philosophy to theology. Yet, it's important to note that the issue here is *not* the familiar dilemma to the West: Which is better—individualism or communitarianism, egalitarianism or hierarchies, and nature or culture? The point is that the Chinese tradition does not often ask this kind of question and there is thus a real cultural/discursive difference. The very habit of viewing this discussion in any way as an effort to decide between the age-old Western polarized options testifies that, by far, whether we choose between dichotomies, for example, good and evil, is one of the most real differences between China and the West. In fact, this difference could be a challenge even to scholars, Western and Chinese, who try to teach the radically relational nature of this Chinese tradition. The following are three cases in point.

Winner of the Ralph Waldo Emerson Award of Phi Beta Kappa and the James Henry Breasted Prize of the American Historical Association, Benjamin Schwartz's *The World of Thought in Ancient China* (1989) helps the reader understand important aspects of dominant Chinese schools of thought in significant ways. Schwartz, for instance, points out that although the Chinese Taoists focus on the difference between the transient/finite on the one hand and the eternal/infinite on the other, there is "no implication that the transient and finite is either 'unreal' or intrinsically 'evil' as such" (200). Using the example of the relation between "conditional reality" and "ultimate emptiness," Schwartz says that neither is more or less "real" than the other (226). In quite a few instances like this in his book, Schwartz clearly explains this Chinese habit to co-relate, a habit that manifests itself in more schools of thought than one. Nevertheless, Schwartz westernizes this very concept in his discussion of the Taoist Zhuang Zi:

> A case can indeed be made that, in the *Chuang-tzu*, the inexhaustible variety and "creative" ingenuity of nature is **more deeply** appreciated than its order and regularity, and that in his case it would be limiting indeed to translate the term *tao* in its "being" aspect as "order of nature." Much of the imagery suggests not so much order and pattern as inexhaustible grandeur and protean changeability. (219–20, emphasis added)

Once again, whether variety/creativity or order/regularity is preferable is not the issue. The issue is how to interpret the Chinese Taoist Zhuang Zi: Does he appreciate one not more, nor less, than the other? Or, does he appreciate one "more deeply" than the other? The former is more holistic and based on some passages in the book *Zhuang Zi*, while the latter is a more dichotomized/westernized take on some passages in *Zhuang Zi*. The Chinese more holistic approach would not permit drawing conclusions from these passages in such a way—even though these passages, in isolation, can indeed be interpreted as Schwartz does.

Similarly, Michael LaFargue, the renowned Taoist scholar in the United States, brilliantly demystifies the simplistic notion that Chinese Taoism is beyond rationality (1998, 266). He says that the Taoist aphorisms "mean to evoke some rational connection" (268), thus deconstructing the dichotomized mysticism on the one hand and rationality on the other and concluding that in "a feelingful way" (272), we *can understand* Taoism. Even LaFargue, however, seems somehow compelled to conclude that "[w]hile the various sayings in this set have different targets and offer different images, there is plausible unity to their *stance* and its motivation. *All favor* a 'low-profile' in the ruler as opposed to a political philosophy that emphasizes a striking show of force to dramatize the fact of superior control" (271, emphasis added). The set LaFargue refers to may very well emphasize as he interprets; yet, the issue remains: How is the reader supposed to *understand* the contradiction between the claim that Lao Zi's book *Dao De Jing* is not teaching philosophical doctrines (263) on the one hand and, on the other, the interpretation that Lao Zi has a dichotomized and "value-motivated stance" in general? Again, the former sounds more co-relational, while the latter, more westernized. If both are in *Lao Zi*, how can an interpretation settle on one while ignoring the other?

Finally, unprecedented is Xing Lu's pioneer work *Rhetoric in Ancient China, Fifth to Third Century B.C.E.: A Comparison with Classical Greek Rhetoric*. She puts it well when she says that "Laozi's skillful use of paradox served the important rhetorical function of changing people's habitual thought patterns and *leading them to see the reverse possibilities*, by appealing to our intuition" (1998, 237, emphasis added). However, it is one thing to be habitually blind to reverse possibilities, and it is another thing to say that these possibilities are absolutely superior—or inferior—to the other possibilities. Therefore, when Lu says that "[u]nlike the Western mode of inquiry, which emphasizes the affirmative, Laozi's emphasis was on the negative" (237), one is at a loss as to what different mode of inquiry she is referring to. Isolated passages may indeed prompt one to interpret Lao Zi's "leading them to see the reverse possibilities" as preferring those possibilities, but the entire book *Dao De Jing* must be taken into consideration, not to mention its historical context. Interpreting the text in context, the interpreter will find a view much more complex than the simplistic notion of picking either side over the other. Had Lao Zi simply flipped the value hierarchy over, his mode of inquiry would not have been different from the hierarchy as is and, I would venture to add, his teaching, not as influential as it has been.

Again and again, therefore, we see interpreters explain the Chinese thinking in one way and conclude their interpretation another way. It almost seems as if they had to bring the interpretation to some cultural protocol, a protocol that is both implicit and very real. The point here is not to dispute the value of dichotomized thinking, which certainly has its place in a myriad of situations where we humans constantly find ourselves. Rather, the point is to show that cultures have a shaping power on discursive practices, and, as with culture, discursive practices, cross-culturally, differ, thus the discursive diversity.

The Space

To most of us who are not philosophers, the philosophical differences we experience everyday are differences in culture; culture, as shown in the first section, molds and channels discourse; and discourse, as I hope to show in this section, helps to shape a culture as well. In fact, philosophy, culture, and discourse together form a powerhouse for a culture's maintaining and improving its well-being. Therefore, I wish to show that there is the need for a legitimate and favorable space for alternative discourses.

How do discursive practices help to mold—maintaining and improving—a culture? Together with many others, we English teachers help with the molding and shaping on a daily basis. When we teach students how to write with clear theses, how to support those theses with supporting evidence, and how to cut irrelevant details, for instance, we are teaching them criteria for judging, for example, relevance and irrelevance. In general, a more dichotomized mode of inquiry will judge fewer things as relevant than a more relational mode of inquiry does. To Plato, for instance, although a living being is the "composite structure of body and soul joined together" (1987, 28), the soul is unquestionably superior to the body. To Confucius as well as to the Taoists Lao Zi and Zhuang Zi, however, this superiority is not as absolute, for the former/latter cannot be understood without the latter/former—and everything in between. By no means do I imply that Plato is not complex; however, I do intend to show that while the Chinese do not oppose Plato by simply turning his value system upside down, they do indeed strike an alternative view. This Chinese move, therefore, complicates the already complicated Platonic view by expanding the relevancy zone and making the boundaries between the soul and the body and, discursively, of the categorical propositions murky at best. At the risk of oversimplification, I will say that to stay within the boundary of the categorical proposition, we teach/maintain the Western tendency to dichotomize. To push the boundary of this practice, we teach/enrich this Western practice.

Certainly, not only is any Platonic tradition already complex, but also, in the West, there are many more traditions coexisting and interacting with all kinds of Platonic traditions. In the rest of this essay, I hope to show, first, that a Western tradition of writing as inquiry, drawing upon Aristotle's concept of the probable, challenges the polarized dichotomies. Then I hope to show how pedagogically dichotomized tendencies, as seen in philosophical inquiries before, can be too obstinate for us to understand the other.

Whether the beginning words in Aristotle's *Rhetoric* should be translated as an *off-shoot* of or a *counterpart* to dialectics depends on the interpreters' views, and a view I have found more compelling helped me recognize an important difference between Aristotle and Plato and, in turn, a similarity between Aristotle and Confucius. As philosopher Martha C. Nussbaum points out, although Aristotle agrees with the *Phaedrus* on the value of appetites and passions to rationality and soul (1999b, 307), he has an overall more active view of these appetites and passions than that seen in Plato's Decree of Destiny.

> Aristotle does not dwell, as does the *Phaedrus*, on the special cognitive function of the sense of beauty. His concern is more *inclusive*. None of the appetites, not even the appetite for food, which Plato seems to hold throughout his life in unmitigated contempt, lacks, properly trained, its cognitive function. (Nussbaum 1999b, 308, emphasis added)

In other words, although like Plato, Aristotle keeps the realm yonder intact, he does not look down upon this changing realm here—as does not Confucius.

> Aristotle has defended the view that the internal truth, truth *in* the appearances, is all we have to deal with; anything that purports to be more is actually less, or nothing. The standpoint of perfection, which purports to survey all lives neutrally and coolly from a viewpoint outside of any particular life, stands accused already of failure of reference: for in removing itself from all worldly experience it appears to remove itself at the same time from the bases for discourse about the world. (Nussbaum 1999b, 291)

There is no doubt many interpreters consider Aristotle as a dedicated student of the knowledge of certainty, as is Plato. Even so, it is beyond question that at the same time he is no less a dedicated pursuer of the knowledge of the probable. The ability to maintain this more *inclusive* perspective is a major similarity between Aristotle and Confucius as well as the Chinese Taoists Lao Zi and Zhuang Zi.

Like the Chinese who complicate Plato's already complex view of the world, Aristotle "argues that the values that are constitutive of a good human life are plural and incommensurable" (Nussbaum 1999b, 294). As with the Chinese, boundaries are often breached in Aristotle's realm of the probable. An example of this realm's incommensurability can be seen in Aristotle's "Book VI" in *Nicomachean Ethics: Introduction to Aristotle* (McKeon 1992), where boundary crossing abounds within a whole network of thought. There, Aristotle uses the concept of productiveness for all three different kinds of knowledge, scientific/philosophical, practical/political, and productive/artistic; he uses the word *truth* as a goal for both scientific and practical knowledge; and he uses the word *reasoned* for both practical and productive knowledge. Further, like the Chinese who do not see virtue and vice as separable, Aristotle sees "a beauty in the willingness to love someone in the face of love's instability and worldliness that is absent from a completely trustworthy love" (Nussbaum 1999a, 420). In fact, Nussbaum concludes that in general each salient Aristotelian virtue seems inseparable from a risk of harm" (1999a, 420). Finally, like the Chinese who see changing as the nature of reality as well as ways of living, Aristotle sees practical wisdom as using "rules only as summaries and guides," as "flexible, ready for surprise, prepared to see, resourceful at improvisation" (Nussbaum 1999b, 305). Certainly, Aristotle does not take, as do the Chinese, this inconstant reality as a defining feature of Reality. Nor, however, does he see this reality as the absolutely inferior and to be slighted as does Plato. As such, the realm of the probable, with all its contingencies, challenges human beings with incommensurable uncertainty and rewards them with unlimited possibilities.

Both theoretically and pedagogically, writing as inquiry follows this Western tradition. The constant change in our life provides opportunities for inquiry. Simply put in Janice Lauer's words, this means writing for the purpose "to go beyond what you already know . . . to gain insight and to share it with readers" (2000, 3). This way, "discourse processes can be initiated by questions or unknowns, as opposed to theses. What is important is that students can pose questions they want to pursue and try to generate new knowledge through writing" (Gale 2000, 4). Consistent with Aristotle's cultivation and training of practical wisdom, Lauer's instructional practices rely on "thinking that's flexible and gives guidance during complex processes" (Gale 2000, 7). Thinking this way could bring the thinker beyond the simplistic black or white, individual or communal dichotomies. As Lauer says,

> Writers as inquirers not only find what is unique in their experiences, they also find patterns and structures in their lives similar to those they have heard or read about. They learn what makes them unlike anyone else who has ever lived, as well as what makes them like all others who have ever lived. They become aware of their cultural assumptions and the ways in which their values have been shaped by larger cultural forces around them. (2000, 3)

In my own practice of teaching college writing, I focus on the process of developing theses from questions, on fostering students' sensitivity to their own dissonance/puzzlement, and on assisting them in braving the unknown, in refining their judgment, and in creating new possibilities. Theses then are developed correlatively because they originate from puzzlement, a starting point that forces the writers to consider two or more differing and possible alternative perspectives. Reflecting upon my own practice of teaching writing as inquiry, I've realized how the process is compatible with my own culture's propensity for correlative thinking, correlative learning, and correlative teaching. In other words, although writing as inquiry is indeed very Western, in a rather important way, it is also Chinese.

In my years of being a Chinese professor teaching American college students to write as inquiry, I have been rewarded with seeing students not only wanting to keep an open mind but also mastering strategies to help themselves to achieve open-mindedness. Students bring their own cultures to college writing. With the help of concrete discursive/inquiry strategies we practice, they learn that their own unexamined deep-seated convictions can be both limiting and enabling; they practice to become more aware of their own need to inquire; they learn to gain different perspectives to answer their own compelling questions; and, eventually, they see how to make a difference in their own cultures. At the same time, however, I have also worked with students struggling with writing as inquiry—because of the impact of more dominant cultural traditions. An example of one of these traditions, for instance, can be seen in a 1999 grammar/style book, where the author says: "Good writing is lean and confident. . . . Every little qualifier whittles away some fraction of trust on the part of the reader. Readers want a writer who believes in himself [sic] and in what he is saying. Don't diminish that belief. Don't be kind of bold. Be bold" (Hale 1999, 92). This is, unfortunately, much more familiar to many students than the concept of defining by correlation or of writing as inquiry. Writing according to this tradition therefore only has to do with the product, the apparently confident, certain, and bold product. As to how writers get to the real confidence, certainty, and assertiveness, is beyond the purview of writing. As a result, many of these students make admirable efforts, yet time and again, their inquiry questions, for example, turn out to be rhetorical questions: theses masquerading as questions.

To be sure, students' difficulty with these rhetorical/inquiry strategies is indicative of the dominating cultural tendency to dichotomize. As well, their difficulty demonstrates the need for contrastive rhetoric. Aristotle indeed provides alternative to Plato, and Aristotle can indeed help students in the West to understand the Chinese. In the end, however, Aristotle identifies with Plato in the autonomous status of the realm and knowledge of certainty. In other words, Aristotle cannot replace the Chinese.

Once again, and for the last time, I must insist that the issue is not the value of certainty, or of dogma, either in the realm of certainty or in the realm of the probable. That is an issue beyond the scope of this paper. As it is in the West, the Chinese view on this is complex, and it is not the simple reversal/the opposite of Western views. Suffice it to share an example from Ames and Rosemont's translation (1998, 46–48) of the Chinese concept *tian*/heaven. *Tian*/heaven, they point out, is indeed critical in various schools of Chinese thought, but the translation of *tian* as *Heaven* is so misleading that the Chinese word *tian* should be kept, as in the case of the [non]translation of the Chinese *dao*. The issue here is differences among cultural tendencies, in particular, the tendency to dichotomize and the tendency to co-relate. Further, the point of identifying differences is to show the need to attend to them so that alternative cultural/discursive practices enrich each other.

Conclusions

In the first part, I discussed how cultures mold discursive practices, while in the second part, how discursive practices can also help shape the cultures that make these practices possible. I believe that the discussion here warrants the following three conclusions. First, indeed alternative discourse often looks ostensibly different from a native cultural/discursive grammar, but sometimes differences can be quite inconspicuous as well. Alternatives could very well reside within the same culture, and differences among alternatives are not absolute. In a way, every cultural/discursive reality is plural and incommensurable, which makes easier the understanding of differences as seen in the case of Plato, Aristotle, and the Chinese.

Second, the obscured boundaries among differences are still boundaries, and differences are very real. To reap from the richness of our cultural/discursive diversity requires that we be sensitive to shades of differences, but this sensitivity comes more from lifelong efforts to understand subtle but significant differences than from the mere good will to be sensitive to these differences. Pedagogically, this means that contrastive rhetoric is indispensable, and courses on contrastive rhetoric available to junior and senior university students are a must. In other words, some firsthand experience with different culture/discursive practices is helpful, but systematic effort is also necessary to the understanding of the other. Since cultural/discursive boundaries are often not clear-cut, contrastive rhetoric can help because it provides the space where specialists of one discourse are pitted against those of another, their more thorough attention to the subject helping students understand subtle but often significant details of differences.

Finally, knowledge of a different cultural/discursive practice cannot be thorough without knowledge of one's own culture. In other words, one's sensitivity to the other and to difference cannot be thorough if one is insensitive or ignorant of one's own culture. Our understanding of different discursive practices is aided by a more thorough understanding of what we have taken for granted of our own cultural/discursive practices or, sometimes, by an awareness of a native practice that we have been, unfortunately, woefully naive about. In the end, therefore, contrastive rhetoric is a must to cross-cultural inquiries only when it is true to its name: enabling differences in full—and fair—contact with one another.

Works Cited

Ames, Roger T., and Henry Rosemont Jr. 1998. "Introduction." In *The Analects of Confucius: A Philosophical Translation*, translated by Roger T. Ames and Henry Rosemont, Jr. 1–70. New York: Ballantine.

Aristotle. 1954. *Rhetoric,* translated by W. Rhys Roberts. New York: The Modern Library.

———. 1992. "Book VI." In *Nicomachean Ethics: Introduction to Aristotle*, edited by Richard McKeon, 451–71. New York: The Modern Library.

Bakhtin, Mikhael M. 1986. "Response to a Question from the *Novy Mir* Editorial Staff." In *Speech Genres & Other Late Essay*, translated by Vern W. McGee, edited by Caryl Emerson and Michael Holquist, 1–7. Austin: Univ. of Texas Press.

Bruffee, Kenneth A. 1996. "Collaborative Learning and the 'Conversation of Mankind.'" In *Composition in Four Keys: Inquiring into the Field, Nature, Art,*

Science, Politics, edited by Mark Wiley, Barbara Gleason, and Louise Wetherbee Phelps, 84–97. Mountain View, CA: Mayfield.

Chuang Tzu. 2001. *Chuang-Tzu: The Inner Chapters*, translated by A. C. Graham. Indianapolis: Hackett Publishing Company, Inc.

Confucius. 1980. *The Analects*, introduced and annotated by Bojun Yang. Beijing, China: Zhong Hua Shu Jiu.

Gale, Fredric G. 2000. "An Interview with Janice Lauer." *Forum* 11(2): 1–12.

Hale, Constance. 1999. *Sin and Syntax: How to Craft Wickedly Effective Prose*. New York: Broadway Books.

Kolln, Martha. 1998. *Rhetorical Grammar: Grammatical Choices, Rhetorical Effects*. Boston: Allyn and Bacon.

LaFargue, Michael. 1998. "Recovering the *Tao-te-ching*'s Original Meaning: Some Remarks on Historical Hermeneutics." In *Lao-Tzu and the Tao-te-ching*, edited by Livia Kohn and Michael LaFargue, 255–75. Albany: State Univ. of New York Press.

Lauer, Janice, Andrea Lunsford, Janet Atwill. 2000. "Introduction." In *Four Worlds of Writing: Inquiry and Action in Context*." 4th ed. edited by Janice Lauer, 1–10. Boston: Pearson.

Lu, Xing. 1998. *Rhetoric in Ancient China, Fifth to Third Century B.C.E.: A Comparison with Classical Greek Rhetoric*. Columbia: Univ. of South Carolina Press.

Nussbaum, Martha C. 1999a. "The Betrayal of Convention: A Reading of Euripides' *Hecuba*." In *The Fragility of Goodness: Luck and Ethics in Greek Tragedy and Philosophy*, 397–412. Cambridge: Cambridge University Press.

———. 1999b "Non-Scientific Deliberation." In *The Fragility of Goodness: Luck and Ethics in Greek Tragedy and Philosophy*, 290–317. Cambridge: Cambridge University Press.

Plato. 1987. *Phaedrus*. New York: Macmillan.

Rosemont, Henry. 2001. Lecture on Confucianism and Human Rights, at University of Wisconsin-La Crosse.

Schwartz, Benjamin I. 1989. *The World of Thought in Ancient China*. Cambridge: The Belknap Press of Harvard University Press.

8

Questioning Alternative Discourses
Reports from Across the Disciplines

Christopher Thaiss
Terry Myers Zawacki

Preface

When we saw the call for proposals for a collection on alternative forms of intellectual work in the academy, both of us noted that this was a project that offered us the opportunity to write about some questions we'd been discussing informally in the context of Writing Across the Curriculum (WAC) and our writing-in-the-disciplines requirement: To what degree do academic writers conform to the conventions of their particular discourse communities? How open are they to alternatives, in their own work and in the writing students do in response to assignments?

At the same time, we were drawn to this call for proposals because we thought we might be able to blend our academic and personal interests by experimenting with style and form, questioning the meaning of the word *alternative* even as we enacted it. We proposed to interview scholars in a range of disciplines outside of English Studies and to experiment with ways to present our findings. Our proposal was accepted, with further encouragement from the editors to take risks ourselves in the writing. And then something very curious happened.

We found ourselves talking mainly about the form of our article as if it were separate from the data we'd begun collecting from our interviews. How, we wondered, could we demonstrate that we were taking risks, employing alternatives? We played with the idea of including dialogue, letting our informants "talk" in an uninterrupted (by us) flow of text, telling our own personal stories, violating margins (literally) by putting boxes of text (short bios for our informants? quotations from their writing?) in the margins or overlapping our central text. As we spun out ideas, we'd look at each other and ask, "Too clever?" "Too obviously performative?" We didn't want to be guilty of "rampant alternative alternativisms," a term used by one of our informants to describe a kind of experimental work in anthropology, which was often "aestheticism without connection to a cause" (Lancaster 2001). What cause did we have for choosing one kind of performance over another? It was not productive, we quickly realized, to talk about form until we had examined the interview data in the context of our hypotheses, which are what, after all, our interview findings were intended to confirm or confound.

Introduction

We are hypothesizing (1) that writing practices by scholars within disciplines will show that the boundaries around disciplinary discourses are far more permeable than we indicate to students when we teach them to conform to the discourse conventions of their majors; however, we also hypothesize (2) that academics working outside of rhetoric and composition are not likely to be aware of the usefulness of certain kinds of rhetorical performances to disrupt dominant discourses, either as protests against hegemony or as assertions of identities typically invisible in the academy.

Our hypotheses are motivated by three main concerns: First, as WAC professionals, we've had ample opportunity to note the contradictions in the way disciplinary conventions are described and subscribed to in practice and in the literature. On the one hand, for example, our experience (Thaiss and Zawacki 1997) reading the proficiency portfolios students submit for credit for our advanced writing-in-the-disciplines course has shown us that, regardless of discipline, students include work in a surprising variety of genres and styles, lending credence to the idea that disciplinary boundaries are permeable, with genres constantly being redefined (Bazerman 2000). On the other hand, texts on writing in the disciplines generally offer prescriptive advice and definitive standards for format and documentation, including the discipline-specific guides Chris and his collaborators have written in theater, law enforcement, and psychology (Thaiss and Davis 1999; Thaiss and Hess 1999; Thaiss and Sanford 2000). We wondered how aware academics were of this apparent double standard.

Second, we'd both been interested in the degree to which academic writers felt free to experiment with the discourse conventions guiding their disciplines and whether they were self-conscious about their relationship to these conventions. How clearly could our informants articulate perceived standards, and to what degree did they feel obliged to follow them, both in their own work and in their advice to those "coming up" in the field? Our inquiry would also give us insights into what Swales terms the "anti-taxonomist" view of genre, about which he notes that genres proliferate and become difficult to describe because of rhetorical and social complexities (1990, 43). To what degree and in what ways did our colleagues see their disciplines allowing and even encouraging new genres or variations on the standard? To what degree did they allow or even encourage students to write outside of these conventions?

Third, if the boundaries of disciplinary discourse are as permeable as we are hypothesizing, then how could we explain that permeability? Did it come, at least in part, from resistance to dominant discourses and hegemonic practices? This question interests us in light of much of the theorizing around the topic of alternative discourses in the academy; that is, in radical/critical/liberal pedagogy, in cultural theory, in feminist theory (as Terry's work [Zawacki, 1992 and 2001] explores), and in contrastive rhetoric. LeCourt in "WAC as Critical Pedagogy," for example, criticizes WAC pedagogy for expecting students to accommodate themselves to disciplinary discourses, thereby silencing their cultural, socioeconomic, and gender differences as well as their alternative literacies; she advocates teaching students to resist those discourses (390). We knew that many fields in the humanities, because they have analyses of discourse at their center, might be more aware of arguments about writing to resist, writing against the grain or including the personal, for example. But we wondered if we would find this same awareness in fields within the social and natural sciences, where the convention is that the data speak, not the writer.

Our Method

For this reason, we chose to interview faculty colleagues in disciplines outside of the humanities; colleagues whom we knew as successful writers in their fields, all of them tenured, with several among them also known for writing for more popular audiences or in media besides print. We knew of these scholar-writers also as conscientious teachers and curriculum leaders, people who had worked with us in varied ways on writing-across-the-curriculum projects, some of them our close colleagues for as long as fifteen years.

We interviewed the following people, all faculty at George Mason University:

Roger Lancaster, professor of anthropology; author of *Thanks to God and the Revolution* and *Life Is Hard: Machismo, Danger, and the Intimacy of Power in Nicaragua* (1992), his study of life in Nicaragua during the Sandinista regime;

James Trefil, professor of physics and Robinson, Professor of Interdisciplinary Studies; contributing writer to *Smithsonian Magazine*, and author or coauthor of popular books on science, typically reviewed in the *New York Times*;

Jeanne Sorrell, professor of nursing and director of the Ph.D. in nursing; author of many articles on writing in the nursing profession; coproducer of videotapes on primary care;

Robert Smith, professor and chair of psychology; author or coauthor of many articles and reports on the effects of substances on animals and humans;

Victoria Rader, associate professor of sociology; author of *Signal Through the Flames*, her study of the homeless advocacy of Mitch Snyder;

Priscilla Regan, associate professor of political science; author of *Legislating Privacy*, on federal debates regarding privacy versus freedom of information and the new technologies;

Daniele Struppa, associate professor of mathematical sciences and dean of the College of Arts and Sciences; author or coauthor of articles and books on differential equations. A non-native speaker of English, his first language is Italian.

Our questions to the informants fell into three broad categories: their perceptions of disciplinary standards, their practices as writers, and their pedagogy related to writing. We've organized our findings into three main clusters.

Findings

Cluster One: How did the informants define "standard" writing in their disciplines and what did they perceive as alternatives to that discourse?

- Each of our informants easily noted a formal center of the discipline or a clear range of acceptable styles in terms of ways of thinking, standards of evidence, and format.

None of them doubted that there were identifiable standards, and could easily tick off a few features. This isn't to say that they gave us minute details of these features, but they didn't doubt that they existed or that they could recognize them easily. Smith, for example, quickly said that all acceptable writing in psychology was "data-driven" and followed the rules of the APA manual. Struppa said that in math most writers followed a "template"—"definition, example, theorem"—so that even if an article were written in a foreign language, a reader could follow the standard order of sections and the universal language of mathematical symbolism in order to see what a colleague was arguing and how the proof proceeded. Sorrell identified a hierarchy: "experimental"—hypothesis-driven—work, either quantitative or qualitative in emphasis, with the quantitative having traditional priority. Regan gave the most complex answer: she estimated forty divisions of research in political science, each with its own standards of evidence and typical methods. Still, she saw them all converging in some basic demands for "good scholarly writing": clear, hypothesis-based, and logically and systematically argued. Lancaster noted Malinowski's influence in framing anthropology as a discipline whose "whole point is to take on the received wisdom, to dislodge the idea of clear, universals, to problematize conceptions of what human beings are like, including the ethnographer," yet even he could identify the "typical ethnography: 7–8 chapters, brief intro and conclusion, recognizable rubrics (kinship, etc.)."

- All informants could readily identify alternative discourses relevant to their disciplines, and all would advise probationary tenure-line faculty to avoid them.

> Sometimes I think I'd sort of like to disappear and write some novel and escape from everything, but that's not what you're asking. There are lots of popular— I guess that's alternative—venues for political writing but, given the range of publication outlets and approaches I can take in Political Science, I don't feel that constrained to fit some mold. Priscilla Regan

When we asked them about their own writing, the informants easily named methods or styles that they or others had explored that were outside the mainstream discourse. All agreed, for example, that popularizing—writing for a nonacademic audience—is outside the standard and, furthermore, usually looked down on. "The idea of engaging the reader is often viewed with suspicion," Lancaster said. "One of the most insulting things you can say in academics is that it reads like journalism. If it's too readable, it's not taken seriously." Trefil, well known as a popular science writer, regards this work as socially valuable and certainly appropriate for a tenured scholar who has already proven that he can do more standard scientific work. Nevertheless, he said, it would be unthinkable for a young scholar to try to achieve tenure by writing like a Carl Sagan. Smith mentioned a psychology colleague who had become nationally recognized as an advocate for community responsibility for the mentally ill, but noted that it took years for his studies of community attitudes to gain acceptance as scholarly work, and he didn't even begin this research until after he had achieved tenure. Rader said she wouldn't have undertaken her book on Mitch Snyder if she had not already had tenure. Too many people outside of academia read it, she noted, so it's considered not academic enough.

> It's like building furniture in your garage, a hobby but not your real work. The best that I could hope for is that they wouldn't hold my popular writing against me. Jim Trefil

- Most of our informants said that it was standard in their disciplines to avoid the personal and to emphasize the clarity and logic of the argument and the strength of the evidence.

Trefil, for example, described the impersonality of scientific discourse as a deliberate tactic to minimize tension in a highly competitive field where violent disagreements and personal animosity must often be contained. Struppa's math "template" corroborates the preference for an impersonal style. In nursing, as Sorrell noted, the "I" of the researcher is still rare, even though in some kinds of qualitative research the "I" of the informant prevails.

Two of our informants, Struppa and Regan, noted allowable exceptions. Struppa cited some uses of the "poetic"—metaphors and tiny dedicatory excerpts from literature—used to preface or conclude articles. Some Japanese mathematicians, he said, use poetic comments, such as one eminent mathematician who writes, after proving his theorem, "How beautiful is the view from the top of the mountain." Struppa explained that his colleague meant that "getting to this theorem was like a huge and arduous climb and now, because of the theorem with its really major result, you can see all of mathematics in a way you couldn't before." But such "flourishes," he warned, should be undertaken only by those who are sure of the quality of their math reasoning; otherwise, they can hurt publication prospects. Struppa also described a doctoral student's work as including "little pieces from Sufi mysticism, Islamic poetry, and Buddhism. I review his work before he sends it out, and most of the time I leave them in because I know his work is good and that people are going to be impressed. If the writer's math is only okay, I wouldn't do that kind of thing; it irritates people."

Regan also saw prefaces and acknowledgments pages in books as sanctioned places for the "I" in political science. For her, there is a sharp distinction: while she might in a preface refer to the five years she spent working for Congress on technology assessment, for example, she would not in the book itself cite her experience as a source or use that experience as evidence. Likewise, Struppa said the only "tolerable" expressions of the personal were short dedications at the start of articles, perhaps including a quote from an author. For example, he dedicated an article to his uncle who had attempted suicide and chose a quotation from novelist Yukio Mishima. "So Mishima's words—'Human life is limited, but I would like to live forever'—were a message from me to him that I knew what he was going through. This is as personal as I get. And that is allowed. But it's not very typical."

Cluster Two: Have our informants sometimes written in alternative forms? If not, why not? If so, why and how did they come to choose a particular alternative form?

While our informants seemed to have a clear sense of standard writing in their disciplines, all but two have written in what they consider to be alternative forms. Whether or not they choose to write in alternative ways (as each defines *alternative*) seems to be based on (1) a tradition of writing outside conventions in their disciplines, and (2) the need to uncover knowledge that they couldn't access using conventional methods or to say something they couldn't say in conventional styles. Underlying both of these is their perception of the risks they take when they choose to work in nonmainstream ways.

- Informants in disciplines with a tradition of working outside the mainstream were clearly most comfortable with the alternative projects they had chosen.

Lancaster described his second book, *Life Is Hard,* as comprised of journalistic and impressionistic passages, raw fieldnotes, chapter-length interviews and life histories, newspaper articles, and letters. We've already noted anthropology's tradition of experimental writing; yet Lancaster said he recalled thinking when he finished, "My goodness, aren't I daring, But then I reread the book a year or so later and thought, 'Oh my god, it's a standard ethnography.'" In contrast to anthropology, the natural and physical sciences do not have a tradition of stylistic experimentalism; nevertheless, there is a tradition of writing outside the mainstream in the form of books and articles translating advances in science for the broader educational, economic, and political community. So a Jim Trefil, for example, can feel, at this point in his career, comfortable writing articles for *Smithsonian* magazine, futuristic speculations like *A Scientist in the City*, and *Why Science Matters*, a book advocating science education.

- Conversely, when a discipline does not have a tradition of alternative discourses, a writer can be very uncomfortable with the risks he or she perceives when choosing to work in these ways.

Because her discipline, sociology, does not provide a model for her highly personal writing on social movements, Rader expressed a strong sense of discomfort about both of her book projects. She explained that she doesn't read mainstream journals in sociology because their emphasis on quantification is not relevant to her approach. When she talked about *Signal Through the Flames*, for example, she described the misunderstandings that came when sociologists began counting the homeless. "The advocates had already created a public issue. Once you start counting, you get an undercount and then everybody thinks there isn't as much need as previously thought. They were well-meaning sociologists but they played a reactionary role." While *Signal* is unconventional (part biography, part news reporting, and part review of statistics), she described the book she's currently working on as "going the full distance, as far as I am able to go, spiritually and emotionally, in terms of risk taking." In it, she blends her own story —"what I've learned along the way"—with the academic so that the book is "both a personal and professional journey." Rader has only recently felt that there is an audience for this writing: "typical people, people like me—white, middle class, educated—who want to get socially involved but have no support. This book is partly to offer that support."

- For our informants, a sense of risk is often outweighed by the need for alternative discourses to uncover and present new knowledge.

This point was vividly made for us in our interviews with Rader and Sorrell. By Rader, who chooses to work within a social action model because, she said, she is not as attached to her image among sociologists as she is to her image among activists. And by Sorrell, who explained that she never thought of anything she did as alternative because the nonmainstream research she was doing met important scholarly and professional goals. Still, she characterized this work as experimental. It's her experimentation that we want to highlight because she seemed to have such a compelling need for a form to talk about data she thought was valid and valuable—data based on nurses' intuitions and stories about their practice—but which could not be expressed within the conventional research paradigms. Sorrell's sense of the risk involved in her research agenda was not mitigated until she heard nursing scholar Patricia Benner describe using nurses' stories as data to analyze phenomenologically how they develop nursing skills. Sorrell thought she could use the same approach to analyze nurses' intuitions, which "had been downplayed because there were too many gender stereotypes to contend with." Nurses always talk among themselves, she noted, about "their feelings, say, that a patient is going bad, but they didn't want the docs, mostly men, thinking that they were crazy to go on intuitions about a patient." To learn how to do phenomenological analysis, Sorrell attended (and continues to attend each summer) the Advanced Nursing Institute for Heideggerian Hermeneutical Studies. Her approach, as she described it, is to ask informants to tell a story in response to a question she asks; she analyzes the stories, identifies themes, and includes parts of their narratives in her discussion of the phenomena she's looking at. She presents this research in conventional articles but also in videos she produces, most recently one on ethical concerns in the care of Alzheimer's patients.

- If our informants said they did not write in alternative styles, it was usually because the work they wanted to do was so tightly tied to disciplinary conventions that there was no need to use alternatives.

For Regan, as we noted in section one, the discipline of political science was sufficiently expansive to allow her to do the work she wanted. In Smith's case, he had achieved such consistent success by following the standard paradigm for experimental reporting in psychology that he really couldn't conceive of alternative projects he wanted to do. At one point, he acknowledged that he might like "one day" to write in a more "text-book style" to explain why his research on the neurological effects of various drugs on mice is "more than just one more experiment." Yet, while he would like to be an advocate in that arena, he doesn't "see the point in doing it unless there's some kind of publication opportunity, unlikely because that kind of work will not be supported in the sciences."

- Informants working in alternative forms expressed a self-conscious awareness of the necessity of developing a different voice for this writing; however, they don't always know if they have been successful.

> I was trying for prosaic and got called poetic (by the reviewers of *Life Is Hard*). But you can't always tell what you're doing when you're in the middle of it. Roger Lancaster

When we asked Trefil how he learned to adapt a physicist's voice to a popular audience, he said he wasn't really conscious of developing a voice: "I don't think about it when I write, which probably means I do have that voice." The hardest thing he had to learn, he told us, was to get rid of scientific style. "I kept repeating, 'Remember, no footnotes. No footnotes.'" Rader told us it has taken her seven years to "get the voice" for her current project, mainly because she has no models. The voice she finally settled on blends the personal and the academic, she said, by a sort of "what I learned along the way" strategy; that is, she talks about the research as part of her own professional and personal journey.

- If informants choose to write about personal aspects of their lives, they do so because the project demands it rather than as a political statement about identity.

Lancaster spoke insightfully about the "organic relationship" between a text and its writer. In talking about *Life Is Hard* he noted his need for "an alternative form to mirror the discombobulation of a failed revolution." In the book, Lancaster also talks about his own sense of dislocation as a new academic looking for work and his conflicting desires as the partner of a military man opposing the revolutionaries. The revelation of his sexual orientation grounds a lengthy chapter about homosexuality in Latin America. While he does "come out" in this chapter, his revelation is used to question his own stance as an anthropologist studying this culture. Even though the whole point of Rader's work is to explore her personal and professional journey as an activist, she is not using identity as a political statement and is, in fact, deeply troubled by how one establishes credibility for a book like this. "I've never written totally in first person. I'm always second-guessing the validity of my experiences as legitimate evidence." It's "repugnant" to her to name drop or seem to be popularizing her self-image through referencing the famous people she's worked with, such as Jesse Jackson and Mitch Snyder, yet she knows that she must write in detail about her activism in order to establish her credentials. Lancaster and Rader are the exception, however, in including personal information in their writing. Even those informants who were writing less formally, like Trefil, or working with others' personal stories in their research, like Sorrell, did not see a reason to include stories about themselves in their work. As Trefil said, explaining why he didn't want to write about himself, "Basically scientists are dull people with interesting ideas."

Cluster Three: Do our informants ever give assignments asking for alternative ways of thinking and writing about the discipline? How open are they to students writing in alternative ways to assignments they give?

As a corollary to our first hypothesis, we expected that the data for this section would show that informants who wrote outside of disciplinary conventions would most likely allow students to do so as well, and, conversely, that those who wrote in standard ways would most likely give standard assignments. We were somewhat surprised, then, at what we found.

- Our informants generally favored generic forms over disciplinary forms because they perceived these to be more accessible and instructive to undergraduates.

> My objective for undergraduates is that they can take a simple mathematical idea related to an issue of interest and write coherently about it for a number of pages. In graduate school, they can learn to write fully formed mathematical papers. Daniele Struppa

With one exception, our informants did not seem to think it necessary or even desirable to train undergraduates to think and write as physicists, anthropologists, sociologists, political scientists, mathematicians, and so on. Graduate school was the time for that work, they believed. More important than teaching undergraduates to imitate disciplinary discourses, our informants said, was teaching them how to summarize and analyze, write clear and logical arguments, situate themselves within the conversations of the field, and engage creatively and critically with these conversations. These goals could best be achieved through familiar genres that would allow students to bring what they already know to their understanding of the content of the course. Regan, for example, assigns letters (to newspapers, politicians), op-ed pieces, talking papers (briefings), and analyses of public events (debates, town hall meetings). These assignments concern ideas and issues students care about while also requiring them to write for different audiences and purposes, to "distill information and be concise and to the point," and to present "clear, organized, and logical arguments." Lancaster, who noted that ethnographies themselves are alternative forms for most students, said he seldom gives ethnographic assignments, preferring instead assignments which "awaken a sense of how to essay an everyday experience and to think critically about it." For much the same reasons, Trefil asks students to summarize articles on science topics and then explain "any effects the topic might have on everyday life."

For all of these informants, clear writing, no matter what form it takes, is the goal, not the imitation of disciplinary forms. Even Smith, who was adamant that students majoring in psychology must "be trained in a data-based mode of thought" and write scientific reports in their writing-intensive course, said that the main thing "we are trying to do with undergraduates is to teach them to think scientifically and communicate clearly. How they use those skills is going to vary a lot. Only about 20 percent of our undergraduates go on to graduate study."

- When our informants gave assignments that seemed more clearly alternative to conventional academic forms, these assignments tended to resemble their own alternative work and/or epistemologies.

And the students read these stories out loud in class, which can be really emotional. I've learned to bring a box of Kleenex to class. Jeanne Sorrell

As a parallel to his self-described "montage" style in *Life Is Hard*, Lancaster asks students to convey course material in forms other than the typical academic paper. These may be visual and written collages, theatrical renderings, short stories, any form that demonstrates "a serious engagement" with the subject matter. He said he tends to get the best writing when students are encouraged to experiment with form and genre. Just as Rader uses her own life stories in her current book project, she also asks students to synthesize their experiences with the course work in order "to make sense of concepts, like community, for example." In giving these assignments, Rader hopes to inspire a commitment to social activism; this commitment, she believes, can occur only when "we understand ourselves in relationship to a social problem."

Interestingly, while cast in quite different terms, Sorrell's aims for her assignments can be seen as pursuing a quest similar to Rader's; that is, to tap into nurses' personal knowledge in order to identify and understand new kinds of professional knowledge. To get at this knowledge, Sorrell asks students to write what she calls "paradigm cases"; these are stories they tell about themselves in relation to patients they have cared for. The stories, which are read aloud in class, tend to elicit tears, even the happy stories—"Perhaps it's the intensity of reading aloud, or maybe we hold the stories differently in our memory." Sometimes, Sorrell told us, she "gets nervous" about the storytelling, "maybe because it feels less academic." Sometimes students get nervous too, she said, because they've "learned to do experimental reports and they think they should be doing more sophisticated stuff."[1] Yet the paradigm cases have yielded a rich pool of data, which students can draw on for phenomenological analysis or for their own personal uses. In May 2000, the stories were published in a chapbook called *Beveled Edges: A Portrait of Caring Nurses' Reflections*. The stories in the chapbook reflect, as the Preface says, "the soul of nursing"; they also reflect Sorrell's collaboration with her students to compile and edit the stories and to find a publisher. In fact, many of Sorrell's most experimental professional projects, she said, have grown out of work she began with students. [2]

- Conversely, when our informants gave students assignments calling for unconventional forms, they expressed a range of concerns about how to respond to and grade the resulting papers.

Clearly, it is easier to grade writing that reproduces standard academic forms. So Smith could say with no compunction, for example, "If a psychology student does something that isn't mainstream, the work is returned and they are told to do the assignment." Then again, Regan, who values logical argument and a systematic presentation of evidence in political science, was unexpectedly tolerant in her response to our question about how she might grade a paper from a government major in Terry's class, a student from Sierra Leone who wrote five long paragraphs describing the beauty of his country before moving on to describe in contrast the terrible upheavals there. His thesis was implicit in the contrasting descriptions but never directly stated; he ended by quoting a number of commentators on "the situation" in several neighboring countries. Regan said she would not reject the paper nor would she ask him to eliminate the paragraphs describing his country; instead she would ask the student to sharpen his thesis and contextualize the description.

Sorrell said she "hated" grading the paradigm cases and "usually gives all A's." Because all sections of the required writing-intensive course in nursing now include a paradigm case assignment, Sorrell is working with other faculty on criteria to use across sections. Meanwhile, some nursing faculty have expressed a desire to "go back to conventional case studies, with traditional lab data and analysis of facts" because this would be "easier to teach and to grade." Rader acknowledged that there is "lots of ambiguity in my style [of grading]. And students can get mad, like 'My story's my story, how can you evaluate it?' so I sometimes grade on how hard they've tried. If I think someone has tried but didn't have a sense of the assignment, that's one thing. But it's another if they have skills problems or can't get the main ideas, I ask them to revise, to practice until they get it." Rader also noted, however, that she includes a lot of work on critical analysis, "one of the skills sociology should be teaching. Students should learn how to build an argument; it's not okay to just start in with their opinions." Lancaster stated that his "core values" are that writing "should be clear, it should be readable, and it should be logical." Nevertheless, he also values student work that defies grading according to these criteria for prose essays. Of his "anything goes" assignments ("I don't allow belly dancing. I don't allow bizarre rituals. And nothing dangerous but almost anything else"), he said, "I grade on content, not aesthetics. But it's hard."

Conclusions, Implications, Recommendations

Framing the conclusions that follow is one of the many insights we gained from our informants, one that became a sort of touchstone for us: Lancaster's assertion of the "organic relationship" between a text and its writer. We'd set out to write an alternative text, which, at our editors' request, would take risks with form and content. Yet, we discovered early on, as several informants have in their own writing, that the alternative in academic writing grows out of a research agenda, the nature of the findings, and the writer's sense of the best way to present these findings to the audience he or she envisions.

- We hypothesized that the boundaries around disciplinary discourses are more permeable than we indicate to students. Our research clearly supports this hypothesis and provides a possible reason: How a writer writes within the disciplines seems a compromise between the conventions of discourse and the idiosyncracies of the writer—differences in personality, shaping experiences, outside influences. We can say that writers choose disciplines because of these turns of mind and heart, and then they negotiate their space within the disciplinary rhetoric. The conventions don't silence these writers, as so much of the theorizing around dominant discourses suggests; rather, we think that conventions provide part of the shape of their individual discourse. In *Academic Discourse and Critical Consciousness* Bizzell argues that we in composition should have as an "overarching" concern the study of the power of a discourse community "to constitute a world view" (1992, 224). Our research begins to address Bizzell's concern in that we see our informants shaping disciplinary conventions—always somewhat indeterminate, as Swales reminds us—to fit their growing and changing needs and desires, their world views, one might say. These scholar/writers succeed, then, not because they've allowed conventions to inhibit their personalities, but because they've had the imagination, drive, and flexibility to find discourse communities, often within larger disciplines, that accommodate their individual visions. For the most part, we see them enacting these same values in the assignments they give students; they want undergraduates to find a way to engage "personally" with the material, hence their emphasis on familiar genres that allow for an "essaying" of "everyday experience."

Our research shows that we in composition studies can't simply provide students formats or sample essays and expect that these will give them an adequate or in any way accurate picture of writing in a discipline. Much less can we generalize about so-called academic writing in any detail. Certainly we can reiterate our informants' insistence on "clarity," "logic," and "evidence," and we can enact these virtues—as we interpret them—in our assignments to students and our evaluation of their work; but we need much more basically to warn our novices of the great variety of ways that teachers will enact and interpret these virtues, and we must arm them with strategies for dealing with this variety. The goal is not that they leave their favorite modes of thinking or expression at the classroom door; rather they should seek ways to blend these with what their teachers expect. It's not silencing, but it might be respectful modulation.

Similarly, in shaping the writing program, there can be no substitute for faculty conversation about standards and acceptable alternatives. We know from many years of working with faculty across disciplines in writing workshops, on collaborative projects, and in conversations, that they often hastily generalize about their colleagues' expectations without in fact having studied them. For example, as a Ph.D. student in English, Chris wrote many of his course and seminar papers in nonanalytic genres—plays, stories, poems—and he was routinely told by his professors that "no one else in the department would accept your writing in this form, but it's fine with me." Yet no professor rejected the work. We can encourage colleagues in other fields to talk with each other about acceptable variety in student work and ways to cultivate this variety while still letting students know that there are agreed-upon conventions that represent ways of thinking in the discipline.

- In defining *alternative discourse* and in honoring students' desires to write in alternative ways, we should distinguish among motives for alternatives. We hypothesized that academics working outside of English studies would likely not be aware of arguments around the use of alternative discourses as a way to disrupt hegemonic discourses and assert marginalized identities. In our informants' responses we discovered that they were well aware of alternative discourses and, in fact, most were enacting alternatives in their own work, not to disrupt conventional discourses but rather as a necessary way to tap new knowledge or to reach new audiences within or on the edge of the general framework of the discipline (e.g., Sorrell's phenomenology, Trefil's popular science, Rader's introspection). Although they were consciously choosing to work in alternative ways, they never talked about alternative discourse as overt resistance to a formal or ideological center or as a way to express an identity being subsumed in the dominant discourse. The closest any of our informants came to such an assertion was Sorrell's statement that phenomenology seemed, to her, a way to tap into nurses' intuitive knowledge, knowledge traditionally marginalized or undervalued in medical science. Although they were often aware of taking professional risks, these alternative enactments were not explicitly performative; nevertheless, we see the alternatives performing political work in that each performance helps to move disciplinary centers.

So what does this mean for us as teachers? We need to work with students who purposely write in alternative ways to discover where, if anywhere, the center of the discipline meets the edge on which they write. We see a process of ongoing negotiation similar to those our informants described in their own scholarly careers. On one side, how might students be taught to accommodate their individual visions to the conventions of the field? On the other, how might the discipline benefit from those unique views or modes of expression. But there is also another reason for alternative student discourse, the one we teachers most often assume in student writers: the student's reliance on patterns of thinking and writing with which they are most comfortable, out of ignorance of academic conventions. These are the students that all of our informants have expressed a willingness to work with, to educate in disciplinary, and their own, expectations, and to let them revise their work. These are students who want to succeed within the discipline, but who can be silenced because they lack the strategies and encouragement to seek what they need in order to improve. It's important that teachers not facilely mistake the reasons for a student's use of alternative discourses. If we assume a writer's ignorance of conventions, we may miss a purposeful way of seeing that can benefit the discipline. If we assume that a student just wants to be contrary, then we may not extend to that person the help or opportunity—or even the simple advice—they might need to succeed.

Our research corroborates Bazerman's view of a discipline as an "ever-changing, complex field where communal projects, goals, and knowledge are constantly negotiated from the individual perspectives and interests of participants within and without the field" (1992, 63). We have seen these negotiations in our respondents' descriptions of their work at the center and/or on the margins of their disciplines. While we are sympathetic to arguments for alternative discourses as self-conscious resistance to hegemonic academic practices, we believe our data, albeit limited, illustrate that resistance may not need to be overt or dramatic in order to move a center. The kind of disciplinary alternatives that our informants have enacted in their own scholarship and in their students' assignments show us that dominant discourses evolve through an accumulation of forces—pressure from other disciplines, pressures from scholars within the disciplines, and/or larger social and political forces which lead to new kinds of understandings and openness to change.

Notes

1. In this point, Sorrell's students echoed the concerns of many of our informants who worried that their work would be thought "not very sophisticated" (Lancaster) by academic readers if the form or the prose was too readable.

2. Now, as she wrote to us in an e-mail following the interview, she's making plans for an "exciting new project": students will write fictional accounts of daily occurrences in their nursing careers for a pre-teen audience, "using not only themselves as characters but also those not as often featured in nursing publications, such as males and minority nurses." An assignment like this, Sorrell hopes, may help attract young people to nursing. Because the current shortage of nurses "is truly frightening," she asserts, this "alternative form of writing in nursing is more needed now than articles written for ourselves."

Works Cited

Bazerman, Charles. 1992. "From Cultural Criticism to Disciplinary Participation: Living with Powerful Words." In *Writing, Teaching, and Learning in the Disciplines*, edited by Anne Herrington and Charles Moran. New York: MLA.

———. 2000. *Shaping Written Knowledge: The Genre and Activity of the Experimental Article in Science.* Academic.Writing Landmark Publications in Writing Studies [online]. Available: http://aw.colostate.edu/books/bazerman_shaping/. Originally published in print: Madison: Univ. Wisconsin Press, 1988.

Bizzell, Patricia 1992. *Academic Discourse and Critical Consciousness.* Pittsburgh: Univ. of Pittsburgh Press.

Lancaster, Roger 1988. *Thanks to God and the Revolution: Popular Religion and Class Consciousness in the New Nicaragua.* New York: Columbia Univ. Press.

Lancaster, Roger 2001. Interview by Terry Zawacki and Chris Thaiss. George Mason University, Faifax, VA, February 8.

———. 1992. *Life Is Hard: Machismo, Danger, and the Intimacy of Power in Nicaragua.* Berkeley: Univ. of California Press.

LeCourt, Donna. 1996. "WAC as Critical Pedagogy: The Third Stage?" *Journal of Advanced Composition* 16:389–405.

Rader, Victoria.1986. *Signal Through the Flames: Mitch Snyder and America's Homeless.* Kansas City: Sheed and Ward.

———. 2001. Interview by Terry Zawacki and Chris Thaiss. George Mason University, Fairfax, VA, February 27.

Regan, Priscilla. 1995. *Legislating Privacy: Technology, Social Values, and Public Policy.* Chapel Hill: University of North Carolina Press.

———. 2001. Interview by Terry Zawacki and Chris Thaiss. George Mason University, Fairfax, VA, March 2.

Smith, Robert. 2001. Interview by Terry Zawacki and Chris Thaiss. George Mason University, Fairfax, VA, February 23.

Sorrell, Jeanne, ed. (2000). *Beveled Edges: A Portrait of Caring Nurses' Reflections.* Fairfax, VA: George Mason University College of Nursing and Health Science.

———. 2001. Interview by Terry Zawacki and Chris Thaiss. George Mason University, Fairfax, VA, February 16.

Struppa, Daniele. 2001. Interview by Terry Zawacki and Chris Thaiss. George Mason University, Fairfax, VA. March 5.

Swales, John 1990. *Genre Analysis: English in Academic and Research Settings.* Cambridge: Cambridge Univ. Press.

Thaiss, Christopher and Rick Davis. 1999. *Writing About Theater.* Needham Heights, MA: Allyn and Bacon.

Thaiss, Christopher and John Hess. 1999. *Writing for Law Enforcement.* Needham Heights, MA: Allyn and Bacon.

Thaiss, Christopher and James Sanford. 2000. *Writing for Psychology.* Needham Heights, MA: Allyn and Bacon.

Thaiss, Christopher and Terry Myers Zawacki. 1997. "How Portfolios for Proficiency Help Shape a WAC Program." In *Assessing Writing Across the Curriculum: Diverse Approaches and Practices*, edited by K. Yancey and B. Huot, 79–96. Greenwich, CT: Ablex.

Trefil, James. 2001. Interview by Terry Zawacki and Chris Thaiss. George Mason University, Fairfax, VA, February 9.

Zawacki, Terry Myers. 1992. "Recomposing as a Woman—An Essay in Different Voices." *College Composition and Communication* 43:32–138.

———. 2001. "Telling Stories: The Subject Is Never Just Me." In *Questioning Authority: Stories Told in School,* edited by L. Adler-Kassner and S. Harrington, 34–52. Ann Arbor: Univ. of Michigan Press.

9

So It Was This Beautiful Night
Infecting the Hybrid

Belinda Kremer

So it was this beautiful night. Daylight savings had just kicked in, everything seemed brighter. Early. Clear blue, midnight blue, 3/4 moon. And I was walking, thinking how many different ways I could come home from the L. How there were all these maps of the way home, how just one of them would emerge.

I thought about simultaneity. How, sometimes, multiple versions live horizontally, planar; an array, and you choose, aware of what's been nixed, or that much gets nixed in order, ever, to choose; to create, to mistake, to fall into the singular construction that is any moment. Then there's the other simultaneity—the obscured kind—where from the beginning there's a plan, a map, an order, a schedule, a vision—& the other ways the thing might occur are, and remain hidden. Some effort of consciousness or will required to see what might be. Not an array, but containment. You don't see what's hidden, not chosen, the layers previous, the choices, the archetypal untaken road, unless what's been obscured inserts itself, a ghoul popping up from the basement. Otherwise invisible as the different words that might have driven this sentence. Let the spell-check por

Not in dictionary:	por
Change to:	poor

pop up what else might	poor	have been, and you might
laugh, you might have a new	pro	idea. You might become aware
of language itself, its branch-	pour	ing, innumerable possibilities,
and if you're in the mood, you	or	remember that life is like
that—that any containment is	pore	construct, perhaps contami-

pork
porn
port
poi
pod
pop
pot
poy

nant; that cracks in the vessel are a cold shower, a wake-up call, what we often love best. How do we let those contaminants, those infections, those cross-pollinations, those unplanned-for hybridities, mistakes, become as much a part of texts and our teaching of them, of the texts that classrooms *are,* while still exacting, enacting enough containment to effectively uphold our end of the college bargain, tuition in exchange for tuition?

I had a plan. You've got to have a plan. I'm not against the beauties of containment, its necessity—its sheer athleticism, will; Frost famously said that writing free verse is like playing tennis without a net—you know. But if we're talking about texts, about so-called hybrid discourse, about challenging how we read & write & teach texts, where, if we're being truthful, can we start but with [not with containment but] mess?

Hybridity itself is such a clean word. I much prefer infection, parasitism. Infection, parasitism—process, not product. Even—especially since it's unlikely we're actually bringing together distinct species—crossbreeding, interbreeding. But I just don't think those will catch on. Hybridize is better than hybridity, I suppose—a little more crawling. A little more aware of the spilled fluids on the table, the occasions of mislabeling, the drama of witness, the outside actors. Still, doesn't this all need to be queered a little? Behind the thin scrim of metaphor, the heterosexual reality—cross a male of one species with a female of another—lurks. Not to mention a creepy shadow of eugenics. And if hybrids are often sterile, can hybridity possibly be a good metaphor for generation?

Anyway. I had a plan. And I wrote it out, on another coast, at a friend's computer, New Year's Eve. We'd made and eaten soba noodles and garlic bread, our own strange combination of desires and available ingredients. Drunk some good wine. Kids in bed. Adults talking, laughing. And it just seemed like time to get this thing out of the way—I'd been procrastinating. I wanted to start '01 with a job crossed off the list, not a job still waiting. I made a plan. It went like this:

Textual Hybridity: A Proposal

Hi Helen & Chris

I'd like to propose a piece, structurally somewhere between a narrative and a collage, in which a creative writing class serves as a text that was written, read, and taught by me. I approach this text with a hybrid reading, as the instructor of the course, as a writer, and as a person who became deeply involved with a student in the class, A—, who was/is HIV+ and who became quickly and dramatically unwell, mainly in response to a first, very rough round of chemo, and in need of response as the class progressed. A— herself, and her hybrid text will be examined, as will the infection and hybridizing of the course material, as it became necessary to overtly acknowledge that the text and genre of our course was being altered (from an assumed normalcy) into an infected or hybridized text and genre. What I mean by this is that most of all of the students in that room seemed to be facing severe illness for the first time, let alone terminal illness (A—'s prognosis was not hopeful; she and her doctors hadn't landed on an effective mix of meds, and certain conditions were progressing at a debilitating rate). The course was interrupted, or the course became about interruption; in fact, the course mirrored the true, disjoint process of creation. I will examine how decisions I made affected my sense of competence and connection in the room; the questions about pedagogy that were raised for me (What was the value, what were the benefits, what were the losses, the in-betweens, of saying, "Part of our subject matter here is that one of you is nineteen years old and is experiencing a terminal prognosis, and most of you are struggling with very basic, important questions about how to be around that"?)

+	1	Feb 18		(2,420)	hmmm
+	3	Mar 3		(7,548)	Fwd: Belinda and K—
+ A	5	Mar 7		(5,279)	yet another email from me
+ A	6	Mar 10		(2,669)	Re: yet another email from me
+	9	Mar 13		(1,979)	Re: checking in
+	10	Mar 12		(4,050)	
N	11	Mar 13	To:	(1,852)	carrying a little bit OK with you
+ A	13	Mar 15		(1,838)	class tomorrow
+	15	Mar 16		(5,685)	Re: class tomorrow
+	16	Mar 16		(2,305)	new poem
+ A	17	Mar 29		(1,546)	nightmare
+	21	Apr 5		(2,670)	paper and winter
+ A	24	Apr 20		(2,189)	up and up and up
+ A	27	Jun 2		(2,046)	twizzlers
N	32	Jun 15	To:	(700)	spillage
N	34	Jun 23	To:	(1,000)	haircut
+ A	37	Sep 10		(2,088)	birdy
N	38	Jul 16	To:	(709)	love to you
N	41	Sep 10	To:	(2,179)	Re: birdy
N	42	Sep 16	To:	(1,433)	Re: a poem?
N	43	Sep 16	To:	(1,858)	Re: nothing at all really
+ A	44	Sep 16		(1,767)	a poem?
+ A	45	Sep 16		(4,271)	nothing at all really
+	46	May 30		(5,246)	letters

In California, L— said she'd attach the proposal and send it for me in the morning, and she did. Meanwhile, F— decided she was ready to head home and promptly, in the darkness outside, making the turn to head up the sharp drive, backed into my rental car, which, since there were a lot of us there, was parked where cars usually weren't. All I'm saying is that "crash," "dent," "buckle" and "you never know" immediately infected my plan, became part of the consciousness of this essay.

Does it matter? Intention must matter. Why we write. And then the sense that it must matter has to go to bat and knock the sliders and inside curves pitched by "it doesn't" out of the park.

The car was driveable. It had, really, just a small rumple in the driver-side rear door. I carried on to my grandmother's house. I was there, at her house, for various reasons, and my proposal went into my travel bag, and its containment, its sense of purpose, its apparent clarity made it a stranger to me when I unpacked it, a week later, at home.

Date: Thu, 18 Feb 1999 08:25:15 PST
Subject: hmmm

Belinda.

I think that people stop seeing when you are sick. I mean they of course see you. Some people see your bald head and tired eyes and glance away as quick as they can; pretend that they didn't. The nurse who has seen your chart and is scared to take your blood sample sees a lost cause and tries to pretend you into a number. The doctor sees your x-rays and numbers and is interested in what course the process will take. The world sees you and doesn't even know that you are there.

I wish, I wish, I wish.

I wish that I could just say to someone. I am. And they would accept everything that came after . . . scared, proud, alone, sarcastic, funny, smart, bitter, caring, dying. I wish that they would see all that and still just see me behind it. I wish that I could just scream to someone "I AM" and they would look at me and be able to see me and be able to say "I know."

I know that there isn't really anything you can say to this. I don't really know why I am writing it to you. Maybe because this is what you do—read things. Maybe just because I need a friend . . . even if it is only in writing . . . only on email.

A—

Date: Tue, 9 Mar 1999 23:47:46 PST

> bkk—

> In class today we talked about Guernica the whole time . . . Sigh. it would have been OK if I

>hadn't done an independent study on Guernica for a semester at george mason.

> ps what does the middle k stand for?

Date: Wed, 10 Mar 1999 10:36:46 -0500 (EST)
Subject: Re: yet another email from me
Hey A—
I just saw Guernica at the Guggenheim; "Picasso: The War Years." Lots of studies for it, too . . . well, of course, I didn't "see" it, but you know what i mean. that was a really good show. too bad about your class, though.

the middle k is for—
—Give it a stab.
—bk

Date: Wed, 10 Mar 1999 08:17:40 PST
Subject: Re: yet another email from me
So Katherine,
I would like to be really witty . . . The only words I could think of were kid, kinship, kill and katty. And I just couldn't string them together into a clever alliteration. guernica at the guggenheim. sounds like the title to a tacky poem.

I read the stories from our class during my i.v.-o-rama this morning. we are a DEPRESSED bunch of kids aren't we? Maybe you should think seriously about the amount of stress you are putting on us. Reads like some of us are beginning to crack under the pressure.
A—

I read the essay proposal again, thinking that in a week, after my surgeon excised the infected gland that was giving me so much trouble, while the anesthesia puffed its way back out of my body and the swelling came down & the flesh began to knit, I ought to similarly begin smoothing the proposed ideas into their own healthy whole.

But so what? I was, in some sense, bored—knowing that I should now take the ideas outlined in the proposal and fill them in. And yet, just this sort of containment, a killing, I think, sort of containment, was precisely what I taught against in composition, rhetoric, creative writing, argument, poetics—so it struck me as absurd that I could possibly express the felt sense, the aesthetic sense and the theory, of teaching the embrace of the rough nap of text and process and textual mess, of changing lanes & blind spots, if I myself were trying to box it up. How much the self resists, even with intention: working against the grain of "normal."

EXPECTATIONS ARE BEING AROUSED . . . THE READER RECAPITULATES "EVIDENCE" FROM THE PORTION OF THE TEXT HE (*sic*) HAS

READ TO PROJECT FORWARD A CONFIGURATION, A TENTATIVE ASSUMPTION OF WHAT THE WORK AS A WHOLE WILL BE AND MEAN ONCE IT IS DONE

SHOWS LITTLE INTEREST IN THE CREATIVE PROCESS AS SUCH AND HAS VIRTUALLY NO INTEREST IN AUTHORS

THE AUTHOR OR HIS OR HER INTENTION OR LIFE, NOR, ON THE OTHER HAND, WITH THE HISTORICAL OR CULTURAL CONTEXT OF THE AUTHOR OR THE READER

THE LITERARY WORK THEREFORE DOES *NOT* EXIST ON THE PAGE

THE EARLY 1960S, WHEN A COMBINATION OF SPACE-AGE PREOCCUPATION WITH SCIENCE AND COLD-WAR FEAR OF IMPLICATION LED TO A VIEW OF LITERATURE AS INTELLECTUALLY CHALLENGING YET SOCIALLY AND POLITICALLY NONCONTROVERSIAL

SO UNIVERSALLY ACCEPTED AS *AT LEAST THE FIRST STEP* IN THE UNDERSTANDING OF LITERATURE THAT IT IS ALMOST EVERYWHERE THE CRITICAL APPROACH TAUGHT IN INTRODUCTORY LITERATURE COURSES

LANGUAGE CONSISTS JUST IN BLACK MARKS ON A PAGE THAT REPEAT OR DIFFER

CONTENT IS LESS IMPORTANT THAN FORM

THE CONVENTIONAL NOTION OF READING . . . THAT A WRITER OR SPEAKER HAS AN "IDEA," ENCODES IT . . . AND THE READER OR LISTENER DECODES IT, DERIVING, WHEN SUCCESSFUL, THE WRITER/ SPEAKER'S "IDEA"

IS THE EXPRESSION OF THE AUTHOR'S PSYCHE, OFTEN HIS OR HER UNCONSCIOUS, AND, LIKE DREAMS, NEEDS TO BE INTERPRETED

THE WORD, THEN, LIKE THE UNCONSCIOUS DESIRE, IS SOMETHING THAT CANNOT BE FULFILLED

(Bain, Carl, Jerome Beaty, and J.Paul Hunter. 1991. "Writing about Literature: Critical Approaches." In *The Norton Introduction to Literature*. New York: Norton.)

I love my new Rhodia pad, I'm writing this on it. Do you know these pads? I've coveted them forever, I admit to a stationery fetish. This is the first time I'm seeing if I can live with Brit commas, usually I'd scatter the semi- and colons all over the page. Also full stops. It leaves me feeling like I need to scratch, I know it's pseudo in a way, tried on. The itch occurs just between "scratch" and "I." This whole paragraph feels rashy.

Date: Wed, 03 Mar 1999 06:51:16 PST
Subject: Belinda and K—

B—

My best friend is dead.

That's the sentence. There's not even any emotion behind it for me to talk about. It's just a fact, a thing.

I wish that you could have met E—. One time we sat out on his steps waiting for a cab to a movie for two hours, gabbing about nothing at all, never realizing that the cab had never come and the movie was almost over. One time he told me that he was trying to tell me all of his stories. Another time he told me that I already knew all of his stories.

Then the funniest thing happened.

E— got sick. And we laughed about that too. I would sit next to his hospital bed in sterilized, blue-grey institution rooms and tell him that this crash diet of his was making me look bad. His eyes would crinkle with amusement at how uncomfortable I would get trying to respond politely to the non-stop chatter of his slightly senile, older than god roommate. Even when we stopped laughing, he would look happy when I talked to him. By that time I would only talk about the things that made his eyes seem less desperate. I think I only realized a little while ago that I ended up just telling all of E—'s stories back to him; because those were the things that would make his knuckles less white and relax all the muscles that I hadn't known existed over his cheek bones and beside his nose.

I told him about the time that he couldn't find his easter basket for two hours after his brother had found his and he started crying so hard that, even after his parents simply gave it to him, he was hiccuping too hard to eat the ears off the rabbit. I told him about how for a month he had his new middle school believing that he was really a girl named E— and how he couldn't talk about sex without his ears turning red. I told him about how for a year he was convinced he wasn't getting any parts because he needed a nose job, when really he just wasn't very good yet.

I am nervous about this appointment today. This guy is a bigshot. My doctor must have written two million letters for him to have this much interest in my case.

all my best to both of you

A—

All I'm saying: it's 1998, '99, 2000, '01, and you're teaching literature or composition or creative writing in a university, and the assumption right from the start is that these genre separations are serious as a heart attack, serious enough to warrant their own division numbers; and it follows, other things that go with your time are a post-post-structuralist hangover that feels remarkably like structuralism itself, like the "post" and "post" cancel instead of double each other—take us backward, into self-contained texts, instead of tearing at the edges—and a retro fear that intention and subjectivity are the de facto failed, sad second cousins to science, the stellar son or daughter always rushed right into the room, first to meet the relatives.

So I was sitting in on my friend's seminar on fractal poetics. A fabulous seminar. During a break, a Ph.D. student, J—, said the reason she studied what she studied, she was looking at Jeanette Winterson, was because she loved the writing.

Everyone laughed.

"No, really," she said.

Everyone laughed.

That was pretty much that. Laugh and laugh canceled each other, and in the absence of investigating laughter as a response, of or seeing J—'s love of the text as a front-edge possibility, the question was dropped.

But it mattered. If there's something we truly need to infect, hybridize, cross-pollinate, it's the values of humanism, which suggest we might come to know from, for example, poetry, something about living in the world, with the literary theoretical values that dismiss intention and meaning and "because I love it" as valid starting points for critical inquiry. Since the admission of a shared affection is essentially a nonprogressive inquiry—a conversation that can be entered and exited at almost any point—this infection of affection also has the positive potential to infect some of the less-productive boundaries of teacher/student genres.

I think we can infect the following: the idea that when a reading comes from love, or is interested in intention, in the generative impulses of the actions of writing and reading, there is something essentially indefensible (because personal) in one's response—it can't be codified—thus it can't be studied.

—WHY NOT?

Isn't it possible that fear stands right behind the avowal that subjectivity makes critical thinking impossible, that fear is part of what drives this distance from the text? It seems excruciatingly difficult, within universities, and particularly within the liberal arts, to justify the worth of, or even admit to the existence of, arguments that can't be solved. There's a problem with what we are often doing in university classrooms: having acknowledged a core of literary critical thinking that's productive and that says texts have inconsistencies, contradictions, gaps; language is inherently unstable, unmappable, etc., we jump—not into a fray of multiple meanings & readings & their articulation, not into the richness that indeterminacy and the hybrid metaphor, at best, promise—but *away* from meaning completely. The objectivity + literature hybrid is a dead cross, essentially based on a false premise; it strives for the controlled reproducibility of the scientific result without acknowledging that the strict controls in place to create reproducible results are controls that dull humanistic questions. It forgets, too, that reproducible results are meant to *serve* theory, not to *be* theory. If this were imported, the cross might be more productive; then we might generate a theory of literature that saw a given text as the control, a reproducible result passion for the text, and that then sought a theory to explain how black marks on a page connect people and experience across centuries, miles, cultures, ages. Instead, we have, too often, been given literary theory itself as the controlled parameter: if I critique it on this theoretical basis, and you critique it on this theoretical basis, we will get the same result.

And this uniformity of result serves what purpose? That we can generate reproducible critical readings of a particular text? And that does what, and for whom? The next infection, the next hybrid that we need to effect, is this: bleeding meaning and intention back into literary theory—they are, at this point, foreign matter. And they are defended against.

A— wrote:

Hitchhiking Sestina

It was a dusty frantic road.
No tree approached to offer shade.
But walking tall along the thin white line,
I felt strong enough to laugh
ferociously at the passing cars' speed
and how none would stop to offer a change

of pace. But I knew that would change.
I had been traveling along that dusty road
so long I thought time would speed
up to match my frantic pace toward the shade
of an unknown destination where I could laugh
without feeling I was crossing the line

between the hilarity and the sanity that were the dashed line
forming a highway traveling life without change
or bills to make a cushion in which to laugh
about a possible lack of food while on the dusty road.
I decided New Orleans would be my place of shade
so I could tell my rides where to go with such speed.

The people picked me up in such speed
and followed one another's Saabs in straight lines,
driving without seeing through their Ray-Ban shades
that I sat next to them with no change
in my pockets, nor the will to laugh
at the jokes they made driving the dusty road

to New Orleans. Where everyone was on the dusty road
to nowhere, and all the kids took speed
or coke in perfect white lines,
so they would be able to bravely laugh

through another night's worth of change
and disaster in a lonely alley's shade.

I did not find my shelter or shade
in New Orleans. I had been on the endless dusty road
too long to leave my life of change
and travel for the Mardi Gras mood of speed
and coke and paranoid laughs.
So I left in search of lines

along a frantic road of dusty shade.
Where I could line my throat with laughter
at the speed of life when you seek to change.

And then there's affection.

The truest contraband in the economy of the university is affection. Contraband in the scholarly sense because theoretical fashion essentially views affection as naive. Contraband in the writerly sense because in a creative writing class, students are actively authoring the course text/s; and as every teacher knows, Lolita grins up, mouth lollipop red, from every encounter of affection with a student, giving yet another reason to subscribe to the excision of the author from the text. We do some packaging, containment of our humanity by containing the humanity of the text—its author/s, whether proximal or far away; its reader/s; itself, its communicative power—to avoid the volatile presence of affection in the room.

Is this what writing is, though?

Date: Wed, 31 Mar 1999 18:32:39 PST
Subject: shopping

hi b,

I was wondering, and if you already went out really don't worry about it, but if you haven't if maybe we could switch the shopping list to food instead of music sometime in the next week or two? I started listening to a Tom Wolfe novel someone lent me today at the hospital. I think that the man just decided that he wanted to write a book that was REALLY REALLY long. He draws every last description out to the n'th degree . . . like he was describing something as tawdry and he just went on and on about the tawdriness, oh the tawdriness, tawdriness, tawdriness of this tawdry thing that seemed so tawdry in its tawdriness (I don't remember what it was now). i started laughing out loud at that point. I think if i finish it I will have to just listen to every other word to get a sense of the plot behind the words.

By the way after reading some of Alice Munro I have decided that I really should just stick to painting . . . I think she already has the writing thing covered. =)

A—

Date: Mon, 31 May 1999 10:26:43 PDT
Subject: Re: tomorrow

Hi b.

It's been a really hard weekend. J— died very late Thursday night which I knew perfectly well was coming and still somehow managed to be surprised by. As if I was expecting him to hold on for courtesy's sake. I guess I just didn't know how to write that when I wrote to you that night.

I never feel as though that sort of thing is real until 24 hours after the fact anyway. I always focus on the inconsequential during that brief grace period.

The session wasn't as bad as I was dreading and I'm doing ok now though tired.

A—

Date: Sat, 19 Jun 1999 21:49:03 PDT
Subject: bad news/happy thoughts

B—

Did ya ever look out the window to the sky
Close your eyes against the bored sun and dopey clouds
And start to wonder how long you'd be stuck here

And were you dreaming of clouds that moved a little faster
In a place where poets weren't poets because everybody was
Where singers weren't talented because everybody was
Ya know, a Judy-Garland-Somewhere-Over-the-Rainbow type dream

Did you learn to spit like a boy
And braid hair like a girl

And did you cry out, "God!"
And not be swearing
and not be wondering if he even existed
Or if he would answer you or not

And can you really sing
And write real poems
And talk to a real God

love, A—

Date: Mon, 21 Jun 1999 22:32:25 -0400 (EDT)
Subject: Re: bad news/happy thoughts

A—

hi you
hey I want to visit the place where no one's a poet because
          everyone is
here's my secret
          I think I visit that place every time I write a poem

gertrude stein said

poetry is really loving the name of anything
& for me, when I write a poem, I take on faith
that I have a community of other lovers with me

          so it's god faith poetry all in one
pretty dreamy yes?

—BK

Via the syllabus, student gets signified: student is the implied subject of a string of imperative verbs; in other words, student is passive: *Bring. Read. Write. Critique. Respond.* Their agency is muted by the series of directives I give, but their best writing, always, is animated by intention, agency, affection for the act of communication, passion about meaning.

For the unhappy intersection, the impoverishing proximity, the sterile hybrid of objective + humanities, I have only an un-solution: this is a place to de- or anti-hybridize, to infect with, rather than immunize against (meaning): to extract this code generated outside the body of the humanities, and better, perhaps, left there.

Anything Is Possible

Last night's wet
     dripping roofline rain
          slowed to stalactites

in this morning's pre-dawn cold
     Yesterday icicles arrived
          the same way

Today anything is possible
     We are ranged
          only by the imminence

of the lengthening days
     & the garden's insistent green

     last night I drove A— to D—'s house we held her

while chemical pain racked her today she sent an e-mail
how?) to say
she just wanted to be seen she needed somewhere
to say "I AM" she didn't know why
she picked me she said "maybe because this is what you do:
you read things"

nudging life's "why" to the rear

proclaiming the mud-suck
song and rage of spring
making its yearly offer:

renewal in exchange
for our faith
or mere existence

I know this: I don't want to read
another single article
admiring the elegance
and blind will of viruses

or mere existence
I promised someone new
I'd go the distance

steady at her side
in the breaking viral slide
coming for her sure as spring

It's said we all need a line
a line to sing through
to sting chaos back
to sense   to sense the disparate
and disparaging

Sometimes we take a hard look
at the ground's open mouth
sometimes we believe

we're not turning the bed
for a last summer
I try to hold these

one in each hand
letting the gaps and troubles
blow like chaff in a bright wind

She's been drawing madonnas and children,
madonna and child. Her own mother
won't see her. Then there are the songs
about Jesus and kids. She's better than this,
more complex; she's been reduced
by the virus and a lack of love,
each impossible to underweigh.
A year ago, before she'd told,
her family's distance could be read
logistical. Pen, pastel, charcoal
in hand, she textured her first chemo
into stark lines, buzzsaw sounds nicking
her head to crewcut, the stubble's surprise of blue-black
gunpowder dusting her skull.
Now everything's transparent: a blank
kind face cradles a child in one, two,
five, seven, endless
iterations of the same longing: all a wish
to go home, to be taken up in arms. A loss
no one can fill. I can record it, and offer
her my arms, which aren't the ones
she wants, but will settle for.
A kind of death: the available
filling in—

Seeds of wishes sift between
—would she call them failure
or dream?—the roof-tight spears

might hold steady and clear
A blanketing snow might push back
late March's imminent leaving

The denial of winter
might rise up and

—A—, friend
these next lines are yours

It's raining, raining, raining, all the wrought iron and windows are beaded up with fat drops. Our own screens are covered with, with, with the water beaded and then running down, running down . . . and in running down, changing the shape of where they are.

That's about as far as we can go with most of this. Truly. I wish you a good day, a sheltering sky, a theory of literature that believes you exist. I hope the rain clears up. Things, in truth, are often less complicated than they seem.

The windows? Thank you, but you're too kind. We usually just let the rain dry itself in the air.

Date: Tue, 30 May 2000 19:15:33 EDT
Subject: letters

B—

I want to tell you something.

I've been writing you these letters this past year. Of course you know that, but I mean letters every day, sometimes 2 or 3 a day. I have a whole diskette saved of writings that begin with "Dear Belinda." You have become my journal of sorts. Lately as I begin something with "Dear Belinda" and know somehow that by using your full name I am compelling myself not to send it, I have begun to wonder why.

I don't know why I am telling you this now. Perhaps it is this feeling of gently floating back into last summer's fatigue and illness. I can feel last summer in my lungs again, that slow filling of liquid that is impossible to cough out and difficult to breathe through. Maybe it is because I have felt so unconnected this last week, so unsure that out in the darkness the world is really and truly still there, and not something I'm making up. My left side, also, becomes less real as I lose a little more feeling in my hand and in my face. Maybe because once again I feel like I am slightly losing my grasp on words and thoughts and coherence, and I always worry that they, too, can be summarily taken away.

Perhaps it's because I want to know that, in the future, when you actually see all these letters, I have said to you while I am here, "This is what I meant." and this is why they are here. Not to put a claim on you, or to make you feel uncomfortable, but to say thank you for being something you did not know you were. I suppose I could just put this letter to file as well, and let you read it then. I know I will feel a lot less silly and pathetic and over-dramatic if I do that. But I hope I do not.

—A

—Being what we write about.

Note: Through tireless research and belief, A— became part of a protocol, and through that a drug and chemo regimen, through which she has stabilized. It is spring 2001. She is currently debating whether psychology or sculpture will next engage her.

10

Re-Clustering Traditional Academic Discourse
Alternating with Confucian Discourse

LuMing Mao

In his recent essay "Literacy, Identity, Imagination, Flight," Keith Gilyard calls our attention again to a double-bind that, "whenever we participate in the dominant discourse, no matter how liberally we may tweak it, we help to maintain it" (2000, 268). However, Gilyard views this double-bind both as inescapable and as "part of a productive tension, a heightening of contradiction" (2000, 268). Such a characterization has enabled Gilyard to remain optimistic and to be "reaffirmed in the notion that being critically careful does make a difference" (2000, 268). In this essay, I intend to take up Gilyard's characterization of this perennial double-bind and apply it to a discussion of alternative discourses. Or perhaps more precisely, I want to use alternative discourses as a *concrete* example to suggest that a dilemma of this nature not only can be turned into a "productive tension," but it also nurtures the very possibility of re-visioning traditional academic discourse or the dominant discourse in ways that will help open up more spaces for other discourses. In other words, I want to reconsider the divide that has become so much a part of our conversation about traditional academic discourse versus other discourses.

From Discourses to a Shifting Discursive Continuum

So, what is traditional academic discourse? Bizzell, in "Hybrid Academic Discourses: What, Why, How," suggests that traditional academic discourse displays a number of distinctive characteristics, such as using a written register (or what she calls "grapholect"), complying with a controlled or rigid structure, and embodying a typical worldview (1999, 10–11). Not surprisingly, these characteristics have also been singled out as being constitutive of essayist tradition, which, according to Scollon and Scollon, can be characterized as decontextualized, fictionalized, as well as structurally controlled (1981, 47–52).[1] In the same essay, Bizzell also tells us that new forms of discourse are emerging, which she dubs "hybrid academic discourses." And these discourses combine previously nonacademic discourses with traditional academic discourses (1999, 11). Bizzell further attributes their emergence and their growing acceptance to our academic population becoming more diverse, and more importantly, to their ability to enable practitioners to "do intellectual work in ways they could not if confined to traditional academic work" (1999, 12). According to Bizzell, their features or traits range from, for example, writing in "non-standard" English, to relying on personal experience, to arguing indirectly or by "offhand refutation," to writing oneself into the story (1999, 16).[2]

The emergence of hybrid academic discourses clearly deserves our attention. As Bizzell has indicated, hybrid academic discourses challenge the dichotomy between traditional academic discourse and students' home discourses (2000, 7). Further, such discourses may provide an empowering voice for those whose home discourses have often been disregarded if not discredited. On the other hand, the term *hybrid* embeds implications that could be quite troublesome, too. For example, as Bizzell herself has acknowledged, the term is "at once too abstract and too concrete" (2000, 7). It is too abstract because it creates an illusion that the use of hybrid academic discourses would make boundary-crossing, cultural or linguistic, both easier and risk-free. It is also too concrete to the extent that it risks pigeonholing people's language—as if to suggest that each one of us must uncover our hybrid academic discourse, one that is necessarily distinguished by its "home discourse" (2000, 7–8).

But what about the term *alternative,* which has been used interchangeably with the term *hybrid,* and which I am using in this essay over the term *hybrid*? While the use of *alternative* may have avoided the kinds of implications Bizzell has uncovered for *hybrid,* it might create some other problems of its own. For one thing, to characterize anything as alternative may have already marginalized it relative to its counterpart, which is mainstream, standard, or traditional. Hence, you have *alternative medicine/therapy, alternative logic,* or *alternative lifestyle*—just to name a few. Although each of these terms does indeed represent a new or different paradigm within its own context, it also, perhaps inevitably, creates a division, if not a hierarchy, between the alternative and what it is presumed to challenge.

Second, the use of *alternative* in *alternative discourse* may also imply that traditional academic discourse is always pure and/or stable, and that it is immune from any alternative influences or intrusions. But this kind of implication certainly is not true. In fact, traditional academic discourse undergoes its own metamorphosis—however imperceptible or slow-going it may be. I suspect that its own instability may have in part contributed to, or created an environment for, the emergence of alternative discourses. Critical discourse analyst Norman Fairclough identifies one particular change in traditional academic discourse—a change he refers to as "conversationalization" (1995, 101). He points to this increasing blurring between our daily conversation and our academic discourse as "part of a process of cultural engineering and restructuring cultural hegemony" (1995, 105). It is this kind of linguistic blurring, according to Fairclough, that presents new opportunities as well as challenges (1995, 106).

Third, there often is this disciplinary temptation to embrace new terms or concepts when they seem to generate enough intellectual excitement or suggest new directions for research. I am certainly not against (the use of) new terms or concepts per se, but I do protest when we neglect to carefully uncover their implications, and to examine larger sociocultural conditions that have nurtured or spurred their emergence. Clearly, the use of any alternative discourse is not going to solve all the linguistic and social inequalities traditional academic discourse presents and perpetuates—though it is an important start. And linguistic and social transformations transcend or demand more than the use of alternative discourses; they call for other cultural interventions that challenge the "*naturalized* hierarchy" or what Fairclough calls "cultural hegemony" (1995, 105).

Now that I've made my disclaimers, can I then claim some degree of impunity for the use of alternative discourses? I am afraid not. To address these limitations that could potentially handicap the use of the term *alternative,* I suggest we reconsider the discursive relationship that has so far characterized traditional academic discourse and alternative discourses. It is a hierarchical relationship—one that places traditional academic discourse on top and alternative discourses at bottom. And it is also an antagonistic relationship pitting one against the other. Therefore, in order to collapse this kind of hierarchy, and in order to neutralize this kind of antagonism, we need to replace this divisive relationship with a shifting discursive continuum that consists of different clusters of discursive tendencies. Further, on this continuum, certain discursive features may be clustered to form a particular discourse (known, for example, as traditional academic discourse), and certain other discursive features may be coalesced to form what have now been referred to as alternative discourses.

What's the payoff, then, for making this discursive move, so to speak? There are several. First, discourses seen now as clusters of discursive tendencies, be they traditional academic discourse or other alternative discourses, can be anything but fixed or stable since they are part of this *shifting* continuum.[3] As such, there is no seamless boundary between different clusters. Thus, it is not unusual for some discursive tendency to be drifting between two different clusters. For example, Bizzell suggests that the use of personal experience as a source of illustrations is one of the characteristics of hybrid academic discourses (1999, 16). On the other hand, traditional academic discourse may also draw upon personal experience to shore up evidence. So, the use of personal experience as a discursive tendency could share its *allegiance* between these two discourses. The point, of course, is that one shifting of association does not traditional academic discourse make. Rather, it is both a cluster of discursive tendencies and its codified recurrence that constitute a particular discourse.

Second, and perhaps more important, the call for a shifting discursive continuum is also a call for foregrounding those ideologies that inform, and are in turn enforced by, corresponding clusters of discursive tendencies. Following Foss, ideology is "a pattern or set of ideas, assumptions, beliefs, values, or interpretations of the world by which a culture or group operates" (1996, 291). As such, ideologies ground our actions, and they "simultaneously explain, often exonerate, and always partially create, in interaction with history and the material bases of society, the distribution of goods" (Gee 1996, 21).[4] Therefore, it seems only appropriate to propose that some cluster of discursive tendencies does not automatically carry more social clout than some other cluster of discursive tendencies. The very reason it does so is that it encodes a set of beliefs and values that is championed by, and has become an integral part of, a dominant community. The longer the dominance of these beliefs and values, the more natural such a cluster becomes and the more acceptable it also becomes within a given society. Alternative discourses, be they feminist rhetoric (Foss and Griffin 1995) or Black Talk (Smitherman 1977), are less acceptable or less valued not because their discursive tendencies are deficient, but because the ideologies they are grounded in challenge the dominant ideology, the status quo. And it should come as no surprise at all when such alternative discourses are not considered appropriate in settings that represent dominant social, cultural beliefs and values, but only at the margins that carry much less cultural capital.

Finally, a shifting discursive continuum affords us a real opportunity to renegotiate or to re-cluster different discursive tendencies so that we can better challenge or denaturalize what is traditional or what is mainstream. For example, we can begin to ask: What discursive features are being used? Who is using them? For what purpose? And for whom? These kinds of questions will enable us to avoid making reductive correlations between discourses on the one hand, and people and ideologies on the other. While discourses and ideologies, as I've suggested above, are intimately related, it does not mean that their mutually reciprocal relationship allows no room for negotiation, for creative engagement. For example, it is quite possible that members of the dominant discourse community use alternative discourses to demonstrate their desire to "go native." By the same token, feminist rhetoricians or African Americans could invoke traditional academic discourse to advance their own causes when they realize that their own discourses may not be able to do so. In short, the use of any given discourse does not automatically transform its user into a spokesperson for its underlying ideologies. Nor does the use of the Other's discourse compromise her/his membership in her/his own speech community. Otherwise stated, while discourses (or clusters of discursive features) may be tied to or reflective of certain ideologies, their users and their immediate discursive conditions ultimately determine if these discourses actually promote such ideologies. There is simply no easy correlation here.

Alternating with Confucian Discourse

As I've discussed in the preceding section, to fully realize the productive tension between traditional academic discourse and alternative discourses, we need to think of them as clusters of discursive tendencies on a shifting discursive continuum. And to further understand the dynamics of this shifting discursive continuum, I believe we need to step out of Western discursive traditions and invite ourselves into other, non-Western discursive traditions. As Bakhtin aptly puts it, "it is immensely important for the person who understands to be *located outside* the object of his or her creative understanding—in time, in space, in culture" (1986, 7; emphasis original). Shifting from Western discourses to Confucian discourse in ancient China may prove to be appropriate and timely as a way of relocating ourselves in time, in space, and in culture.

So, what about Confucian discourse? Does it have anything to do with alternative discourses? To begin with, there appears to be a family resemblance between, on the one hand, discursive tendencies attributable to alternative discourses in the West, and discursive tendencies prominent in Confucian discourse, mainly in the *Analects,* on the other. Alternative discourses or hybrid academic discourses, according to Bizzell, may include such tendencies as: coming at one's main points indirectly, using personal experience to evoke the reader's emotional response and sympathy, and employing what she calls "appropriative history" (see Note 1). Interestingly enough, such tendencies have also found their way consistently into the *Analects.* Of course, as I've noted above, some of these tendencies may temporarily slip into traditional academic discourse, and/or some of them may shift out of the cluster with which they are usually associated. What is important to remember is that it is the regularized clustering of these tendencies, as well as their concomitant cultural capital, that sets alternative discourses apart from traditional academic discourse.

The *Analects* is a collection (twenty books or chapters) of sayings attributed to Confucius (551–479 B.C.E.) sayings put together by his disciples after his death. It took them over three centuries to complete the entire work. Because this text involves the work of many of his students, and because it spans several centuries, the *Analects,* according to Ames and Rosemont in their introduction, "can initially give the appearance of being fragmentary, disconnected, and occasionally, in conflict with each other" (1998, 9). Its apparent disunity could almost make the *Analects* a fitting example of our contemporary alternative discourse—though, ironically, the *Analects* later became the premier text by which "Chineseness" was defined (Ames and

Rosemont 1998, 9). In this sense, it has become more traditional and mainstream than Confucius ever anticipated in his lifetime. As a philosopher, an educator, and a politician, Confucius was deeply concerned about the pressing problems of his day, and the *Analects* contains many references to people, places, and events that are unfamiliar to contemporary Western readers. In spite of these kinds of differences, we may not fail to spot a number of recurring discursive tendencies throughout the whole text. First, we find Confucius in the *Analects,* to be quite fond of speaking by metaphor or analogy—both of which are examples of indirection, and both of which enhance his rhetorical effectiveness. For example, the Master said:

> Governing with excellence (*de*) can be compared to being the North Star: the North Star dwells in its place, and the multitude of stars pay it tribute. (76; bk. 2, par. 1)

Here, by comparing governing with excellence to being the North Star, Confucius effectively highlights the need to command absolute authority and to exert total control in governing. Confucius provides us with a similar example of indirection in the following passage:

> There are indeed seedlings that do not flower, and there are flowers that do not fruit. (131; bk. 9, par. 24)

In this passage Confucius speaks again by metaphor: he uses seedlings to describe students who never grow into maturity, and flowers to characterize students who fail to accomplish anything even though they grow up. These are just a few of the examples one finds in the *Analects,* and these examples illustrate how extensively Confucius uses the strategy of indirection to convey his teachings to his students. While the issues he addresses to his students are local, the manner in which they are being addressed are not local at all, but metaphorical.

Second, Confucius is seen in the *Analects* to be alternating a lot between speaking in the first person singular and speaking as a sole representative of the rich cultural Chinese past. To put it somewhat differently, he likes to alternate his personal stories with impersonal, doctrinal pronouncements. Using our contemporary terminology, we might say that Confucius is intent on mixing genres by way of juxtaposing his individual narratives with public pronouncements. He does it in such a way that they could be perceived as examples of narrative disunity.[5] Let me cite a few examples of this discursive tendency. In Book One of the *Analects*, addressing the issue of filial responsibility and the cultivation of the Way, Confucius has this to say:

> While a person's father is still alive, observe what he intends; when his father dies, observe what he does. A person who for three years refrains from reforming the ways of his late father can be called a filial son. (74; bk. 1, par. 12)

In this passage Confucius is being quite impersonal. Speaking from a third person's point of view, he is assuming the voice of an authority—a voice that is unyielding and unequivocal in defining filial responsibility. Likewise, when asked about the role of ritual propriety, the Master once again invokes this authorial persona:

> Deference unmediated by observing ritual propriety (*li*) is lethargy; caution unmediated by observing ritual propriety is timidity; boldness unmediated by observing ritual propriety is rowdiness; candor unmediated by observing ritual propriety is rudeness. (120; bk. 8, par. 2)

These kinds of impersonal teachings are a central part of the *Analects,* and we see them almost everywhere in each of the twenty books. At the same time, Confucius never hesitates to apply his doctrines to his own life, to his own conduct. He is always ready and willing to be quite self-reflective in his dealings with his students. The impersonal ethos now gets infused with a heavy dose of his own personal narrative. For example, the Master said,

> To fail to cultivate excellence (*de*), to fail to practice what I learn, on coming to understand what is appropriate (*yi*) in the circumstances to fail to attend to it, and to be unable to reform conduct that is not productive—these things I worry over. (111; bk. 7, par. 3)

Here, and as in many other places in the *Analects*, Confucius is performing an introspective speech act, sharing with his students his concerns over how to cultivate excellence. He shows no fear of exposing his students to his worries. These kinds of personal reflections constitute another major component of the *Analects.* They become part of Confucius' own life, of his triumphs and disappointments.

Third, Confucius lived in a time of turbulence and instability in Chinese history—one that both challenged and threatened the existing social, cultural, and economic order. One central mission for Confucius was to restore the rich culture of the past, and to bring back harmony and ritual propriety to his time. Against this backdrop, we find in the *Analects,* a major effort on Confucius' part to defend the tradition and to promote a past that champions his ideology. I see a compelling similarity between this strategy and what Bizzell calls "appropriative history"—where the writer tries to write him/herself into the history. For example, in the first two paragraphs in Book Seven of the *Analects*, Confucius stakes out his role in relation to the culture and tradition at large. The Master said,

> Following the proper way, I do not forge new paths; with confidence I cherish the ancients —in these respects I am comparable to our venerable Old Peng[6] (111; bk. 7, par. 1)

> To quietly persevere in storing up what is learned, to continue studying without respite, to instruct others without growing weary—is this not me?(111; bk. 7, par. 2)

In these two passages the Master makes it quite clear that his job is to preserve and enhance the rich Chinese cultural past. But that does not mean Confucius is a passive thinker, blindly worshiping the tradition. Several paragraphs below in the same book, Confucius explains to his students why he is a creative thinker and an earnest discoverer. The Master said,

> I am not the kind of person who has gained knowledge through some natural propensity for it. Rather, loving antiquity, I am earnest *in seeking it out.* (115; bk. 7, par. 20, emphasis added)

For Confucius, the best way to preserve and transmit the tradition is to seek it out, to participate fully in rediscovering it. In other words, the process of seeking the past out is a creative, re-visionary process—where Confucius aims to recover and restore what has been lost, and where he is trying to construct a symbiotic relationship between himself and the larger, ever-expanding community.

As Ames and Rosemont point out, in their introduction

> (p)ersons are not perceived as superordinated individuals—as agents who stand independent of their actions —but are rather ongoing "events" defined functionally by constitutive roles and relationships as they are performed within the context of their specific families and communities, that is, through the observance of ritual propriety (*li*). (1998, 29)

This kind of relationship further reinforces the discursive intermixing between the personal and the communal in the *Analects*.

As a result, we witness in the *Analects* many times when Confucius is trying to restore ritual propriety and to redefine what constitutes authoritative or exemplary conduct (*ren*).[7] According to Ames and Rosemont, the fact that Confucius is asked very frequently what he means by the expression *ren* suggests that he is reinventing this term for his own purposes (1998, 50). In Book Four, Confucius spends a great deal of time trying to redefine *ren*. For example, the Master said,

> Those persons who are not authoritative (*ren*) are neither able to endure hardship for long, nor to enjoy happy circumstances for any period of time. Authoritative persons are content in being authoritative; wise persons (*zhi*) flourish in it. (89; bk. 4, par. 2)

> The authoritative person (*ren*) alone has the wherewithal to properly discriminate the good person from the bad. (89; bk. 4, par. 3)

By defining what it means to be an authoritative person (*ren*), Confucius is re-authorizing those ancient sage kings who epitomize authoritative conduct; at the same time he is also repudiating those who claim to be authoritative in their behavior, but fall way short of the standard he has set up. To the extent that he succeeds, Confucius is rewriting a history that purges the imposters from the real sages, and he is rewriting a history that embodies and enforces his own ideologies.

From Alternative Discourses to Critical Language Awareness

So far, I've identified three discursive tendencies in the *Analects*. As one would expect, these tendencies—speaking by indirection, mixing the personal with the impersonal, and writing oneself into history—have certainly not been characterized, by Confucius' friends or foes, as examples of an alternative discourse. On the other hand, these tendencies have been singled out in our time, on this side of the Pacific, as part of alternative discourses. What does this interdiscursive similarity mean? Does this kind of discursive resemblance make the *Analects* more equalizing than its contemporary texts that did not exhibit these characteristics? Or does it make our own alternative discourses more Confucian than the *Analects*? The answer to either question is, of course, negative. Such a resemblance, though, confirms the need to construe different kinds of discourses, on either side of the Pacific, as clusters of discursive tendencies on a shifting discursive continuum.

How these tendencies are characterized is not determined by any particular clustering of discursive tendencies. Rather, it is their underlying conditions and ideologies that serve as the basis for their name. In other words, there is nothing inherently alternative in, for example, performing a genre-mixing speech act or in speaking indirectly. By the same token, to be objective or impersonal in our writing does not make us necessarily traditional either—even though such a characteristic is often branded as part of traditional academic discourse. The central issue here has to do with whether or not a certain cluster of discursive tendencies becomes codified and valorized, and whether or not the ideology it fosters eventually assumes doctrinal hegemony. Should this be the case, it becomes only *natural* to accord these tendencies both their proper name (like "traditional" or "normal") and their proper place (like a classroom or a courtroom). On the other hand, if some other clustering promotes an ideology that aims to compete with, and better still to subvert, the dominant ideology, such clustering will probably be characterized as "alternative" or by some other marked nomenclature. And the choice of one discourse (like traditional academic discourse) over another (like alternative discourse) turns into a moral issue if what is *natural* gets equated with what is good. Not to adopt traditional academic discourse, thus, becomes unnatural (not good) at best, and perverse at worst.[8]

For example, we tell our writing students that their home discourses, while valid, are only appropriate for nonacademic purposes because these discourses are associated with different sets of appropriateness conditions. This kind of reasoning, of course, is an indirect way of saying that they are not fit for academic purposes. And our students do get the message, too, since they often feel apologetic, if not embarrassed, for the intrusion of their home discourse into their academic discourse. It becomes only natural for them to leave their home discourse at home. Now, given the fact that these discursive tendencies evidenced in the *Analects* embody no inherent or immanent values, what are the values or social conditions that are associated with them? What, if any, can Western readers of the *Analects* – students and teachers alike —gain in their efforts to redefine the relationship between traditional academic discourse and other alternative discourses?

Let me here focus on two conditions that may have contributed to Confucius' choice of these discursive tendencies. On the one hand, Confucius lived through one of the most formative periods of Chinese culture, and both politically and intellectually the landscape was quite diverse. Commenting on the social conditions that Confucius witnessed and experienced, Mote puts it this way:

> In such a time the opportunities for a creative response to the unusual strains and pulls tended to produce reflective, systematic thinking about human problems—or philosophy—and the peculiar risks of public life tended to urge the even marginally meditative toward the reflective life. (1989, 31)

No wonder Confucius himself set a pattern for the "Hundred Schools" and promoted a society that encouraged learning and social mobility (Mote 1989, 35–36). On the other hand, Confucius was part of the history that saw vital, divisive changes. Many of these changes concerned and dismayed him because they represented a serious threat to a cultural order that he cherished. To reverse this trend, he set out to restore this order, and to recover a past where social harmony was preserved and protected. For him, more specifically, there was a serious, if not crippling, discrepancy between name and reality, which to him was ample evidence of breakdown at the very top (Mote 1989, 44). It was this kind of discrepancy that led him to "rectify the names."

These two competing conditions, as a result, had provided enough opportunities for Confucius to be discursively creative in the social, cultural, and moral deliberations of his time. Yet, as they gradually assumed doctrinal supremacy and moral hegemony, his teachings ultimately drowned out all other intellectual, philosophical voices. They became the only legitimate voice replacing all other non-legitimate, and illegitimate voices. In this sense, Confucius' teachings became too traditional as they were being used to champion a conservative ideology that only appealed to the rulers of China. Once again, there is nothing alternative about them at all.

A similar tension now appears to be in place in our profession, too. Namely, these days we hear a persistent call from certain quarters in our society to enforce the standard and to teach Standard English. Sometimes one feels that it has grown into hysteria. As teachers of English, we feel the pressure to teach our students traditional academic discourse so that they can function adequately once they join the work force. Meanwhile, multiculturalism, and a push for linguistic and cultural diversity on college campuses nationwide are gaining more momentum than ever. Out of this growing awareness of the need to foster diversity has emerged a conducive environment for other, nondominant voices to be heard and to be validated. It is this kind of tension that has in large measure contributed to the emergence of alternative discourses in our time.

Alternative discourses, as clusters of discursive tendencies, provide both opportunities and challenges. They are agents of opportunities when they make it possible to foster and promote a particular set of ideology seeking to challenge the ideological positions held by traditional academic discourse. And traditional academic discourse, as another cluster of discursive tendencies, becomes just as constructed and shaped by relations of power as are alternative discourses. Because discourses are contingent upon power relationships, and upon social conditions, it becomes only necessary to critically evaluate them, and to heighten our awareness of how language or discursive tendencies function in some most opaque manner.

Fairclough refers to this kind of language critique coupled with reflective analysis "critical language awareness" (1995, 221). It is crucial to point out, however, that achieving critical language awareness or effecting certain discursive changes is not the only source of challenge to traditional academic discourse, and to asymmetrical distribution of cultural capital. And sometimes there is no necessary correlation between the two. Nevertheless, it is no less crucial to be able to intervene, and to be able to flout traditional academic discourse in order to help bring about positive interventions. It is these kinds of interventions that can lead to new discursive practices, and that can open up spaces for the nondominant communities. In turn, these new discursive practices will set in motion the process of realigning or re-clustering the discursive tendencies on this shifting discursive continuum.

What are the material consequences of undertaking such a project? There are quite a few. For one thing, traditional academic discourse may now be constituted by some other discursive tendencies. Likewise, alternative discourses could assimilate tendencies that have been primarily associated with traditional academic discourse. This kind of re-clustering may eventually yield enough of a discrepancy between name and reality (that is, between traditional academic discourse and the tendencies that the former is expected to command)—so that traditional academic discourse may stop being traditional. Their realignment will help challenge the dominant ideology traditional academic discourse has been associated with. While the introduction of the *Analects* into our writing classroom may not necessarily provide immediate strategic actions for challenging social conditions or ideological assumptions—and it is not meant to—it does seek to foreground the shifting, contingent nature of our discourses.

And I want to suggest that it is this kind of heightened awareness that will spur us for transformative actions. Contrary to this desire of Confucius, the kinds of alternative discourses I am trying to nurture in this essay and in my own classroom should only welcome and embrace other voices, other discourses. In fact, it is these voices and discourses that constitute the very existence of our alternative discourses. As part of this shifting continuum, alternative discourses thrive on their own shifting characteristics, and genre mixing becomes their only stable tendency. Such an outcome will therefore help us promote a real sense of mixed, emergent community—where the disadvantaged, the nondominant, may begin to feel comfortable and competent. Only then can we begin to claim that the process of uncovering this tension is becoming more productive and more proactive—a tension that I referred to, à la Gilyard, at the beginning of this essay. To the extent that my going East is a temporary, but necessary, journey across time and space, I have then come full circle—only with a fuller appreciation of the role of underlying ideologies, and of their relationship to different clusters of discursive tendencies.

Postscript: A Not-So-Direct Response

One may ask, by now, "What exactly is your manner in which you've presented your case? Is this essay an example of indirection, the blurring of the personal with the collective, and/or an appropriative history?" Such questions certainly put me into a discursive dilemma. To answer them is to violate the principle of indirection, but not to answer them risks obscuring my message and alienating my readers. Let me, then, try to offer a not-so-direct response. I have to admit, directly, that my essay is informed by indirection, which, I hope, has allowed me to playfully challenge our current discourse paradigm. I wonder about its effectiveness as well as its legitimacy—after all, my essay is still operating within the current discourse paradigm. While I've inserted a lot of first-person pronouns, singular and plural, into this essay, coupled with many conversational structures, I really haven't included any personal stories as we now understand them. At the same time, I have to confess that the writing of this essay and the journey that the act of writing has taken me through has turned into a personal story of sorts—however indirectly. For it has now fundamentally changed the way I look at different discourses, and at their legitimacy and their values. Finally, I think this essay is, discursively speaking, a mixed bag: while indirection certainly is a major subtext, my essay has appropriated discursive features that are closely associated with traditional academic discourse rather than with alternative discourses. Such appropriations only reaffirm, perhaps indirectly, the fact that it is discourse users and their immediate discursive conditions that help shape their ideological content. There is, directly put, no simple correlation.

Notes

1. For Scollon and Scollon, these characteristics in essayist tradition correspond to, if not exactly embody, the defining properties of the modern consciousness (1981, 49–54).

2. Bizzell also refers to this last trait as "appropriative history"—in which the writer retells traditional history in creative ways that highlight her/his agenda, ideology (1999,14).

3. According to the *Oxford English Dictionary*, the literal meaning of the word *discourse* is "to run to and fro, to traverse over a space or region." My call for this shifting discursive continuum aims in part to highlight and reinforce that very meaning. Similarly, Spellmeyer, attempting to uncover the dialectical tension between oneself and the other, between an inside and outside, between constraint and desire, draws upon the very meaning of the word *discourse*, which, Spellmeyer states, by conveying the meaning of "running back and forth," "implies the need for such a doubleness" (1989, 722).

4. By "goods" Gee means "anything that the people in the society generally believe are beneficial to have or harmful not to have, whether this be life, space, time, 'good' schools, 'good' jobs, wealth, status, power, control, or whatever" (1996, 21).

5. This kind of genre mixing may have also been induced in part by the fact that the *Analects* is a compilation of Confucius' sayings by his students over many years.

6. The identity of this person in Chinese history is unclear.

7. Ames and Rosemont have opted to translate the Chinese character *ren* as "authoritative person," "authoritative conduct," or "to act authoritatively" depending on the context —instead of the traditional English translation "benevolence" or "humaneness." Their choice is a considered one. For their detailed explanation, see Ames and Rosemont (1998, 48–51).

8. By connecting the use of different discourses to moral significances, I am drawing upon Cameron's critique of plain English style in her *Verbal Hygiene* (1995, 68–72).

Works Cited

Ames, Roger and Henry Rosemont, translated 1998. *The* Analects *of Confucius: A Philosophical Translation.* New York: Ballantine.

Bakhtin, M. M. 1986. *Speech Genres and Other Late Essays*, translated by Vern W. McGee; edited by Caryl Emerson and Michael Holquist. Austin: Univ. of Texas Press.

Bizzell, Patricia 1999. "Hybrid Academic Discourses: What, Why, How." *Composition Studies* 27 (Fall):7–21.

———. 2000. "Basic Writing and the Issue of Correctness, or, What to Do with 'Mixed' Forms of Academic Discourse." *Journal of Basic Writing* 19:4–12.

Cameron, Deborah 1995. *Verbal Hygiene*. London: Routledge.

Fairclough, Norman. 1995. *Critical Discourse Analysis: The Critical Study of Language*. London: Longman.

Foss, Sonja K. 1996. *Rhetorical Criticism: Exploration and Practice*. 2nd ed. Prospect Heights, IL: Waveland.

Foss, Sonja K. and Cindy L. Griffin. 1995. "Beyond Persuasion: A Proposal for an Invitational Rhetoric." *Communication Monographs* 62 (March):2–18.

Gee, James Paul. 1996. *Social Linguistics and Literacies: Ideology in Discourses*. London: Taylor.

Gilyard, Keith. 2000. "Literacy, Identity, Imagination, Flight." *College Composition and Communication* 52:260–72.

Mote, Freedenck W. 1989. *Intellectual Foundations of China.* 2nd ed. New York: McGraw-Hill.

Scollon, Ron and Suzanne B. K. Scollon. 1981. "Narrative, Literacy and Face." In *Interethnic Communication.* Norwood, NJ: Ablex.

Smitherman, Geneva. 1977. *Talkin and Testifyin: The Language of Black America.* Boston: Houghton.

Spellmeyer, Kurt. 1989. "Foucault and the Freshman Writer: Considering the Self in Discourse." *College English* 51 (November):715–29.

11

Vernacular Englishes in the Writing Classroom? *Probing the Culture of Literacy*

Peter Elbow

I'm wrestling here with a conflict in goals—a conflict I know is shared by many teachers of first year composition. My strongest desire is to invite all students to write in whatever dialect or variety of English is theirs. As the 4Cs statement on "Students' Rights to Their Own Language" (see Committee 1974) points out, these dialects are full, sophisticated, rule-governed languages with all the bells and whistles of any language. On the other hand, my desire is vulnerable to strong criticism that takes various forms: (a) I hear Lisa Delpit saying that such an invitation is a white liberal way to keep Black students from getting power (1988). (b) I hear teachers (like me!) saying, "But what about helping students satisfy writing program assessments and other faculty?" (c) I hear critics of so-called expressivism saying, "We must concentrate on academic discourse." Summing up this conflict: How can we change the culture of literacy yet also help all students *prosper* in the present culture? A good strategy for handling contradiction is to introduce the dimension of time (see Elbow 1993): to work for the long-range goal of changing the culture of literacy, and the short-range goal of helping students now.

The long-range goal. What would we see if we waved a magic wand? We'd see a culture that accepts and even welcomes a multiplicity of dialects for writing; and lots of publication in many dialects that used to be oral, stigmatized, and associated with backwardness or stupidity. Even prestige writing and academic discourse would be published in these heretofore low dialects. And finally, standard written English itself (SWE)—what is now the grapholect—would actually wither away.

A fantasy. But it's already happened. It's the history of literacy in Europe. Not so long ago, Latin was the only acceptable medium for writing. What we think of as English, French, Italian, and Spanish were oral vernaculars: low, common, "vulgar" (vulgar = "of the people")—and unfit for writing. Dante argued powerfully for the eloquence of the vulgar tongue (*De Vulgari Eloquentia*) and made an even stronger political statement by writing his *Commedia* in the vernacular of a particular and restricted culture. Chaucer and many Medieval and Renaissance authors—now revered —wrote in oral dialects that were looked down on by intellectuals and academics. Even in the eighteenth century, Robert Burns wrote in a disparaged dialect. (The flowering of rhetorical studies in eighteenth and ninteenth century Scotland was partly driven by the effort of some intellectual Scots to avoid stigmatization because of their dialect.)

And now? Latin has virtually disappeared. The upstart, oral, low vernaculars are now official literacies. And they (such is the culture of literacy) try to forbid writing in vernacular dialects *they* consider low and of the people. This complicated process took a long time (Menocal [1994] gives interesting insights), but we are moving surprisingly fast toward a similar end. Four hopeful signs:

1. There is already a growing body of published writing in various vernaculars (examples in appendix). Most of it is not academic, but many readers have come to value this writing and realize that literacy—the world of letters (literally)—poorer without them.
2. In academic writing, the rhetorical conventions have opened up fast in the last few decades. I sense that deconstructive and postmodern scholarship cracked things open first, but then various rhetorical and structural styles have flowered and become respected—often with a personal dimension. (Two 4Cs presidents, Keith Gilyard [1991] and Victor Villanueva [1993], provide notable examples.) This collection and Helen Fox's *Listening to the World* (1994) are powerful reminders of how many people are beginning to see the parochialism and limits of what have tended to be felt as "normal" or universal canons of thinking, logic, and organization.
3. Even the grammar and syntax of conventional academic discourse shows a crack. Geneva Smitherman has written respected academic discourse using not just the rhetoric of African American Vernacular English (AAVE or Black English or Ebonics) but many features of its grammar and syntax (in her 1974 article "Soul 'N Style" and her 1986 book *Talkin and Testifyin*).
4. In 1994, Smitherman led a small research team that analyzed AA Vernacular English in hundreds of student essays on the nationwide literary tests (NAEP). In the latest exams they looked at (1984 and 1988), they found

that "Students who employed a Black expressive discourse style received higher NAEP scores than those who did not . . ." (2000, 186). In earlier exams from 1969 and 1979, Black discourse style did not correlate with higher scores. To explain these findings, Smitherman writes: "As cultural norms shift focus from 'book' English to 'human' English, the narrativizing, dynamic quality of the African American Verbal Tradition will help students produce lively, image-filled, concrete, readable essays . . ." (2000, 186). This correlation between high scores and a Black rhetoric or discourse style held up across persuasive, comparison/contrast, and informative essays.

The Short-Range Goal

But the news was not so happy in the short term. Even though students benefited from using African American rhetoric or discourse style, they did not benefit from using AA grammar and syntax. The good effects of AA rhetoric turned out to be a function of primary trait scoring. Holistic scoring presented a different picture. "With holistic scores, there continues to be what we found in 1969–79 . . . the more BEV, the lower the holistic score. This finding is not surprising given the holistic method, which includes assessment of grammar, mechanics, and syntax" (2000, 174). In addition (and this is an important finding for what I will suggest later), "BEV syntax and BEV discourse are not co-occurring variables" (2000, 183, her italics). That is, AA students were as likely to write with only one or only the other or both dimensions of AA language. So the liability of AA grammar and syntax was more apparent when students used it alone—without AA rhetoric and discourse style.

This is sad but not surprising. We have anecdotal evidence that teachers (and the general public) sometimes penalize AAVE "wrong grammar" more heavily than garden variety (white?) mistakes or ESL mistakes. Villanueva tells of learning that he could get top grades on his undergraduate papers by making his grammar flawless—even though his rhetoric was "Sophistic" or "Latino" and far from what his teachers called for as "logical thinking and organization."

Thus, virulent stigmatization of dialects attaches more to grammar and syntax than it does to rhetoric. Is this because grammar and syntax are more internalized and automatic—and experienced more as markers of identity? In any case, this situation is built into literacy itself. Literacy as a culture or institution almost always implies just one dialect as the only proper one for writing: the "grapholect." (Some dialects are closer to the grapholect than others, but all dialects other than the grapholect are oral. Standard Written English is no one's mother tongue.)

One more problem for our short-term goal. Students are mostly not yet benefiting from the recent rhetorical flowering of academic writing. Most faculty won't accept from students many kinds of rhetoric and structure that they happily write and read from their colleagues. (The term *academic discourse* doesn't really apply to student writing. We need a term like *school discourse* for what academics demand of students—as opposed to what they accept from peers [see Elbow 1991].)

So the short-range goal is clear: help students in our classrooms today whose comfortable dialect is not "Standard" American English (SAE) to meet the demands of most teachers and employers. We can't wait for a new culture of literacy.

The commonest approach to this goal is to get these students to use only SAE or even SWE for writing—and restrict their nonSAE dialect to speech. Marcia Farr, a notable champion in the fight against the stigmatization of so-called nonstandard dialects, took this view (in an e-mail response to my 1991 "Inviting the Mother Tongue" essay): "I worry a bit about trying to get them to write in their 'mother dialect.' . . . [U]sing it in the classroom (unless in creative writing) confuses form with function. I think it's more important to get them to *fully* realize the adequacy of all dialects. 'Leave their oral language alone,' as it were, but teach writing in SE."

This approach has worked for many students and teachers. Perhaps I will be convinced that it's best when I've had as much experience as she's had with lots of nonSAE students in lots of contexts. But I can't resist a different approach: inviting teachers to explore ways to invite students to experiment with vernacular dialects in writing. I find support from two important sources. Geneva Smitherman writes: "once they have produced the most powerful essay possible, then and only then should you have them turn their attention to BEV grammar and matters of punctuation, spelling, and mechanics" (2000, 186); Lisa Delpit writes: "Unlike unplanned oral language . . . writing is more amenable to rule application—one may first write freely to get one's thoughts down, and then edit to hone the message and apply specific spelling, syntactical, or punctuation rules (1997, 7).

Part of my motivation is short term and pedagogical. How can we help speakers of a nonSAE dialect ever feel fluent or comfortable in writing if we have to force them to write in a grammar and syntax they don't feel as their own? And in particular, how can we help speakers of stigmatized dialects (like AAVE or Puerto Rican English or Hawai'ian Creole English or various Caribbean Creole Englishes) develop their best skill on paper if we enforce a dialect that they correctly feel is bent on wiping out their own language and culture? After all, we experience our language or dialect—our natural grammar and syntax—not just as something we use but as a deep part of us. How can students get energy, vitality, and voice into their writing—deeper resonances—if they can't use the dialect that has access to their unconscious?

But part of my reason is aesthetic and ideological. As a longtime cheerleader for writing as a mode, and as an observer of all the excellent writing published in nonSAE dialects, I feel literacy is impoverished if it's restricted to SAE—even at the level of grammar and syntax. And I feel dialects and varieties of English are precious; I suspect they are more likely to thrive against widespread dialectal leveling if they are used for writing.

But let me stress my earlier phrase, "invite students to experiment." I think we should invite, not demand or even pressure; and our invitation should be to experiment and try out options, not settle on a single approach. We need to recognize and respect (and talk about) the various reasons why students might *not* want even to try out a nonSAE "home" dialect in writing—particularly if it is a stigmatized dialect. Maybe some won't want to use a home dialect for *any* classroom task; maybe some won't want to use it for those academic rhetorical tasks that they experience as impersonal, abstract, square, or clunky—alien to home rhetorical traditions; maybe some will want to work on developing fluency in *producing* SWE and therefore be willing to pay a price of reduced comfort, fluency, and power; maybe some will feel that they have too few allies in the class and so will need to use vernacular dialect only for private writing (if at all); maybe some will actually disapprove of their vernacular—just as Jesse Jackson called Ebonics "trash talk."

But how can we invite students to write in nonSAE dialects and still produce writing to satisfy most of their teachers and employers—readers who often see stigmatized grammatical features as signs of laziness and stupidity? As I continue to strategize, I see two tasks: first to help students learn that they *can* write in their most comfortable dialect—for most assume they must try to use SWE when they write; second, to help students learn how to take some of these pieces written in the vernacular and revise them into SWE.

First Task: Helping Students Write in Their Most Comfortable Dialect

Here are some things I've found useful.

1. Provide students with published examples of powerful writing in vernacular dialects (see the appendix). Students need to know that writing in vernacular dialects is not some weird experiment but something proven by some of our best published writers. They also need to know that much prestige literature of our culture was written in vernacular dialects that were considered low and unsuitable for writing (e.g., Dante, Chaucer, *Sir Gawain and the Green Knight,* Robert Burns).
2. Be more careful about introducing freewriting. I used to say, "Write quickly and use whatever words come easily. Don't worry about mistakes." I finally realized that when I phrase it (and think it!) this way, I am reinforcing the idea that when words come easily that differ from SWE, they are mistakes. In short, I was inadvertently reinforcing the idea that writing belongs only in one standard dialect. A more thoughtful introduction:

> Try to use this freewriting for whatever language comes most easily and naturally to your mouth and ear—that feels most comfortable, most yours. If it's different from school language or formal writing, that doesn't make it

wrong. Do you remember the powerful published writing we read together—where eminent authors used various home dialects of English?"

3. I think we should require a good number of assignments to be in SWE, but that needn't be the goal for *all* assignments. We can ask students to revise some of their freewrites and low stakes pieces and personal essays into final corrected drafts in their comfortable or vernacular dialect. It's easiest and most natural to do this with more personal or creative pieces (which campus literary magazines will often publish). But it also makes sense to do this with some academic essays. I often ask students to revise midstage drafts in two directions—both into SWE and into vernacular—even when it's an essay trying to do academic work. Some of Smitherman's academic writing in AAVE makes a good model (see "Soul 'N Style").
4. When an essay has to end up in SWE, we can invite the vernacular beyond the earliest drafts into later (but not final) drafts. Consider the criteria that most teachers look for in good writing: effective ideas, reasoning, organization, and clear sentences. Of course these are highly contested concepts: what most U.S. faculty find "effective" and "clear" often doesn't match what respected readers in other cultures call effective and clear (as has been so well shown by Helen Fox's *Listening to the World* and some other contributors in this book). Nevertheless, we can shape our feedback to help students revise their essays to meet even staid versions of "good thinking and rhetoric" *and still totally ignore matters of dialect or grammar and syntax.* That is, students can achieve every one of those strengths—even parochially defined—without having to think about grammar and syntax.

After students have revised their essays as much as possible to meet the desired rhetorical criteria, they (and we) can finally turn attention to grammar and syntax. It's encouraging to see fewer surface problems—syntax that is mistaken or tangled or both—when students write in their most comfortable dialect through the middle drafts of an essay. As most ESL teachers know, many mistakes in English grammar and syntax are "production errors" that result from students stretching to write in language that is alien to them—additional and different mistakes from those they make when not trying so hard to be correct (as in comfortable speech). Similarly, plenty of mainstream SAE students make fewer grammatical mistakes in their freewriting than in their carefully crafted writing. So nonSAE speakers who write comfortably in their vernacular will of course retain all the "wrong" grammar and syntax of their dialect, but they won't be so likely to make production errors or to tie up their syntax in knots.

But some teachers have trouble ignoring grammar and syntax and responding only to thinking, organization, and clarity. Grammar and syntax we experience as wrong grabs our attention and blinds us to substance. Here's a sad but understandable comment by a dedicated teacher (from a list serve): "Only now can I really address the underlying thinking and understanding problems—because previously the writing was so atrocious that I couldn't see them." If we want to help all our students, we have to get over this. Nancy Sommers (1982) pointed out that even mainstream dialect students need us to read *through* grammar and syntax to the content since so many of them have a hard time moving from their spoken vernacular to an alien SWE (even if their vernacular is called "standard"). Countless students of all sorts get too little feedback on their thinking, organization, and clarity because they've mostly been pushed about their "wrong" language.

Second Task: Helping Students Revise Late Drafts into SWE

Where our first task for the short-term goal is to help students learn to be comfortable writing in a dialect that feels like theirs—even while working on important essays—our second task is to help them revise or copy edit late drafts of some important essays into SWE. Here are some techniques I've used.

5. We can directly teach some of the grammar and conventions of SWE. College and university writing teachers don't have much time for this because we generally have our students for only one semester—and often ours is their only writing course in college. Nevertheless we help them a lot by sprinkling in some *mini-workshops* of only ten to twenty minutes to treat the most frequently troublesome matters in grammar and syntax. These mini-workshops are more effective and interesting if they highlight contrasts between the grammar and conventions of SWE and various other dialects (including *spoken* SAE). Mainstream students are usually quite interested to learn the logic of, say, African American or Latino grammars, and to learn that they are just as regular and sophisticated as the grammar of SWE and not at all limited or defective. (See Palacas [2001] for an account of how Black English has a more sophisticated system of tense and aspect than "standard" or "white" English. He builds a first year writing course around the study of AAVE as it compares to SAE and SWE.)
6. I have found it enormously productive to make a simple but major change in my calendar of assignments: to add an extra "final final draft" or "copy edited draft" assignment. *After* students have revised their essays on the basis of feedback from me and from classmates to strengthen the ideas, reasoning, and evidence, and to increase the clarity of structure and sentences (however defined)—but not yet worrying about grammar and syntax or spelling—*then* they have one more draft assignment. Their only job now is to give *all* their attention to matters of grammar and syntax. At this point, the final process of copy editing and changing to SWE is less daunt-

ing. A good number of surface problems have disappeared, and it's easier than expected to change the so-called "nonstandard" dialect features of grammar and syntax into SWE.

I find this extra draft assignment helpful for all my students because it finally teaches them at a behavioral level the crucial difference between revising and copy editing. In preparation for this "final final" draft, I usually give a bit of feedback. For most students, I'll circle deviations from SWE on a couple of paragraphs or the first page. For a few students where it seems appropriate, I'll actually suggest corrections—but only on the first or second essays of the semester.

Readers of earlier drafts have said, "But Peter, you blithely skate over this huge job: how can nonSAE speakers 'just' copy edit into SWE?" I agree, it's a daunting job, even for SAE speakers. But my point is that there's no way they can avoid it. That is, the copy editing difficulties aren't caused by using a nonSAE dialect for early and middle drafts. Sooner or later, nonSAE speakers have to translate their most automatic dialect into SWE. Their only choice is whether to do that translating during earlier stages of writing when it is likely to distract them from the task of coming up with thoughts and developing and clarifying them—or at the very end after they've finally got their thoughts the way they want them. So the only life buoy I can offer to nonSAE speakers is the one that I find helpful for SAE speakers: "Experiment to see whether it isn't easier to achieve SWE at the very end when you can give your full attention to it and you have no other tasks to distract you."[1]

An Objection

All my suggestions lead to an obvious objection:

> You can't use vernacular dialects like AAVE for academic discourse. These dialects carry a whole culture and rhetoric—involve ways of seeing and thinking—that conflict with the practices of academic discourse.

A clarifying distinction is needed here. If we look at traditional AAVE *rhetorical habits and styles* (such as the heavy use of narrative [Ball 1992, 524] and the use of proverbs and aphorisms, sermonic tone, direct address, and conversational tone [Smitherman, 2000, 181]), these may indeed conflict with traditional Western academic rhetorical habits and styles (such as impersonal or detached abstract reasoning and certain styles of point-based argument and organization). But AAVE *grammar and syntax* do not preclude any of these academic rhetorical practices. Remember that Smitherman's research found no necessary correlation between students' use of AAVE rhetoric and AAVE grammar and syntax.

Let me digress to make my argument more concrete. Consider the process that I, like many other teachers, try to follow in helping all students write a persuasive or analytic essay, even if it is intended to be wholly impersonal. I invite them to start with freewriting or journal writing about the topic (sometimes even playing with genres such as a "rant" for the seed of persuasion or "angry letter" about some issue to be analyzed). Next I ask students to change the rhetoric or discourse style or structure; that is, I ask them (sometimes by reading to each other in pairs) to find and articulate the "points" that are already embedded in the writing, and to figure out other points that are needed in order to make a piece of analysis or persuasion that is fairly impersonal rather than an expression of their feelings. This creates the midprocess draft that gets feedback and is revised to a final draft—*but still* there is no attention yet to grammar and syntax. Then for the final final draft, all attention goes to grammar and syntax.

Notice how this process, when used by speakers of nonSAE dialects, leads to an interesting theoretical puzzler: At what point would a speaker of (say) AAVE "stop using the vernacular dialect"? Was she no longer using the dialect when the rhetoric was no longer AAVE?—or only when she expunged AAVE grammar and syntax? I don't care so much about the theoretical conundrum; my point is pedagogical and phenomenological: that such speakers get a chance to put all their attention on new rhetorical tasks (tasks that are often new to mainstream college freshmen too) and not waste any of the considerable attention that would distract them if they were also trying to change their grammar and syntax.

Of course, I've described the extreme case where the goal is a completely impersonal essay. More often I and most teachers are looking for an effective piece of analysis or persuasion that doesn't have to be so cold and square. For that goal, we can show students the model of an essay like Geneva Smitherman's "Soul 'N Style." She creates strong analysis and persuasion (and it was published in an academic journal); but she mixes this academic rhetorical style with a vernacular rhetorical style involving direct address and a personal tone. And of course she uses plenty of AAVE grammar and syntax (though not exclusively)—even for final publication.

Concluding Reflections

It seems as though I have been dealing with controversial issues of ideology, cultural theory, and pedagogical theory. But in the end, I'd say that it all boils down to a concrete personal and political choice that each student should be invited to make:

> Which is better for you: using the grammar and syntax of your most comfortable vernacular dialect for composing and developing essays that are trying to do standard academic rhetorical tasks? Or would you rather start out with the dialect of SWE if you are going to have to end up in that dialect? Which is more important for you: the comfort of not having to think about grammar and syntax while you're trying to accomplish new difficult rhetorical and cognitive tasks? Or the possible confusion of using two different dialects for writing?

I repeat that students needn't try to answer this question beforehand or once and for all. The crucial invitation is to *experiment* and *try out* alternative ways of arriving at final drafts in SWE —to see which ways are most productive for them. We need to respect their reasons for declining the invitation, but let's not refrain from *making* the invitation. I can't believe it's right to leave students with the sense of no choice—with the sense that there is only one way to go about writing, namely to leave their most comfortable vernacular out of it—that writing itself necessarily means trying to use SWE.

Choice turns out to be an ideal fertilizer for discussions of the realities and politics of language. But of course in a classroom, it's never full choice. I find I promote discussions by making clear to students the ways in which I as a teacher am using my authority to create what many of them experience as a tricky combination of choice and *no-choice*. Let me summarize this combination. I invite choice as to whether to use vernacular dialect for a good deal of writing—and even some final drafts. Yet (as a teacher of first year writing in today's culture of literacy) I try to enforce *no-choice* in my requirement that students copy edit successfully at least three or four out of the five or six main essays into the grammar and syntax of "correct" SWE.

I also provide choice and no-choice about rhetoric or discourse style. On at least a couple of persuasive or analytic essays, I restrict choice and try to insist on a generally point-driven rhetoric and structure rather than allow something purely narrative or associative. But I invite rhetorical choice about whether or not to meet conservative standards of "school writing" (first paragraphs with thesis statements &c. &c. &c.). In fact I don't hide my bias toward more organic and less rigid conventional structures for point-driven rhetoric—yet I try to get students thinking about, and feeling, the difference between stricter and looser school conventions for point-driven rhetoric. In my comments, I often find myself writing, "What you have here works well for me, but lots of teachers would find it too 'loose' or undisciplined." Of course when it comes to more informal or personal essays, I invite non-point-driven rhetorical structures where you don't necessarily even "say" what you are saying.

This combination of choice and no-choice—along with the readings of published nonSAE dialects and the explicitness about my teacher authority—all this leads naturally to discussions of crucial topics: the reality of vernaculars as full sophisticated languages in their own right rather than "bad English"; the stigmatization of dialects; policies of institutions and teachers on various dialects and the present unfair burden on speakers of nonSAE vernaculars; and signs of change in the culture of literacy. When there aren't many speakers of nonSAE dialects in the class, it's helpful to start off with discussions of the way literacy works. I like to show students that at present, *no one* can write without moving from their spoken vernacular to the grapholect —but that my preferred process for myself and all students is to do most composing and revising in one's own oral dialect. It helps students to realize that literacy's chosen dialect, SWE or the grapholect, is no one's mother tongue—and yet that they nevertheless can write in their mother tongue. The political point is that it's noncontroversial for speakers of SAE to write in their vernacular and afterwards revise and copy edit into SAE. (They need to know that when Ken Macrorie and I first began to publicize freewriting, it *was* controversial.)

These thoughts lead to a summary of my whole essay: everyone should be able to do what SAE speakers can noncontroversially do: compose in their vernacular dialect. But in the short term – for the few decades till we achieve the long term-goal of a more inclusive culture of literacy—nonSAE speakers will have more work to do on essays that need to end up in Standard Written English.[2]

Notes

1. K–12 English teachers can spend more time teaching the grammar and conventions of SWE. We college teachers of one-semester courses can't teach writing if we make grammar and syntax a major focus. By the way, when I make a separate final final draft assignment where the only task is to copy edit to SWE, I openly allow and indeed invite students to get help with this process. This bothers some teachers, but it makes perfect sense to me. If we invite students to get feedback and help in making substantive revisions to their essays, why shouldn't we do the same when it comes to surface revisions? Figuring out what one needs to do to produce a final draft in SWE is a realistic, important, and writerly skill: one of the main ones I'm trying to teach.

2 In this essay, I draw on and build from my longer essay, "Inviting the Mother Tongue." I've shared various versions of that essay and this one in various settings and I'm grateful for the good ideas and criticism I received. I'm particularly grateful for extensive and cogent feedback from Patricia Bizzell, Marilyn Cooper, and Helen Fox, and from the participants in the 2001 UMass Symposium on Writing and Dialects and Varieties of English.

Appendix: Examples of Published Writing in Vernacular Dialects or Varieties of English Other than Standard Written English

AAVE or Black English

Hurston, Zora Neale. 1937. *Their Eyes Were Watching God.* Philadelphia: J. B. Lippincott.

Sapphire. 1996. *Push: A Novel.* New York: Knopf.

Geneva Smitherman wrote academic discourse in AAVE in "Soul 'N Style" and some essays in *Talkin and Testifyin.* (See Works Cited.)

Walker, Alice. 1982. *The Color Purple.* New York: Harcourt Brace.

Caribbean Creole English

Lovelace, Earl. 1984. *The Wine of Astonishment.* New York: Vintage.

Sistren, with Honor Ford Smith, ed. 1986. *Lionheart Gal: Life Stories of Jamaican Women.* London: Women's Press.

Hawai'ian Creole English ("Pidgin")

Lum, Darrell. 1990. *Pass On, No Pass Back.* Honolulu: Bamboo Ridge Press.

Yamanaka, Lois-Ann. 1997. *Blue's Hanging.* New York: Farrar, Straus and Giroux.

———. *Saturday Night at the Pahala Theater.* 1993. Honolulu: Bamboo Ridge Press.

Hispanic or Latino/a English

Anzaldua, Gloria. 1981. *Borderlands / La Frontera: The New Mestiza.* San Francisco: Sisters-Avat Lute.

Treviño, J. S. 1995. *The Fabulous Sinkhole and Other Stories.* Houston: Acte Público.

Cisneros, Sandra. 1991. *Woman Hollering Creek and Other Stories.* New York: Random House.

Works Cited

Ball, Arnetta F. 1992. "Cultural Preference and the Expository Writing of African-American Adolescents." *Written Communication* 9 (4):501–32.

Committee of the Conference on College Composition and Communication. 1974. "Students' Rights to Their Own Language." *College Composition and Communication* 25:1–18.

Delpit, Lisa. 1997. "Ebonics and Culturally Responsive Instruction." *Rethinking Schools* 12 (1) (Fall): 6–7.

———. 1988. "The Silenced Dialogue: Power and Pedagogy in Educating Other People's Children." *Harvard Educational Review* 58 (3):280–98.

Elbow, Peter. 1991. "Reflections on Academic Discourse: How it Relates to Freshmen and Colleagues." *College English* 53 (2)(Feb):135–55. Reprinted in *Everyone Can Write: Essays Toward a Hopeful Theory of Writing and Teaching Writing.* New York: Oxford University Press, 2000.

———. 1993. "The Uses of Binary Thinking." *Journal of Advanced Composition* 12(1) (Winter):51–78. Reprinted in *Everyone Can Write: Essays Toward a Hopeful Theory of Writing and Teaching Writing.* New York: Oxford University Press, 2000.

———. 1999. "Inviting the Mother Tongue: Beyond 'Mistakes,' 'Bad English,' and 'Wrong Language'." *Journal of Advanced Composition* 19 (2):359–88. Reprinted in *Everyone Can Write: Essays Toward a Hopeful Theory of Writing and Teaching Writing.* New York: Oxford University Press, 2000.

Farr, Marcia. 2001. Email to the author.

Fox, Helen. 1994. *Listening to the World.* Urbana, IL: NCTE.

Gilyard, Keith. 1991. *Voices of the Self: A Study of Language Competence*. Detroit: Wayne State Univ. Press

Menocal, Masia Rosa. 1994. *Shards of Love: Exile and the Origins of the Lyric*. Durham, NC: Duke Univ. Press

Palacas, Arthur L. 2001. "Liberating American Ebonics from Euro-English." *College English* 63 (3)(Jan):326–52.

Smitherman, Geneva. 1974. "Soul 'N Style." *English Journal* 63 (4):16–17. Reprinted in *Talkin That Talk: Language, Culture, and Education in African America* (New York: Routledge).

———. 2000. *Talkin That Talk: Language, Culture, and Education in African America*. NY: Routledge.

———. 1986. Ta*lkin and Testifyin: The Language of Black America*. Detroit: Wayne State Univ. Press

Sommers, Nancy. 1982. "Responding to Student Writing." *College Composition and Communication* 32:148–56.

Villanueva, Victor. Jr. 1993. *Bootstraps: From an American Academic of Color*. Urbana, IL: NCTE.

12

Full (dis)Course Meal: Some Words on Hybrid/ Alternative Discourses

Laura Lai Long

LANGUAGE AT THE TABLE

> **chop suey** (chop' soo' I) [<Chin. *tsa-sui*: various pieces], a Chinese-American dish of meat, bean sprouts, celery, etc., cooked in a sauce served with rice.
>
> —*Webster's New World Dictionary*

Hybrid. The word spilled onto the table of books and ingredients as she examined the topic proposal for her final research paper. "Of mixed origin," quoted back *Webster's*. She thought about her maman. Chinese. Tahitian. French. American. Four languages, spoken over the phone with Auntie Marcie. "Mixed together," Maman would say. "Like chop suey." Of the four tongues, she had only understood the words of one and half the words of another. Great portions of information, conversation, invitation were left out when Maman and Auntie spoke. She'd snatch the words that she could, like catching flies with chopsticks. They would tease her, dodge each other around her young head, never making clear sense when put together. Later, she read that this had a name. A multilingual household. She thought about how it felt to be tossed into this wok of language. To know so clearly what words meant when stated in their native language, their home. She still heard the words sounding like "Soy Ngay" whenever she went to bed with wet hair. "Les piques assietes" rang in her ears whenever she felt taken advantage of. In her mind, her stomach was still an "opu." When translated, these words were raw—a term for scolding bad behavior in Chinese, a French term for freeloaders, the Tahitian word for belly. They lost her mother's voice and the original sensation they caused in her when spoken. The meaning as known to she in her childhood.

She also thought about how it felt *not* to understand. The beginnings, middles, and ends of stories were missing, as Maman and Auntie chatted in the kitchen. Words fractured, lost. Chop Suey was a language that would take years to learn, she sometimes thought. By not knowing, somehow, she felt excluded from the conversation, like an unwelcome guest at a dinner party. Sometimes she tried to participate, but the attempts were meager and put on like the warmth of the dinner party host. French—the language she couldn't fully perform in. She knew what she *meant* to say, but was never sure if the meaning was clear. Or acceptable to the invited. She is reminded of her own students in ESL classes and their frustration with language everyday. The struggles to define themselves and defend their opinions in words whose meanings are dubious. The hopes that the words they choose express their intended meanings while capturing the flavor of what those words meant in their native tongues. The assumptions that they have made themselves understood. The end of the foreign meal. All the question marks left on the plate.

INVITATION ONLY

Socrates: *But I do think you will agree to this, that every discourse must be organized, like a living being, with a body of its own, as it were, so as not to remain headless or footless, but to have a middle and members, composed in fitting relation to each other and to the whole.* (Plato, *Phaedrus* 134)

Also, traditional academic genres shape whole pieces of writing, determining what the parts are and what the structure is. (Bizzell 1999, 10)

The investigators had gathered a set of 20 objects, 5 each from 4 categories: food, clothing, tools and cooking utensils . . . [W]hen asked to put together the objects that belonged together, [many of the tribesmen produced] not 4 groups of 5 but 10 groups of 2. Moreover, the type of grouping and the type of reason given were frequently of the type we regard as extremely concrete, e.g., "the knife goes with the orange because it cuts it." Glick . . . notes, however, that subjects at times volunteered "'that ***a wise man would do things in the way this was done.****' When an exasperated experimenter asked finally, 'How would a fool do it?' He was given back groupings of the type . . . initially expected—four neat piles with foods in one, tools in another."* (anthropologist Glick, as retold by Jacqueline Goodnow) (Rose 1988, 291)

> *[D]epartures from the typical performance pattern of American adults are not necessarily deficits, but may indeed be excellent adaptations to the life circumstances of the people involved.* (Cole and Means) (Rose 1988, 290)

The eve of 2000. A scholar changes her mind. Significant. Composition scholar and social constructionist Patricia Bizzell addresses her colleagues in a *Composition Studies* article entitled "Hybrid Academic Discourses: What, Why, How." Modifications on teaching tradition, a standard. *I would no longer want to defend a pedagogical position that sees its inculcation as a one-way street* (Bizzell 1999, 8). Concession that defining "academic discourse" is **more complex than earlier realized** (Bizzell 1999, 8). Standards can be revised, tradition can be broken, and the dress code for writing redefined. Perhaps soon, all will be welcome.

1970s. Rutgers University. A scholar reads. Paulo Freire's *Pedagogy of the Oppressed.* Mina Shaughnessy's *Errors and Expectations* (1977). A new pedagogy for teaching writing emerges. Words ring through her ears. **Political oppression. Academic advantage. Group membership. Critical consciousness** (Bizzell 1992, 5). *An analytic vision first acquired through literacy schooling can be turned on the inequities in the larger social order* (Bizzell 1999, 7). Result. *Demystification of academic discourse conventions* (Bizzell 1992, 7). ***Groundwork for major social change through preparing previously marginalized students to speak with powerful voices against the mainstream*** (Bizzell 1992, 7–9).

1980s. A term emerges. *Discourse Communities.* Whose discursive practices constrain the ways they structure meaning (Nystrand 1993, 281). *Groups of society members can become accustomed to modifying each other's reasoning and language use in certain ways* (Bizzell 1982, 368). The different tables we sit at. *An individual can belong to more than one discourse community, but her access to the various communities will be unequally conditioned by her social situation* (366). Members only. Access denied.

1982. An article is published. Patricia Bizzell's "Cognition, Convention, and Certainty: What We Need to Know about Writing." A scholar argues for joining unfamiliar discourse communities, putting the tables together. *Examining and teaching patterns of language use and reasoning common to given disciplinary or interpretive communities* (Nystrand 1993, 289). *Focusing on idiosyncratic forms and conventions of academic communities* (290). Examining the menus.

In short, educational problems associated with language use should be understood as difficulties with joining an unfamiliar discourse community (Bizzell 1982, 375). We should share, eat off each others' plates. *Putting meaning into words cannot be seen as a mechanical process of finding the right size containers* (Bizzell 1982, 375). Language spills over.

1990s. New ideas have been formed. Making voices heard. Making academia accessible. Accepting variance. *The academic population is becoming more diverse* (Bizzell 1999, 11). Scholarly papers become more interesting. 1989. Mike Rose's *Lives on the Boundary* is published. An Italian-American of working-class background describes struggling college writers. Breaks myths. Raises issues. Gains acclaim in the popular press as well as within the academic community.

More texts emerge. 1991. African American Keith Gilyard's *Voices of the Self.* 1993. Puerto Rican American Victor Villaneuva Jr.'s *Bootstraps.* 1994. Helen Fox's *Listening to the World.* The *Borderlands* series by Mestiza Gloria Anzaldua.

1997. Werner Sollors. Harvard University. "For a Multilingual Turn in American Studies." Essay published in the June 1997 *ASA Newsletter. Recently voices have been raised that propose, in Mary Louise Pratt's words, "expunging the term foreign to refer to languages other than English" for it applies neither to Spanish nor to "French, Cantonese, Italian, or Japanese; to say nothing of Lakota, Navajo, or Cree"* (Sollors 1997). The guest list gets longer.

Discussion ensues. Composition theorists engage in the new texts. 1998. Andrea Lunsford's "Toward a Mestiza Rhetoric." Published: *JAC: A Journal of Composition Theory. And indeed, much of Anzaldua's work has been devoted to making a space where such multiplicity could be enacted* (Lunsford 1998, 1). *She learns to juggle cultures . . . Not only does she sustain contradictions, she turns ambivalence into something else . . . a new kind of writing style . . . a rich mixture of genres . . . weaving images and words from her multiple selves . . . into a kind of tapestry or patchwork quilt of language* (Lunsford 1998, 1). More talk. Dinner table rhetoric.

Writes Lunsford, "*During this interview, Anzaldua remarks that she has been shocked to 'find composition people picking me up' . . . given that composition has long been equated with hegemony of "standard" English and with gatekeeping*" (1998, 3). A surprise guest has arrived.

Spring 2000. Embracing variance. Redefining academic discourse. Bizzell's notion of hybrid sticks in the researcher's mind. Thoughts arise: hybrid as standard, not Standard as standard? This evening's set meal: Variant, Cultural, Personal, Offhand, Humorous, and for dessert, Accepted. Open invitation only . . .

BORDERLAND COOKING AND KITCHENS OF THE CONTACT ZONE

Translating the Menu

Academic Discourse Translation: This section will discuss alternative discourses and representation, exploring the "contact zone/ borderland" sites for doing alternative discourse work. By means of example, this section will possibly discuss the author's personal attempts to find "located" texts in her own site of work, the Hawaiian Islands, exploring the work of "experimental" borderland writers.

In search of alternative discourse work, she finds herself looking for writers and writing in her own backyard; the site—University of Hawaii, Honolulu, Oahu. There is cooking being done here behind closed doors; borderland cooking in kitchens of the contact zone. According to Gloria Anzaldua (1987), "A border is a dividing line, a narrow strip along a steep edge. A borderland is a vague and undetermined place created by the emotional residue of an unnatural boundary. It is in a constant state of emotional transition. The prohibited and forbidden are its inhabitants" (25). She thinks about how the concept of a "borderland," based on the work of Henry Giroux (Giroux 1992; Giroux and McLaren 1994) and "border pedagogy," works well in locations like the U.S./Mexico borders, where the language, though multivocal, is essentially bilingual and the cultural referents most likely fall behind the lines of primarily two countries. When applying this concept to her own site of research, the Hawaiian Islands, she finds the "borderland" concept to be problematic for one principal reason—the diversity (ethnically, linguistically, etc.) of Hawai`i. As opposed to a single line making one area binary, Hawai`i is made up of a plethora of borders—potentially undefinable and limitless.

She also keeps in mind the kinds of cooking that can be done in what Mary Louise Pratt has called "contact zones," or "social spaces where cultures, meet, clash, and grapple with each other, often in contexts of highly asymmetrical relations of power" (1991, 444). These spaces, Bizzell suggests, can "create conditions in which students are encouraged to experiment with their own forms of hybrid discourse." She stumbles across two writers; Samoan writer Jacinta Galeai and local Hawai`i writer Lisa Linn Kana`e. Young, experimental writers willing to advocate new and different forms of cooking, integrating regional language, text, and experience into new forms of cuisine. "*Let's talk about your cooking,*" she says, "*what's been bubbling over behind these walls.*"

In her "alternative" literacy narrative entitled "Lagaga Tala: Weaving an American-Samoan Writing Life," (2000) writer Jacinta Galeai begins in her introduction, "This mat is woven with stories of growing up in Samoa. These stories, woven with very fine *laufala* strips—dried panadus leaves used to make mats—stay with me and reveal moments that both sting and define my existence as a Samoan-American woman, writer, thinker and user of language." Galeai weaves multiple discourses in her prose, blending untranslated Samoan words and phrases with Standard English, and uses variant forms of writing, from song lyrics to religious hymns, to represent her own cultural way of knowing. Jacinta is from Samoa, has taught English at the American Samoa Community College, is completing her Ph.D. in English at the University of Hawai`i, and has short works published in *Bamboo Ridge* and *Chain.*

In her essay "Sista Tongue (2001)," Lisa Linn Kana`e uses mixed and blended forms, including the use of Hawaiian Creole English, to give a history of and advocate the validation of home languages, especially the use of Pidgin, or Hawaiian Creole English. By drawing parallels between her younger brother's speech disorder and the historical representation of Hawaiian Creole English, Kana`e uses her own dual experiences with language (Standard English and Hawaiian Creole English) to produce multivocal, mixed form prose, "alternative discourse," that continues the ongoing dialogue about Standard English and Pidgin. Lisa is the author of "Sista Tongue" and numerous poems and prose pieces that have been published in issues of *Bamboo Ridge: Journal of Hawai`i Literature and Arts, `Oiwi: A Native Hawaiian Journal, Hybolics* and *Tinfish.* She is a lecturer at Kapi`olani Community College and an editorial assistant for *`Oiwi: A Native Hawaiian Journal.*

Kana`e states, "It is necessary to consider the positive social value of all types of language. Speakers of Creole languages should never be perceived as mere casualties of insularity, ignorance, and social isolation. The history of Hawai`i Creole English has inspiring accounts of resourcefulness, intellect, and competence that both reflect and sustain local Hawai`ian culture." *When local Hawai`i students hear the rhythms of their own voices in their own literature, a literature that validated their identity, they get excited about their reading. It is as if they never imagined their world was significant enough to be in the pages of literature. Afta dat, dey talk up. Dey not so scared fo talk anymoa.*

On Defining "Alternative Discourses"

Jacinta: *The term "alternative" is a bit problematic for me because I don't see my voice as alternative. It is my voice and therefore it can't be alternative for me. But to answer the question, I see "alternative discourses" as forms of expressions (or communication and ways of being) that express a person's voice. For me this voice constitutes everything about me: identity, culture, experiences, values, knowledge, language and so forth.*

> **As I clutched my `api, a tall medium-sized woman, whose gray hair was fastened in a tight bun at the base of her neck, walked in and sat on a chair next to the blackboard. Dressed in a green mu`umu`u with large white flowers, she looked at me and asked, "Na sau lou tina e momoli mai oe?"**

> ***"She must be the faletua—minister's wife—she knows my mother," I thought, feeling a warm wave wash over me. "Leai. Na matou o mai ma Ti'afua ma Naiama," I answered.*** (2)

Lisa: *There have been times when I felt as if speaking, writing, and thinking in Standard English was actually my alternative discourse . . . Speaking Pidgin comes naturally to me.*

> *I was born and raised in Honolulu, Hawai'i and am an ethnic mixture of Japanese, Filipino, Hawaiian and Chinese ancestry. I am not fluent in any of my ancestors' native tongues. Instead, I heard and spoke Hawai'i Creole English, or "Pidgin," as it has been popularly called since its inception. For many Hawai'i residents, Pidgin' is the epitome of the term "local." To speak HCE validates the history and experiences of immigrant plantations, laborers, the progenitors of Hawai'i's now ethnically diverse culture.* (5)

On Using "Alternative Discourses"

Jacinta: *The most important way this discourse has helped me is that it has liberated me from the constraints of academic writing, allowed me to place my culture at the center as opposed to the periphery, and provided me the opportunity to access and reflect and thus interpret my views and ideas. How it has hindered me is a complex question because most of my professors have been open to my work. But I sense that they have other responses to my work that are not clear to them right now or are best left unsaid.*

> *(from introduction): Because the stories I've chosen to weave my narrative come from two cultures—Samoan and American—with multiple spaces, they will be difficult to read at times. But patience and effort in understanding and creating stories have their rewards. Experiencing the weaving of my narrative, you will be part of my contribution to a current postmodern movement that seeks to change how we write and create knowledge. But the greatest reward will be emerging with a greater understanding, and, I hope, appreciation, of the multiple spaces I move in and out of as a Samoan-American writer, thinker and user of language.*

Lisa: *For the most part, I can "go in and out of" Standard English and Pidgin with ease. That's the reality behind the piece, which is why I chose to write Sista Tongue with both languages. It's the way I think, talk, and write.*

> *Local Hawai'i people are raised to believe that Pidgin' is reserved for less formal social environments, i.e. family gatherings or lunch hour conversation, but should never be spoken in "formal" or professional and academic settings. Pidgin' also functions as an identifier of in-group and out-group populations (Yamamoto 21). In other words, HCE is a social marker indicating who is and who is not local. We are conscious of our power to include*

> *and exclude whenever we choose to speak HCE. Jus try bus out da pidgin fo wen you like one Kama'aina discount at one rent-a-car counter da next time you like travel to da outah islands.* (4)

On "Alternative Discourses" and Audience

Jacinta: . . . *the main audience consists of people who are specifically interested in Samoan or Pacific cultures, teachers, students, writers, artists, women, little old ladies (some have been very responsive), and those who just want to participate in opening up spaces for new voices.*

> *As a young Samoan/American girl, she was beginning to become a victim of her own mind/body split—split from her culture, native language and family. Fortunately, however, she was reunited with her culture, language, and family. She chose to begin her journey—examining the moments that formed her development as a writer—with A'oga Samoa because a Samoan person is defined by family, cultural values, and language, and she would not have been able to give voice to her experiences of growing up in American Samoa without this reunion.* (7).

Lisa: *There are so many published works on Hawai'i Creole English that ultimately say the same thing—Pidgin deserves validation because of the value of its social history. I wanted to write a paper that was artistic while expressing my personal stake in the issue, so my "envisioned audience" was my family, especially my brother. My ideal audience? The plantation families and Native Hawaiians and any Creole speaking people who understand the effects of the politics of language.*

> *Studies done on sociolinguistic attitudes in Hawai'i indicate that "HCE is associated with low academic achievement and low socioeconomic status" (Sato 652) . . . local Hawai'i students and teachers participated in these studies. Such is the paradox of local pride and self-loathing that is characteristic of Hawai'i Creole English speakers. Pidgin' is not only the emblem of the Hawai'i plantation era; it has also been perceived as a stigma including low social status, ignorance, and* **local identity.** (7)

On "Alternative Discourses" and Language(s)

Jacinta: *I've been learning the dominant discourse my entire life and I never said, "You're imposing on me" because they did a good job of keeping me in the dark. Now that I know better, I'm not saying, "Get rid of academic discourse." I'm just saying, "Let me write this way." Wait, let me rephrase that. I'm saying, "I'm going to write this way PERIOD."*

> *The first language she learned to write was English. As a result, she experienced the painful "disjuncture" that most Samoans experience when learn-*

> *ing how to write in Samoan . . . The writing included mere copying and repetition of Biblical facts and therefore did not help her to learn to write the academic discourse in her English classes.* (3)

Lisa: *I grew up learning how to live in two worlds; the Standard English speaking world and the Hawai`i Creole English speaking world. I've been pretty fortunate, because I've learned to exist successfully in both. Well, let's say I had to learn. Those who either refuse or haven't learned to shift in and out of these worlds should never feel the lesser for it.*

> *Stigma has made it necessary for Pidgin speakers to learn how to code shift from HCE into Standard English for more formal situations (i.e., job interviews, boardrooms, research papers). This "learned necessity" tacitly perpetuates the assumed superiority of Standard English over Hawai`i Creole English, which in turn reinforces the assumption that speakers of Pidgin' are intellectually and socially inferior to speakers of Standard English . . .* (7)

On the "Blending of Discourses"

Jacinta: *I prefer to use the term "weave" to describe what I do. In fact, my work opens with a poem called "The Weaver" where a Samoan woman is alone weaving a mat, her legs are folded, her eyes fixed on the mat, and she is envisioning the end product. To retain my Samoan identity—writing is a practice founded on Western values—I think of that image and thus use the term "weave" to describe this act that I now embrace. This problem that academics are getting all anxious about implies that our style of writing and even our voices are wrong. Otherwise it wouldn't be a problem. Like I said before I'm not saying, "Get rid of academic discourse." That would be wrong because then I'm guilty of what I'm advocating. I'm saying, "let other voices be heard." Again, they are scared of losing ground, control and power. That's what happens when a group of people with the same perspective holds all or the majority of the power. When you feel that anxious you experience what we in Samoa call, "moe te`ite`i"—tossing and turning in your bed.*

Jacinta: *I suppose the last thing I want to say is that in order for me to engage or enter the dialogue I have to speak my voice. That voice includes Samoan language, jokes, songs, proverbs, Biblical verses, myths, legends, history and so forth. I have to be at the center. My ancestors from Manu`a (my father's family) believe that Tagaloalagi (Samoan God) created the first person above the skies of Manu`a so center is very important to me. People from Manu`a would never buy this periphery stuff. (I know that sounds so egocentric. Well, it is.) Gloria Anzaldua writes about being on the border. Having established my position and having understood my voices, I then speak to/with/against the academic discourses and even poke fun with and at them (as you can tell). I can't help it. Samoans don't like being too serious. We fall asleep easily. We like* *laughing and joking. That's why we say, "E happy lava le teine"—We are into being happy. Well, we are until somebody pushes us to the periphery.*

THE POLITICS OF FUSION CUISINE

The researcher finds herself wondering about issues of fusion cuisine, tasty and variant discourses elevated to a new sense of gourmet. With two clicks on the Web, she is transported to an imagined and virtual community, a technological kitchen. **SEARCHED THE WEB FOR "FUSION CUISINE." RESULTS 1–10 OF ABOUT 5,280. SEARCH TOOK 0.06 SECONDS.**

WEBSIGHT: Rogov's Ramblings: Once Upon a Time in America, The Dubious Past of Fusion Cuisine. She is told that "fusion cuisine" has been called **"literally a fusion of cultural, ethnic and culinary styles that are either native to or eventually immigrated to America."** She is also told that American chefs will all describe how fusion cuisine is a style from which all chefs, no matter their origins, draw strongly on the culinary traditions of their cultural and ethnic roots (as well as on the abundance of raw materials in America).

American chefs have a bubbling, sometimes even raging enthusiasm to experiment with new ingredients. Depending partly on their own cultural and ethnic backgrounds, [they] sometimes apply[ing] Asian, Caribbean, Mediterranean or sometimes even familiar Western methods into what they are convinced is a uniquely American culinary style. [Researcher's note: *a blending of discourses.*]

Fear has run rampant through kitchens, classrooms and conferences that a call is being made for an abandoning of "traditional" discourses. Familiar, Western methods of cooking are being displaced by spicy, exotic dishes, ones that may cause adverse reactions in diners everywhere. That these foreign meals have always been present, steaming and bubbling over in the back of traditional kitchens has been overlooked. Many serving have been eating their own kind of "fusion," mixing up variant home cuisines and blending discourses amongst families and friends, different eating communities. When and where needed. This cuisine now being given the name "fusion" is not something novel nor exotic. Only more expensive in restaurants of fine dining.

Is "Fusion Cuisine" Really a Cuisine?

Cuisines do not just happen because one, two, or one hundred chefs decide that a particular flavor or style is going to be popular. Cuisines are the result of evolution, an intermingling of forces over centuries or even

millennia. A national or regional cuisine develops and changes as part of a living culture, affected by historical forces, geography, geology, climate and technology as well as by the raw materials that are available.
[Researcher's note: *conditions in which discourses are created.*]

Discourses, like cuisines, are situated in a time and place. The conditions of our cooking is as important as the process itself, as critical as the product, the final dish, which has been traditionally presented on a tray of silver, garnished with a sprig of parsley. Now we have chopsticks, wooden kabob spears, fish egg garnish. No utensils; bare hands even. We don't know how to eat this food—we look at it mouths agape and at a loss for words. We can't give it ratings; our criteria don't apply. It is powerfully strong—seductive even—we want to read, eat, swallow. But it's strange, it's new, it's foreign; perhaps an "acquired taste."

Cuisines evolve and are not fads that less than a decade before vanishing to make room for "something new" . . . what is being wrongly called "fusion cuisine" is little more than a sometimes noble series of experiments in the kitchen—often original, often tasty, and often inventive, but little more than experiments that will be forgotten in even less time than they took to develop.
[Researcher's note: *the longevity of hybrid/alternative discourses.*]

Chefs from coast to coast are skeptical about the "trendiness" of this new kind of cooking. Experiments in discourse are not going to change the great cuisines of the world. We are, in fact, keeping some chefs "sous" by not teaching them the real culinary arts. How can they perform in kitchens with their strange utensils for discourses, foreign spices as languages, untraditional ingredients for ideas? We are not *enabling*, we are *disabling*. We are hoarding real culinary power to ourselves by asking others to "experiment." These experiments will not garnish them with success. They will only provide us with the satisfaction of running democratic kitchens, where all voices are heard and all cuisines represented. It's a lost cause, chefs might argue. Until the customers crave a new kind of cooking, "great cuisine" will prevail in the kitchens of the powerful.

Even the very definition of fusion cuisine stands on not too solid ground, for fine chefs have always, consciously or otherwise, been influenced by their cultural and social backgrounds as well as their personal experiences.
[Researcher's Note: *defining discourses.*]

Fusion. Hybrid. Alternative. Untraditional. Nonstandard. Variant. The problem of naming and defining the concept has been more difficult than writing about it. Traits of "fusion cuisine." Examples of "variant forms." Many seek to deny that there is any cooking "traditional" enough to have an "alternative." But some chefs would agree that there were methods and recipes and all kinds of ingredients they learned to make them heads of their own kitchens. This is the discourse, the knowledge, the language, the dominant kind of cooking valued in society. Whatever the name, it exists as a gatekeeper, exists as a convention, Exists.

Another reason to doubt that fusion cuisine is a genuine cuisine is in its very need for originality, each individual chef looking for his or her own individual expressions of just what "fusion" is about.
[Researcher's note: *methods of experimentation.*]

There are no cookbooks for alternative discourses.

A MENU OF TEXTS

SPECIAL OF THE DAY: Variant texts as a generative force for alternative discourses

> TEXT: In its most usual sense, *text* refers to any written or printed document, whether literary or not.
>
> —*The Columbia Dictionary of Modern Literary and Cultural Criticism*

Addition to the Menu: "not only written texts but also any human artifact that can be 'read' or interpreted, including visual representations" (Bizzell 1999, 19).

Revision to the Menu: anything around which you can put a conceptual frame.

Below is a menu of the types of possible "variant texts" which may be a potentially generative force for hybrid discourses. [Note: The list includes suggestions of Patricia Bizzell and Mary Louise Pratt along with an extended list of my own.]

THE MENU

- letters
- poetry
- journals
- comic books
- fashion
- print/engravings

- song lyrics
- case studies
- literary criticism
- journalism
- pamphlets
- asylum/prison writing
- advertisements (copy)
- signs (text)
- sermons
- autobiography, biography
- captivity narratives
- political/government documents
- proposals
- laws/regulations
- magazines
- newsletters
- hypertext
- postcards
- handbooks/manuals
- translated texts
- graffiti
- drawings
- websites
- crafts
- music
- theater/dance
- advertisements (images)
- signs (images)
- murals
- posters
- sculpture
- multimedia
- design
- frescoes
- collages
- architecture
- mosaic
- photography
- mandalas
- film

Message to the management/waithelp: Some advice on serving meals

Course one—expose students to variant forms
Course two—serve texts as models and words to play with/inspire
Course three—encourage experimentation and production of alternative discourses

A NOTE ON HOME COOKIN'

. . . it has become a commonplace to hear the world itself referred to as a text.

—*The Columbia Dictionary of Modern Literary and Cultural Criticism*

Home cookin' is all about finding the ingredients in your own backyard. *The ocean as text. The city as text. Reading the countryside.* Please note: students are literate in different ways without being aware of it. *Plucking words from our gardens.* The main dish for those involved in the classroom is recognizing the importance of locating home-cooked texts as a generative force for hybrid/alternative discourses.

The texts can be "home-cooked" in two ways: (1) showing or demonstrating regional dialects/discourses in expository[1] writing models (Howcanweaskthestudentstofeelcomfortablewritingintheirhomedialectsiftheydonot seemodelsofotherswillingtodosobymeansofexample?) AND (2) derived from the classroom site's regional habitat (by this, I mean the "environment" surrounding the class/location of teaching)(Drawingfromexperienceor theexternalworldaroundthem,studentsneedtextswhichspeaktothemtovalidate/ provoke/createhybrid/alternativeforms). This gathering of texts ain't easy. It requires some digging around, taking a look at what's been growin.' *It might be better for the teacher to do some research before the class begins . . . to find a good crux to explore and collect, if not all, at least a substantial amount of reading material before the class begins, TO WHICH THE STUDENTS CAN ADD (*Bizzell 1999, 18*). Whatever crux is chosen should be carefully derived from local conditions* (Bizzell 1999, 17). Integrating home-grown texts into the classroom.

There are a number of approaches to take when digging for texts. An expressivist might dig from within, having students generate texts from their own experience. A social constructionist might have students dig around in the yard, identifying texts from their environment or their "socially constructed" reality, and analyze or deconstruct how these texts function—how they are considered alternative, how they support or oppose existing values and ideologies. Both kinds of texts are "regional," derived from home sites (*ourselves, our native habitats*). Both are valid. Both serve to potentially generate new forms of intellectual work, opening up the space for new types of cookin.'

NOTE

1. Beware of "take-out" food: fiction as opposed to essay or nonfiction writing as dialect/language models—when students only see their home dialects in fiction models, it can influence the way they see that dialect used/modeled in forms of work in the Academy (mostly in dialogue, rarely in argument).

LEFTOVERS

She enters now a cooking class full of students, writers, publishers and scholars. All capped in tall hats and armed with pens, these chefs are writing, experimenting, revising. For each, it is a beginner's class, although some have been cooking for some time now. The space is active, open, unfinished. She finds a seat at a table. The class begins . . .

The Unconclusion on Hybrid/Alternative Discourses

NOT THE END.

WORKS CITED

Anzaldua, Gloria. 1987. *Borderlands/La Frontera: The New Mestiza.* San Francisco: Spinsters/Aunt Lute.

Bizzell, Patricia. 1982. "Cognition, Convention, and Certainty: What We Need to Know about Writing." In *Cross-Talk in Comp Theory: A Reader* edited by Victor Villaneuva. Urbana: National Council of Teachers of English. 365–389.

———. 1992. "Introduction." *Academic Discourse and Critical Consciousness.* Pittsburg, PA: Univ. of Pittsburg.

———. 1999. "Hybrid Academic Discourses: What, Why, How." *Composition Studies.* 27(2):7–21.

Childers, Joseph, and Gary Hentzi, eds. 1995. *The Columbia Dictionary of Modern Literary and Cultural Criticism.* New York: Columbia Univ. Press.

Fox, Helen. 1994. *Listening to the World: Cultural Issues in Academic Writing.* Urbana, IL: National Council of Teachers of English.

Freire, Paulo. 1970. *Pedagogy of the Oppressed,* translated by Myra Bergman Ramos. New York: Seabury.

Galeai, Jacinta. 2000. "Lagaga Tala: Weaving an American-Samoan Writing Life." Master's thesis, University of Hawai`i at Manoa, Honolulu.

Gilyard, Keith. 1991. *Voices of the Self: A Study of Language Competence.* Detroit: Wayne State Univ. Press.

Giroux, Henry A. 1992. *Border Crossings: Cultural Workers and the Politics of Education.* London: Routledge.

Giroux, Henry A., and Peter McLaren. 1994. *Between Borders: Pedagogy and the Politics of Cultural Studies.* New York: Routledge.

Guralnik, David B., ed. 1971. *Webster's New World Dictionary of the American Language.* New York: World.

Kana`e, Lisa Linn. 2001. "Sista Tongue." Master's thesis, University of Hawai`i at Manoa, Honolulu.

Lunsford, Andrea. 1998. "Toward a Mestiza Rhetoric: Gloria Anzaldua on Composition and Postcoloniality." *JAC: A Journal of Composition Theory* 18 (1):1–27.

Nystrand, Martin, Stuart Greene, and Jeffrey Wiemelt. 1993. "Where Did Composition Studies Come From?: An Intellectual History." *Written Communication* 10 (3):267–333.

Plato. "Phaedrus." *The Rhetorical Tradition: Readings from Classical Times to Present,* edited by Patricia Bizzell and Bruce Herzberg. Boston: St. Martin's.

Pratt, Mary Louise. 1991. "Arts of the Contact Zone." In *Ways of Reading: An Anthology for Writers* edited by David Bartholomae and Anthony Petrosky, 442–460. Boston: Bedford Books of St. Martin's Press (1993).

Rogov, Daniel. 2001, March. "Rogov's Ramblings: Once Upon a Time in America. The Dubious Past of Fusion Cuisine." [Online]. Available: <http://www.stratsplace.com/rogov/once_in_america.html>

Rose, Mike. 1988. "Narrowing the Mind and Page: Cognitive Writers and Cognitive Reductionism." *College Composition.* 39 (3) (October):267–98.

———. 1989. *Lives on the Boundary: The Struggles and Achievements of America's Underprepared.* New York: Penguin.

Shaughnessy, Mina. 1977. *Errors and Expectations: A Guide for the Teacher of Basic Writing.* New York: Oxford Univ. Press.

Sollors, Werner. 1997. "For a Multilingual Turn in American Studies." *ASA Newsletter.* [Online]. Available:<http://www.georgetown.edu/crossroads/interroads/Sollois1.html>

Villanueva, Victor Jr. 1993. *Bootstraps: From an American Academic of Color.* Urbana: National Council of Teachers of English.

13

An Essay We're Learning to Read
Responding to Alt.Style

Michael Spooner

I.

How many copyeditors does it take to screw in a light bulb?

Not sure whether you mean "change a light bulb" or "have sex in a light bulb." Consider revising for clarity?

Will have to check house style for the joke balloons. Is there a way you could work these into the body text instead?

When I started on this chapter I had a little vignette at the beginning, about how my office building was marked for demolition by the university's master plan. It made a nice lead into what I wanted to become a theme about master plans, which, if you were with me through the end, became a comment about convention in writing for the academy. I also liked it because it really happened to me. It had personal meaning. I gave a brief but affectionate description of the office, with its view, its fireplace, its apricot tree and rose bushes, and its general suitability to its setting and to the small needs of my small staff (who were, of course, kept in the dark about the master plan until all the decisions had been made).

That's where I wanted to begin, because it was an important part of my life this past year and because I thought I could make something out of it that would relate to the dilemma we have as writers when we want to break with convention. Then I wanted to bring in Christopher Alexander, the architect who argues that master plans are exactly the wrong way to design campuses. You need to start with the people who work there, he says, privilege the small things, and build your design from the bottom up with a view toward a sort of emergent order instead of the totalitarian approach favored by the current U.S. campus-cum-corporate culture. So this became my allegory for dealing with alt.style in academic writing. The same small values can guide how one responds to alt.writing as a teacher or, in my case, as an editor.

But then, on the listserv that was set up for contributors to this book, Chris Thaiss asked what really is convention, anyway? And Pat Bizzell answered well here are fourteen things that are common as dirt in conventional academic writing, and she identified this as one of them: "personal experience used . . . as a dryly humorous opening anecdote." She just tossed that off on the way to class as something we all *know*. Which is true, I suppose; we do know that. It's not her fault. Still, what chance does that leave me? I thought I was being alt to open with a personal story, but now I see what I should have realized about both the postmodern and the avant garde—the impossibility of *beginning* anything and the hopelessness of trying to build a stance *against* anything. I'm already co-opted before I don't begin.

I notice you're beginning with stream of consciousness. Will the academic reader be okay with this? Won't they expect a more expository approach? You seem to drop this voice later. Will you come back to it? Glancing ahead, not clear to me how you'll segue smoothly into the argument. . . .

In addition to all of this, our volume editors are interested in questions of the legitimacy of academic discourse/s, and they think, more or less reasonably, that as a publisher of discourse that serves the ends of academe, (1) I am invested, by role at least, in institutional convention, and therefore (2) I should have an articulated stance on the tension between tradition and innovation in that discourse. So, in one sense, part of my assignment is to discuss how I can ethically serve my institutional role and at the same time use my role to legitimize (by publishing) discourse that the hermetic institution traditionally resists. The trouble for me, however, is that, from my position, academic discourse looks far leakier than it seems from my volume editors' position. I didn't want to deal with this; generally, I think it's better to leave theory to theorists and not encourage editors to mess with it.

I'm not complaining. Editing is creative and rewarding, plus I don't have to disrupt my work with those tedious sabbaticals and semesters abroad that professors have, don't have to write for publication, don't have to go to over-stimulating world-class cities for MLA in December. But I do notice one disadvantage in my field that more scholastic vocations don't suffer so much. Professional editors generally spend little time in reflection—on editing. There's a great deal of lore (which is no pejorative), but there isn't a large body of scholarship in this field; consequently, editing knows relatively little about itself theoretically. I don't want to overstate this, since there certainly is work published in editorial theory. Some of it, for my money, attends too much to the metaphors and cultures—one might say the master plan—of American business (with its users, information, skill sets, goals, teams, functionality), but some also draws from the best of allied fields like rhetoric and composition, communication, and graphic design. Still, unlike practitioners in those allied fields, unlike composition teachers especially, *professional editors themselves* tend not to pursue or create scholarship in their own field. It's not a publish-or-perish field, or not in the same sense, heh heh, so the practice of editing too often is guided by rather simple formulations, by conventions that are too seldom interrogated.

This is especially so compared to pedagogy (maybe theory is the difference between profession and discipline), and more especially compared to the field of teaching composition. I think this may be part of why I feel nonplussed when asked to reconcile my service to the traditional structures of academe (say, refereed publishing) with my advocacy for alternate discourses within those structures. Still, perhaps the chapter allows me to explore some of both. I've always liked composition as a field because it is, like editing, an occupation preoccupied with response, with the small things of purpose and balance and fit, and what I'll propose here is that editing scholarly writing can be theorized in terms like those of response to student writing. And then I'd like to try that theoretical approach in a demonstration edit of an article written in alt.style.

Did you consider turning this around? I mean, you're saying here that editors could learn from comp studies. But you're not writing to editors, obviously, because they don't read theory, if you're right. (Which you are.)

But then, given the real audience (comp folks) it seems like what you want to say is that comp teachers could learn a thing or two from editors. They could be better teachers if they knew a thing or two about editing. That's your point, right?

At my university, I have taught and regularly visit editing classes in the tech writing program; I also employ editorial interns and other student workers in my office every semester. For me, one of the hardest ideas to convey to students is that editing (I would argue that *any* response to writing) works best when it proceeds from a stance of sympathy or alignment with the writer—not from a stance of Correction or Remediation. Editorial lore, like teaching lore, is full of Correction, and editors complain about their authors like teachers complain about their students. I think this unfortunate persona is encouraged by textbooks and instruction that emphasize the editor's role vis à vis The Reader—or, as in some tech editing books, The User. It seems sometimes that editors believe that there is a particular idiom, a master plan of finite conventions, through which reality prefers to be conveyed. I'm glad to see awareness of audience, some rhetoric-based theory, in teaching editing, but the rhetorical situation I see most often described is a surprisingly flat one, oriented most toward audience and text, strangely erasing the rhetor. They do a Henry Higgins on the writer. They love the language—or is it readability measures?—to a fault. If, as lore, textbooks and teachers often claim, the editor must be the *reader's advocate* , then it's no wonder that editors behave so often as the *writer's adversary.* It's not unlike the argument in composition over the need to teach students to assimilate conventions of academic discourse, where the teacher is positioned not as a responder so much as a gatekeeper. You should hear university press directors talk about what important gatekeepers they are.

EVEN WHEN A WRITER IS SOPHISTICATED IN THE USE OF LANGUAGE, AN EDITOR CAN BRING OBJECTIVITY TO THE READING THAT THE WRITER MAY LOSE BY KNOWING THE SUBJECT TOO WELL. THE EDITOR WORKS WITH THE TEXT FROM THE PERSPECTIVE OF THE READER. THE EDITOR SERVES AS A READERS' ADVOCATE. (RUDE 12)

> Editor
>
> Do you love the English language to a fault? Do you always find yourself editing for correctness in grammar, punctuation, spelling, syntax, etc.? If you possess at least two years' editing/proofreading experience and a degree in English/Journalism, we need your expertise to edit K-12 educational tests.
>
> Advertisement
> Harcourt Educational Measurement
> *Education Researcher*
> 29:9 Dec 2000

House style, again. We don't usually allow violations of the margins like this. I'll check. Just in case, wouldn't it be possible to integrate this advertisment with the body of your text? Introduce it, set it up like a standard block quote? Wouldn't this make more sense to the reader?

Brock Dethier's book, *The Composition Instructor's Survival Guide*, got me thinking about the relation between teaching and editing in this regard. Dethier argues for a stance of respect toward college students—a generous attitude that relates to them not as "kids" but as adults whose writing, logic, responses, even excuses, deserve genuine respect and serious consideration. I'd argue that the editorial stance (whether taken by teacher or editor) should be the same: all writers and their texts deserve to be handled with respect by those who respond. This is perhaps obvious to scholars like Dethier and the contributors to this book. It's consistent with the spirit of composition pedagogy since at least the 1970s, when, with position statements like "Students' Right to

Their Own Language" and other motions toward critical practice, (many in) the field began to question traditional discourse in teaching and to grant a certain authority to students' own discourse(s).

Do you know Schroeder's book ReInventing the University? *His stance toward students is essentially the same, and, importantly for the transcending argument of this present volume, he's oriented specifically toward alternate literacies.*

More specifically, research in composition has developed useful language through which to explore issues in response. I'm thinking here of well-known handles like "facilitative" versus "directive" (and shades between: e.g., Straub), along with more general principles of response from the Rogerian to the postmodern; respecting the (student) writer's ownership; deliberately "reflecting" the writer's position/s in text-specific comments; losing "awk," "ww," "frag," and replacing them with fuller, more accessible comments. I won't review the literature here; I'll just assert the uncontroversial notion that feedback in writing instruction was more than a 1970s platitude. It was a serious move away from Correction and toward Response.

And Helen Fox's Listening to the World, *in case you haven't seen it, is equally attuned to the "alternative" discourse of her international students. And one of Bizzell's purposes is to highlight the contingent nature of what is accepted in the U.S. as definitive convention.*

All of these scholars exemplify the stance you're advocating. (Then there's Smitherman, Villanueva, Elbow, and others.) In addition, not to put too fine a point on it, S, F, & B are the volume editors here; it would be politic to give them a plug.

My own perspective is often dual or ambivalent. Or shifty. It's eclectic, surely. It is informed pragmatically by the lore of editorial professionals, so it's attentive to readerly perspectives and to issues of what Phelps (extending Eisner's ideas) calls "connoisseurship" and "criticism" (99 ff). But it is also grounded in academic studies of response like those to which I alluded earlier. In fact, perhaps obviously now, editorial work is to my mind fundamentally a matter of response to *writers*. It *involves* advocacy for the reader, but ultimately, I think the best editing actually privileges—it's the only way I can see not to erase—the writer.

II.

How many proofreaders does it take to change a light bulb?

Proofreaders should never change a light bulb. They should only query them.

Of course, the professions of editing and teaching are not the same. Still, importantly, teachers who honor their students' own discourse and editors who do not wish to erase the rhetor share an interest in seeing the text develop and succeed on terms of the writer's choosing. That's why I think the first challenge of editorial response to writing, like teacherly response, is not to correct a text toward what the handbooks or readability indices allow, but to understand the writer's ideas and processes. After that, the job is to imagine small ways to help the writer deliver those ideas effectively. I'd argue that such a sympathy for the text is fundamental to the ethics of response (see Spooner 1997 for more on this).

However, I don't want this to be confused with uncritical acceptance of every writerly choice. Novice writers, student writers, even when they may have textual issues (syntax, lexicon, etc.) well in hand, frequently struggle with other dimensions of writing. Experienced writers also miss or exceed the mark. To point out insufficiencies in particular areas can be a thoroughly sympathetic service, then. I'm simply recalling that our commitment to the writer's right to their own language is basic to ethical response.

```
From: Christopher Schroeder
To: Michael Spooner

as for your gatekeeping function, i see you as much
more in the middle—encouraging these challenges
and, at the same time, constrained by the institu-
tional structures of publishing, such as your
review board. as you know much better than i, you
can only do so much before you run up against
institutionalized structures designed to resist
challenges.
```

This book is supposed to address institutional constraints—on literacies, on discourse, on democracy—but I don't think I *do* know those constraints better than Schroeder does, at least not from publishing. He and I have struggled with this dimension of the chapter, because I am not sure I can speak to the issue. I'm not sure it's my issue. What he implies above that I should see as constraint often looks more like collaboration to me. One might think the system of peer review in academic publishing, for example, is (as in his phrase) a structure designed to resist challenges, but my experience wouldn't support that view. Members of my review

Just a query on voice: You seem to make many self-deprecating gestures in this chapter. Do you think these will undermine your authority with the audience? Consider revising toward a stronger statement of your position?

board resist *me* from time to time, but that's not the same as resisting change. I know that Schroeder has met institutional resistance to his pedagogy, his writing, and his research. But even as we readied his own manuscript (*ReInventing*) for publication, I found the review process very supportive, or, at worst, no more resistant than usual. This has been my general experience. I do have disputes with my institution, yes, but I don't think I can complain when it comes to publishing books that challenge the status quo.

What I'd rather do is understand institutional processes in publishing as part of a larger system and larger theory of response to writing. I think we should see each remark by an editor, each peer review, each vote and comment from an editorial board member, as situated and invested in a sort of ecology of response, instead of, from the inside, as a defensive gatekeeping system or, from the outside, as a set of constraints or obstacles to surmount.

> *Oh, I see where you're going—feedback. Situate editorial work within response theory. That's a good move. Can you pull it off?*

Let me play this out in some detail for a minute. Viewed, say, from above, reviews and votes and editorial comments are obviously response documents: they can't be comprehended beyond their interaction with the text to which they respond. Further, in performing their response, editorial comments take, as teacher comments do toward student texts, a complex of stances that response theory is currently addressing: (1) they're *composed and invented* texts, in that they replay to the author the narrative of a reading experience; (2) they're *hermeneutic*, in that they represent a systematic interpretation of the text; (3) *rhetorical,* in that they often advocate a course of action for the author to pursue; (4) *transactional,* in terms of reader-response theory, since they actually respond to the virtual text that is conjured by their own reading; (5) *critical*, since they unfold the intellectual complexities of the text; (6) *contextual,* because of their interdependencies with the larger process of manuscript development and the publishing decision: "other readers may disagree"; (7) *aesthetic* or *appreciative*, and so on. You can see that I'm trying to think about this in the way Phelps recommends in "Cyrano's Nose." Phelps is focused on response to student texts, and it's tempting to see (8) a *pedagogical* dimension in editorial response, too, but ultimately it's not a step I'm comfortable taking. As didactic as peer reviewers and working editors can be, and though one can argue they're responding to "texts in transition" as student texts are, I choose not to see the context of editorial response as a pedagogical one, because I feel the roles of writer and editor are not more than superfically comparable to the roles of learner and teacher. Strange as it may seem, I don't see intervention—at least not as that term is used in education theory—as part of the editorial process.

I HAVE NO COMPUNCTION EDITING THE HELL OUT OF A [WRITER'S] COPY . . . COPY IS ALWAYS BETTER WHEN I GET THROUGH WITH IT. (DTALLMAN, COPYEDITING-L LISTSERV)

So I'm not in tune about institutional constraint on discourse as it applies to academic publishing. I don't deny that the system of refereed publishing is always exclusive. I'm only suggesting the exclusivity has little to do with conventions of discourse. I offer the following list as evidence: *Bootstraps; Listening to the World; Home of the Wildcats; Passions, Pedagogies and 21st Century Technologies; ReInventing the University.* That's a sample of successful alt-oriented books that came through referee processes with which I was personally connected over the past fifteen years. You have your own list of favorite alt.books in academe; I'm saying some(institutional)body approved those books. (In fact, I'm usually and self-destructively inclined to believe there are *too few* rejections in academic publishing, not *too many.* We would improve the academy faster if *teaching* were rewarded more seriously and if publishing ever more books for the audience of scholars were granted less weight. But that's another matter.)

Part of this may have to do with a yet larger context, the culture of publishing, which is decidedly different from the culture of the disciplines in a university. While in the academic department there may sometimes be pressure to conform, in publishing—even academic publishing—novelty works. The pressure is to Innovate, or at least to catch the trend wave. And if you can get Celebrity in there too, that works even better. Why was Heinemann interested in this book you're holding? Start with a marketable subject (say academic discourse). Give it a provocative spin (say critical practice). Now add the Big Names you see in the table of contents, and hey, alt discourse, challenging the status quo, is not a problem. If there are constraints, they come from an institution called the Market, not from the referee process.

Did you want to point out that academe is not consistent? That is, while you're expected to obvserve the discourse conventions, you won't get your dissertation approved or your article published, unless you can show that it is "unique, original, and significant."

"Originality" is a cultural issue that Fox explores. Again, you might give more attention to the work of your volume editors. Just a thought.

READERS NEED TO KNOW MAIN POINTS BEFORE DETAILS; THEY NEED TO UNDERSTAND THE STRUCTURE OF THE ARGUMENT BEFORE THE ELABORATION OF SUPPORTING ARGUMENTS. BUT MANY WRITERS, CAUGHT IN THE TECHNICAL LOOP OF THEIR EXPERTISE, BEGIN THE DISCUSSION AT FAR TOO DETAILED A LEVEL FOR ANY BUT THE MOST EXPERT. (EISENBERG 5)

To step toward a different sort of context, I think I don't identify with Schroeder's stance on academic/alternative discourse for philosophical or maybe temperamental reasons. Don't get me wrong: I think the politics of inclusion and exclusion is a deeply important and interesting subject. I'm sympathetic to the perspectives of Schroeder, Fox, Bizzell, and others writing here. (I think it's fair to note that most of the folks here advocating alternative discourses don't normally write in any other than the prestige dialect of American English. But does that make them phonies, Holden Caulfield?) Further, I do understand that given my role in the institutional structure, I am implicated in the politics of academic discourse, and trust me, I'm happy to encourage such iconoclasms as come my way. My point is simply that the politics of discourse in the American university is not my issue in the way it is my volume editors' issue. "Transformation," even in the post-Freirean era, is still too theological for me. I'm very skeptical of utopian projects, even though I'll gladly sponsor them through my publishing program. Accordingly, what I attend to most, and what I think is the most ethical editorial interest, is not the politics of alternative discourses but their poetics and the epistemologies they embody. The interface of design and critique, in Kress's terms; of connoisseurship and criticism, in Eisner's (per Phelps).

III.

How many marketing directors does it take to change a light bulb?

I hope it's not too late to make this neon?

My thought here is to work out some of the implications of this approach as it applies in response to writing that is composed in "alternate" or "radical" or "alt" style, something that both editors and teachers increasingly face (cf. Bishop). (I'm referencing only print writings here, but, of course, much writing appears in digital spaces; I'd advocate the same editorial stance in either case.)

Will we need to get permission to use these jokes? And again, on voice. I understand your purpose here, but don't you think your audience will take you less seriously for including these light (bulb) touches? Why take the chance?

First, a fairly mainstream example. Here's an excerpt from a letter by May Swenson to Elizabeth Bishop. In a previous letter, Bishop has chided Swenson for using no punctuation in a recent poem. "Are you trying to be like the French?" she snorts. Swenson replies this way.

> It doesn't make things easier, certainly. An extra discipline is imposed in the manipulation of language . . . the whole burden being on the *words* and how they are combined. The reader is induced to concentrate a little harder, too . . . Doesn't it . . . force him to follow more subtle clues to understanding? (September 1953)

"An extra discipline." It's not uncommon for teachers and editors to respond to alt.style as if it were easy, casual, un-serious—not unlike the way

Elizabeth Bishop must have reacted to Swenson. It may be play (of language) on the serious page that they interpret that way, but I'm convinced with Swenson that to manage play toward an important effect in the reading experience absolutely requires an extra discipline from the writer. It can be done frivolously, yes, or badly, or unsuccessfully; but to make it work *well* is anything but easy.

"The reader is induced to concentrate." Alt.style inevitably draws attention to itself, inevitably makes the reader give up some ideas for a moment and accommodate some new ones. A reader has to concentrate, as Swenson suggests, to discover the rules by which the writing works. Editors and writing teachers are used to knowing what the rules are, and we're used to enforcing them; but when you encounter alt.styles, your first task is to figure out a new set of rules in each piece of writing. No wonder some of us resist or feel unprepared. Alt.style draws from what has been called Grammar B (Weathers, of course, Bishop, and others), combines genres and/or media, mixes conventions from various disciplines, messes with typography like a visual poem does. If Myka Vielstimmig is right, even "standard" forms are moving toward more experiment and visuality than they have in the past: "It's an essay the academy is learning to write" (2001). So if you edit alt.writing from Correction, you're going to be very busy, indeed. And even if you edit from Sympathy, you can find yourself at sea.

PREFER THE STANDARD TO THE OFFBEAT. . . . ERR ON THE SIDE OF CONSERVATISM, ON THE SIDE OF ESTABLISHED USAGE. (STRUNK AND WHITE 84)

I think the fluidity of alt.writing recommends that we respond to it from a slightly longer distance. We need to divine the world in which the text imagines itself. What is permissible in this world? What is effective? What's the grammar of this world? From this long view, we see that the editorial task with alt.writing or Grammar B is actually not much different from the task with Grammar A. At least, a fundamental part of the job is to envision the rhetorical situation of the text. Until we know that—audience, subject, occasion, author, and the relations among them—we really can't begin to know what the text needs from an editor.

Not to interrupt the flow of your argument here, but why are you layering these block quotes behind the text? I'm afraid your readers (especially the "senior" ones) will not be able to read them well.

In addition, they seem to contradict rather than support your general positions. What's the point of giving dissenters equal time?

When faced with unfamiliar discourse, many student editors, or even experienced ones, feel the impulse to paraphrase, to recast the text into a style as (putatively) transparent, say, as a newspaper—as if conventions do not change from context to context, as if the primary readers for all texts are readers *like themselves*. This raises an interesting point of difference between teacher and editor, viz., the editor *is never* the audience, to which I would append a corollary:

the editor must always *imagine* the audience. Students often don't have experience with the kind of audience they need to imagine, so they default to an audience they knew very well—themselves.

It becomes a question of repertoire, then—how many audiences can you impersonate—or, from another angle, it's a question of context. How many nested writerly contexts can you perceive? Straub gets into this in his "The Student, the Text, and the Classroom Context"; his idea is that there are principles a teacher can practice that are flexible and useful enough to address a variety of elements in the context of the writer's work—beyond the assignment, that is. McComiskey gives us another handle with his taxonomy of layers (textual, rhetorical, discoursal) and his attention to each layer as he responds to student work. All must be noticed.

This gets us from conventional writing to work that negates convention. When combined with a fundamentally sympathetic stance—instead of a fundamentally corrective one—our repertoire is in a position to help an alt.text become more effective in reaching its own purposes, whatever they might be. But this requires the responder to imagine the text as the writer, not the reader, sees it. With alt.writing, the purposes of the text quite often involve getting the reader to loosen their pants, to accept degrees of variation in language and style that they might normally resist. The editor's or teacher's role, then, is not to bring a radical style back toward convention, but to allow variation to flourish, maybe even to push it farther in the direction of the alt, perhaps even to imagine an alt.style application for a writer whose text doesn't use it.

(A confession here, not for catharsis but because it's relevant to pushing the alt. I was Villanueva's aquiring editor for *Bootstraps*, and when I look at that book now, I can see—even more than I did ten years ago—how rad his concept was. And I'm having this attack of regret. See, Victor, if computers had been where they are now, or if I'd known more about visual composition, or if I'd had more imagination, I could have cajoled people at NCTE to *format* the book in radical ways, to liberate that alt.text from the conventional page. I

This is William Gass's phrase, isn't it: "Getting prose to loosen its pants"? Do you need to cite him?

He's a writer who comes to mind throughout this piece. He derides convention but doesn't believe in the avant garde, either—it's already co-opted, as you point out on page two.

And Gass wants the structure of a text to emerge from the structures of language itself. Do you need to this tie back to Phelps? Alexander?

Not sure why you're including this personal message. Delete? Add a last name, so the reader will know who you mean: Victor Who?

If you keep it, do you want to set it in a different font, so the general reader will know to skip it? Other format suggestions, or leave as is?

mean, as long as I was reassuring them it was okay to "allow" multivocality. *Now*, too late, I can see that those shifting selves need to emerge *visually* on the page as well as rhetorically. Damn. . . . You think I can get the reprint rights on that book?)

So with all this facilitative sympathy and alignment and warm fuzziness, does a responder dare to offer a criticism, suggest an edit? Yes, of course. All the time. All the way through. What the writer needs from a response is, as always, a friendly critique—but it must be one that proceeds from a valid understanding of the text, its purposes, its audience, its traditions, and both *acceptable and questionable* conventions within those parameters. Textual, rhetorical, and discoursal issues vary from text to text, and the responder needs to be broad enough in repertoire to recognize those issues, or honest enough to ask the writer about them. That means, however, that the teacherly or editorial or tutorial queries are in the vein of "how can we help the reader get this?" instead of "sorry, MLA style doesn't accommodate this." Or, as I've seen one editor write, "I never allow my authors to. . . ."

IV.

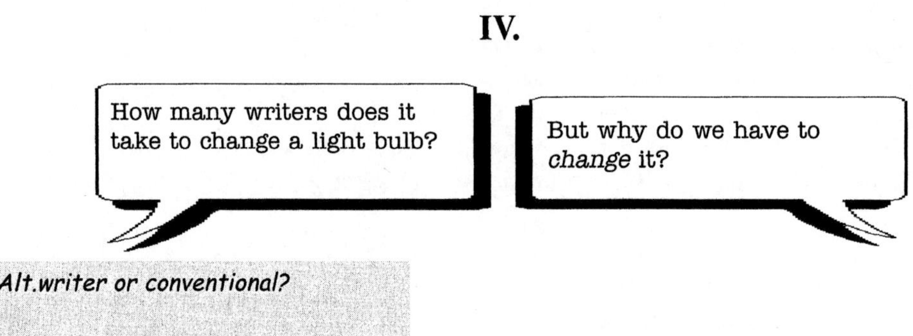

Alt.writer or conventional?

So it's an essay we're learning to read, too. Academic readers, for all their sophistication with critique of content, are more used to looking *through* style than *at* it. Alt comes close enough to invite participation, but after that, as in Swenson's phrase, "the reader is induced," by the unfamiliarity of the alt, "to concentrate" on the process of reading. In departing from the predictable, alt.style depends on the reader to engage and complete it and bring it fully to form. Theoretically, at least since Rosenblatt, we can say that *all* reading is *participative*, inventive. (In fact, we know experientially—from being *mis*-read—how inventive readers can be.) However, alt.writing raises participation to a new level by deliberately disorienting the reader. Alt.style will not be taken for granted, even if that means risking rejection or misunderstanding by its readers.

Still, an alt.essay wants to be read, and this means it must give the reader some purchase, a handle, a perceptible structure or procedure through which to enter. All is not random. (Alt is not random.) But if this purchase on the text doesn't come from convention (and if Bakhtin is right that no utterance is possible without genre), then it must come from within the text itself, where clues to how it combines or re-forms genre can be found. The writer might invent a structure and impose it on the text. But a more successful approach, in my view, is to allow the form to emerge as an organic and coherent feature of the text.

I want to suggest provisionally that these two principles—the *participative* and the *organic*—are features of alternate style at its best, and that we should be guided by them as we respond to writers of alt.style.

I'm appropriating the concepts of the organic and the participative from Christopher Alexander, whose ideas have challenged many accepted conventions in architecture and community planning (see, for example, *The Oregon Experiment*, in which he explores and applies his philosophy to the building program at the University of Oregon). I am tempted to use a word like "emergent" or "implicit" or "systemic" because I know that "organicism" is a concept discredited by postmodern theory, along with the autonomous self and the designated hitter. I should admit that in my view postmodern theory, with its kneejerk aversion to metaphors like this, has abandoned some useful recognition of how systems (conceptual ones and physical ones, too) actually function. However, this is not my fight, so let me try to sidestep it this way. If we can agree that a subject position is a *position,* then I think we've already acknowledged the idea of at least a provisionally coherent subject. And if we can see a genre or rhetorical situation as an ecosystem, with all its tendencies to socialize a text toward conventions, then I think we're already in the realm of the organic. All I want from the word "organic" is this ecological/rhetorical image. I don't think postmodern thought has any quarrel with the plant kingdom. So what I mean by "organic" in relation to structure in writing is the embodiment of context in a manner that is congruent *with* that context. I'm not suggesting that a single structural essence resides by nature or magic within a set of thoughts on a page. Neither would I suggest that the scum in my fishbowl will produce one essential algae. But I *am* saying that those fishbowl nutrients, no matter how decentered, fractal, or intertextual, will not sustain a hippo.

Don't you need to rationalize the "organic" here? It's a devil-word among postmoderns, you know. Alexander himself has been criticized as a modernist.

To Alexander, the principle of organic order requires that "planning and construction be guided by a process which allows the whole to emerge gradually from local acts" (26). What one might call the current traditional in architecture privileges "large lump" projects—multi-story, multi-million-dollar buildings that are too static or "perfect" in conception to accommodate user participation in design or to be corrected toward user needs after construction. Such buildings proceed from a master plan, and master plans inevitably treat users—i.e., unique individuals, people—as too small to consider. Users have to be conceived generically as predictable elements moving within a scheme too large and long term for them to perceive, and to which they will accommodate themselves, like it or not. So parking terraces and heating plants will trump small local office staffs every time.

STYLE AND RULES ARE THE BASIS OF EDITORIAL CRAFT. THE WAY THESE ARE USED IS THE BASIS OF THE ART OF EDITING. (BOGREN, COPYEDITING-L LISTSERV)

Alexander's alternative is to conceive a building program not through a template or master plan imposed from above, but by inverting this scheme. He advocates a process that privileges the concrete needs of users and that proceeds piecemeal, via small, local, user-attentive, user-conceived building designs and decisions. Alexander is not without his critics, of course, though I find him fascinating. But my interest here is to only analogize alt.style in writing with Alexander's alternate approach to building.

In departing from convention, alt.writers are resisting the "master plan" of conventional essayistic literacy. They want to privilege the local needs and aims of the text, *this* text, over the efficient dictates of the "perfect" models approved in the present tradition, in textbooks or pedagogies. Therefore, the order alt.writers achieve in their texts will not necessarily be accessible via the dominant, top-down, hermeneutics to which readers of traditional academic discourse are habituated. Rather, they build order piecemeal, bottom-up, through individual acts of composition that attend to the particular needs of the (textual, rhetorical, discoursal) contexts in which they are writing. And when they are successful, alt.writers achieve a structure that emerges—not magically but—organically from their local acts page after page. When it works, they achieve, in Alexander's terms, an organic whole, not a generic totality.

Similarly, their process depends on a more explicit sense of participation. Perhaps *because* they're consciously resisting convention, alt.stylists need to write in a readerly fashion. When May Swenson drops the punctuation from a poem, she does it knowing that it will "induce the reader to concentrate." Or, appropriating *Hamlet on the Holodeck* (Murray) for a moment, alt.style texts are interactive because, like computers, "they create an environment that is both procedural and participatory." Murray argues that "procedural environments are appealing to us not just because they exhibit rule-generated behavior but because we can induce the behavior" (74). By inducing the reader to participate and discover the order (the "procedures") by which they're written, alt.style texts also respond to the *reader's* inducing;

Personal History: Researching Literature and Curriculum (Literal, Alter, Hyper)

Nicholas Paley and Janice Jipson

Suggest you insert a subhead here, as you introduce this demonstration. Do you have any more light bulb jokes, or shall we use a more conventional approach?

Editing Alt.Style: a Demonstration?
Editing Alt.Style: a Performance?

We began working together in 1974. At that tim
20s, teaching as a two-person education departm
college in southern Wisconsin. Our responsibilities
tary and secondary undergraduate teacher prepa
cluded foundations courses and field placements
curriculum theory. We supervised student teache
responsible for the administrative management
concomitant concerns with ensuring appropriat
teacher certification for our students and with me
quirements. We both had previously earned our Masters degrees in education at the University of Wisconsin and, before

(N: All those paths taken and abandoned, methodologies current and discarded, identities shaped and blasted away, all those words that wear away over time . . . what's their connection with research?)

that, had taught in elementary and secondary schools in this country and abroad. Our undergraduate preparation included coursework in literature, language study, the humanities, and the arts. Surprised—but also delighted—by many of the parallels in our backgrounds, we worked together in the college's teacher education program, taking

When we work *now,* we

don't know where we're
,go;ing *tn* @@@ @^, @v@

(J: Does there always need to be? Leigh Gilmore (1994) suggests that "autobiography (personal history?) wraps up the interrupted and fragmentary discourse of identity, those stories

---

Nicholas Paley is Professor of Education at George Washington University, where he teaches educational foundations, language arts, and curriculum in the Graduate School of Education and Human Development.

Janice Jipson is an Associate Professor of Education at Carroll College in Waukesha, Wisconsin.

English Education, Vol. 29, No. 1, February 1997

with readerly participation, texts reveal their order, in a sense writing themselves before the reader's eye.

Let me point out a few things in this alt.style article from *English Education* (Paley and Jipson).

First of all, you can see from the format that these authors are writing in multiple voices. They're using the layout of the page to coordinate that effect:

different fonts for different voices; one voice is flush right, one is flush left, one is full justified. And so on. I like the approach: using a visual effect to reinforce a rhetorical choice. It works. In fact, I like many things about this article, so you'll have to forgive me if it looks like I can only find fault in what follows. (Paley and Jipson, wherever you are, I think it's a dandy essay; I'm just illustrating how sympathetic response to alt.writing isn't *non*-response.)

1. If you could read the entire article, you would see that, though they interrupt each other, the voices here do not interact with each other on the page. The main sections—in the wide body-text—are written in a joint authorial voice ("We began working together in 1974" etc.), and if you read only those sections from the first page to the last, you would have read essentially a short, linear, conventional essay. Let's call this Voice A. In this voice, we hear a report of two professional careers and of how two people came to reconsider their approaches to the literature education curriculum, ultimately choosing to involve more of the personal, the aesthetic, the narrative, the collaborative, and the political. Here is a sample of Voice A:

> that, had taught in elementary and secondary schools in this country and abroad. Our undergraduate preparation included coursework in literature, language study, the humanities, and the arts. Surprised—but also delighted—by many of the parallels in our backgrounds, we worked together in the college's teacher education program, taking (59)

I want to be clear that this excerpt is set off as a "paragraph" in the printed text. It begins in just this way with a broken sentence, the first part of which had been left several lines above: "We both had previously earned our Masters degrees . . . and, before" break. See how this works? Then, similarly, this partial paragraph ends where I've broken it (". . . taking"), and it will complete its thought on the following page, after a long interruption by the other voices.

2. Then there are sections in first person singular, signed with the initials of the author who (it seems) wrote them—"N" or "J." These are short pieces, and they intrude into the main body as brief sidebar quotations from various sources (from researchers, poets, others). They're usually flush with the right margin, and they're always in parentheses. Occasionally, the voices here talk to each other: N asks a question; J answers. However this is not often. Instead, normally, these sections involve quoted material, not original material, as their main substance. I'm not objecting to this, just pointing it out. Here's an example (61).

> (N: Are academic researchers,
> as Donnmeyer (1996) suggests, "permitted to advance
> all sorts of nontraditional ideas, [but] expected to do this in relatively
> traditional ways, that is, in a way we have come to recognize as academic
> as opposed to some other form of discourse" (p. 20)?)

Good question. On the same page, J offers this quotation from another writer.

(J: Madeline Grumet (1992) writes that "our stories are masks through which we can be seen, and with every telling we stop the flood and swirl of thought so someone can get a glimpse of us, and maybe catch us if they can" (p. 69).)

We'll call this Voice B. Again, as with Voice A, you could skip the other sections, and you would find reading these N and J parts relatively smooth going. It's a fairly conventional dialogue, though depending heavily on quoted excerpts. We hear primarily the words of other scholars—theorists, poets, teachers—who also advocate the stance that Voice A takes regarding the literature curriculum.

3. The third voice—shall we call it C?—offers a more literary, occasionally poetic text, but written once again in first person plural. Like the others, sections in this voice could be read linearly independent of the other sections without loss of meaning or interest. This voice is disrupted on the page frequently by random non-English characters like the @ sign, and primes / ' /, and periods out of place, broken words, broken type, broken lines, and lots of *non-signifying* italic and boldface type. An endnote explains that this effect was introduced by an OCR scanner, and the authors decided to leave it: "The variant form of this essay was produced by chance through the processing of a text scanner intruding its own force" (67). I *think* they mean only Voice C here; the whole essay is in a variant form, but I don't believe a scanner would by chance produce anything but the stuff in Voice C. Here's what it looks like:

Just a note here about length. The requested word-length for chapters in this volume was 5,000 words. Did the volume editors convey that to you? I think you're probably over 6,000 at this point, and wonder if you can trim. We could simply delete a section—your choice, but I'd suggest either the first or last. Or perhaps this little demonstration section. That would get you closer to the limit, and your readers would likely not miss a "practice" section as much as a theory one.

When we work *now, we*

don't know where we're
,go;ing tn @@@ @^, @v@
@ "I,'@ and

up wi th something very ***different*** We begin with **an** idea that
interests us, but **very** quickly **it becomes *many ideas. It***
splits apart i . **nto** pieces. We split **a *part*** into **pie ces.** (59–60)

This is the quasi-poetic voice—or it becomes so in certain sections—and I like the disruptive noise of the textual junk in it. Well, I like it for the most part. I think it works in the bit I'm quoting above, because it acts out the distraction and fragmentation they're describing; I have my doubts about this textual noise in other sections. In any case, to summarize, we hear through Voice C another treatment of the same ideas treated in A and B, but this time we hear them in a highly personal, often poetic style; we hear about dreams, internal logics, inner and outer space; about friendship that grows with collaboration into love and commitment; we hear the refrain "when we work now," which accumulates, as it repeats, into a center of gravity around which the whole essay begins to rotate.

Okay. If you read all the Voice A paragraphs, then all the Voice B paragraphs, then all the Voice C, you can see that these writers composed the texts separately and *afterward* broke them into short units which they then laid out

A
B
C
A
B
C

A query on content here. If, with alt.style, all bets are off re structure, then on what ground can you say that Paley's and Jipson's arrangement here invokes a "flow" from one section to the next, or even a dialogic reading?

This organization leads a reader to think there is a flow from one voice to the next, or from one "speech" to the next, as there is in a dialogue or as there is when one voice comments on what was just written in another. If you try to read them this way, however, you'll be frustrated. The voices do address related issues, but they do not acknowledge each other, comment on each other, dispute, confirm, etc.; it's as if they're simply broken arbitrarily, or cut and shuffled like cards. Unfortunately, I'd argue that broken-ness, disruption, or fragmentation is not an issue under discussion within the article. (You'll have to trust me on this, unless you have a copy of the *EE* journal on hand.) Thus, to me at least, the breaks between voices don't seem either organic or substantive. They look arbitrary. This disappoints me.

Therefore, my first alt.editorial question is: why break the Voice A text in mid-sentence, as these authors often do, just to insert the second and third voices? *Why are we alternating paragraphs*—even interrupting mid-paragraph—*if the voices are going to ignore the alternations* and the interruptions and each other? They're not aiming for dialogue among the voices. But they're not using crots or a list technique, either, as we can see because the discussion carries on from each paragraph in one voice to the next paragraph in the same voice. What are Paley and Jipson after?

One possible answer is that the authors may be more interested in juxtaposition than interaction; maybe they want us to read this essay as three different versions of the same text/argument/narrative, versions that are dove-tailed together physically but are not intended to interact with each other specifically at the places where they juxtapose.

This leads me to a stylistic thought. I wonder if the juxtaposition wouldn't be enhanced by setting Voice B and Voice C in text boxes and pushing them into the flow of Voice A, letting it wrap around them. This would accomplish the interruptive effect and the juxtaposition, but without suggesting a flow from one voice to the next, as a break in the text does. I wonder if that would help. A possible problem with that suggestion is that if we're supposed to read not just Voice A as one long flow, but also Voice B as one, and then Voice C as another long flow, we can't do that very well. (Besides, Voice C has some lengthy sections that won't fit too neatly into boxes that way.)

See, one option would be for Voice B and Voice C to shove in like this, instead of chopping Voice A in mid-sentence, to pick it up later as if nothing had just happened.

Here's another option: columns. We could set this essay like a "harmony" of ancient texts. Do you know what I mean? Sometimes, where variants of the same antique narrative exist—e.g., written by different witnesses—scholars will publish them in parallel columns, aligning the similar sections side by side. We could try the same thing here, comme ça:

Donnmeyer argues that "our first option sets up Voice B to read like a mere gloss" to Voice A.

Isn't the @@! trou .ble with the first *suggestion that it still bre . aks up* the flow from Voice C to Voice C? What can we do to *pre-serve* ***the sense*** **that all** of C needs to be read in sequence, just like **&@@# A does?

Neither of these ideas might work, but, in consultation with the writers, I'd suggest that either one would serve their purposes better than the original formatting.

Second, I notice that the Voice B "dialogue" between N and J doesn't seem quite authentic. Because these bits primarily function to convey the words of other scholars, to get some useful block quotations into the piece, they don't seem like much more than a gesture at dialogue. N and J do sometimes address the same topics; they are aware of each other; they do sometimes refer to each other and to this article. But they don't seriously interact. You see what I mean in the excerpt above? To me, the format of the page and the signatures "N" and "J" say this is a dialogue, but the voices within the text are never truly *in dialogue*.

In that sense, one could argue that the alternative style here is a bit of a sham. To the authors, I would have said, let's either (1) rework this stuff so that the voices are truly communicating, instead of merely packaging block quotes—that is, let's put these ideas in your own words and have N and J discuss them, or (2) let's drop the artifice of dialogue and simply juxtapose these quoted voices on their own. The essay likes juxtaposition, so maybe I'd recommend option #2 here. Again, we could do it with text boxes pushing in from one side or the other, or I think this would work nicely in columns, too. They're already using a distinct typeface (or font), which enhances the effect of changing voices. But either way, my instinct is that the Voice B sections aren't yet functioning the way these authors want them to function.

Finally, I would want to question these authors on the need for the textual noise they've retained from the scanning process in Voice C. Here again is what they say in their endnote. "The variant form of this essay was produced by chance through the processing of a text scanner intruding its own force" (67). Fine, and I think they're using this to enhance the participative dimension in the essay—or they're trying to use it that way; unfortunately, it lacks a sense of procedure that readers look for. Still, is it organic? Does the "variant form" embodied emerge from the conceptual mix in this essay? My sense is that No, the essay makes very little point of either chance or technology intruding its own force. In brief, Voice A recounts a history, Voice B contributes scholarly support, and Voice C turns and turns on the pivot of reflection and change—"when we work now." But it's *change*, not *chance*. There is, in each of these voices, a passing reference to chance, or to fragmentation, or to postmodern theory, or to experimental art, but these references do not aggregate to form a major strand of thought here. There is no reference to the technological, or to its intrusion.

So I don't know. I'd say that what's organic is the poetic or lyrical, and that Voice C is being held back from reaching its full potential by the static and white noise of the scanner. On the other hand, this "variant form" is the hippest, most "alt" effect in the essay, and clearly these authors love the effect. I don't like to cold-water that commitment, but there it is. As a sympathetic reader who wants to see this essay succeed, this is something I would have to mention to the authors. I don't think it kills anything, so I would never say "lose it or we don't publish," but my editorial advice would be to choose between either developing the strand of chance in the other voices or letting it disappear in Voice C.

V.

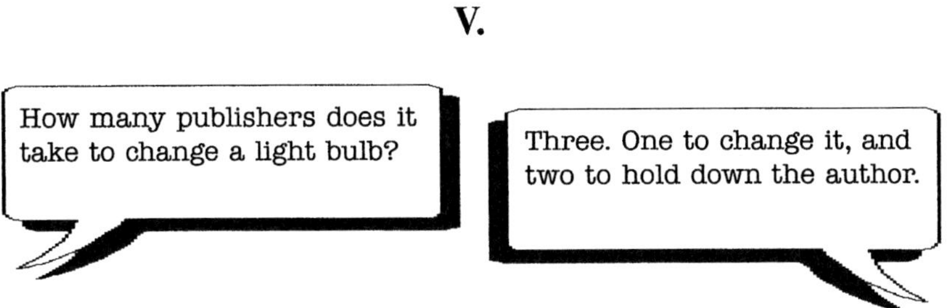

How many publishers does it take to change a light bulb?
Three. One to change it, and two to hold down the author.

Writing across the grain of convention does require an extra discipline from the writer, and I'd argue it takes another discipline from the one whose role it is to respond. While composition studies has come far enough now through the academic-discourse tunnel to appreciate the diverse lights beginning to show in certain scholarly journals and books, still, to be of any real use to students or other writers exploring alternate discourse and styles, we who respond need to expand our repertoire. Even sympathy to alt.work, though necessary, isn't sufficient; writers still need a friendly and informed resistance from their readers. They need an Elizabeth Bishop to say "are you just trying to be French, or what?" Writers and responders will continue to test each other as we invent new grammars of style, as we explore the new essays that the academy is learning to read.

In my new office building, the pipes are still working, though it's been near zero every night for months. The wiring is up to code, and I didn't need to drill through the wooden floor to jerry-rig a phone line for the fax machine. There's no ghost to chill the back of my neck when I'm working late. But the UPS driver hates the stairs into our shipping room. Students come by every day asking where the parking office has moved. City buses charge by our south windows, churning the snow into gray velour, and on the north side, seven satellite dishes from

Though my personal belief is that academic audiences are still not ready for either visual poetry or magazine layouts in scholarly work, it seems odd that you chose a basically conventional, linear approach here.

I know that the jokes and the special formatting in places are contributing to a sort of alternate style. Even the occasional (what seem to me) lapses into the confessional and expostulatory could be seen as a departure from convention. Still, I'm wondering at the end of this piece, why you didn't try something more radical. Did you consider even just going multivocal?

In any case, alt.style of some sort seems an option, if there's time to reconceive the paper.

You decide.

the campus radio station search our building curiously. Don't ask me, I tell them. You'll find the answers in the master plan.

Notes

The letter by May Swenson is available in the Swenson Collection, archived at Washington University, St. Louis. Excerpt quoted here by permission of the Literary Estate of May Swenson.

Do you really think readers will understand that you've created me? I'm a little afraid they''ll think I'm a real person, like, at the publisher. I'm trusting you on this you know.

Thanks to Chris Schroeder and Helen Fox, as well as the following other friends for their encouragement and thoughtful readings of drafts of this chapter: FHE research/writing group, Katherine Fischer, Louise Phelps, Ona Siporin, and Kathleen Yancey.

Works Cited

Alexander, Christopher, et al. 1995. *The Oregon Experiment.* New York: Oxford Univ. Press.

Bishop, Wendy, ed. 1997. *Elements of Alternate Style.* Portsmouth, NH: Boynton/Cook Heinemann.

bogren. 2 Mar 1995. "plural vs singular." Copyediting Discussion List [online]. Available email: COPYEDITING-L <LISTSERV@CORNELL.EDU>

Cutuly, Joan. 1993. *Home of the Wildcats.* Urbana: NCTE.

Dethier, Brock. 1999. *The Composition Instructor's Survival Guide.* Portsmouth, NH: Boynton/Cook Heinemann.

dtallman. 5 Oct 1995. "untitled." Copyediting Discussion List. [Online]. Available: E-mail: COPYEDITING-L <LISTSERV@CORNELL.EDU>

Eisenberg, Anne. 1992. *Guide to Technical Editing.* New York: Oxford Univ. Press.

Fox, Helen. 1994. *Listening to the World.* Urbana: NCTE.

Kress. Gunther. 1999. "English at the Crossroads." In *Passions, Pedagogies and 21st Century Technologies,* edited by Gail E. Hawisher and Cynthia Selfe. Logan: Utah State Univ. Press.

McComiskey, Bruce. 1999. *Teaching Composition as a Social Process.* Logan: Utah State Univ. Press.

Murray, Janet. 1997. *Hamlet on the Holodeck.* New York: Free Press.

Paley, Nicholas, and Janice Jipson. 1997. "Personal History: Researching Literature and Curriculum (Literal, Alter, Hyper)." *English Education.* 29 (Feb):59–70.

Phelps, Louise W. 2000. "Cyrano's Nose." *Assessing Writing.* 7 (1):91–110.

Rude, Carolyn. 1998. *Technical Editing.* 2nd ed. Needham Heights, MA: Allyn and Bacon.

Schroeder, Christopher. 2001. *ReInventing the University.* Logan: Utah State Univ. Press.

Spooner, Michael. 1997. "Sympathy for the Devil." In *Elements of Alternate Style*, edited by Wendy Bishop. Portsmouth, NH: Boynton/Cook Heinemann.

Strunk, William Jr., and E. B. White. 1979. *The Elements of Style*. 3rd ed. Needham Heights, MA: Allyn and Bacon.

Straub, Richard. 1996. "The Concept of Control in Teacher Response." *CCC* 47:223–251.

Swenson, May. 1953. Unpublished letter to Elizabeth Bishop.

Vielstimmig, Myka. 2001. "A Play on Texts." In *New Words, New Worlds*, edited by John Barber and Dene Grigar. NJ: Hampton.

Villanueva, Victor. 1993. *Bootstraps*. Urbana: NCTE.

Weathers, Winston. 1980. "Grammars of Style." In *Rhetoric and Composition*, edited by Richard L. Graves. Upper Montclair, NJ: Boynton/Cook, 133–47.

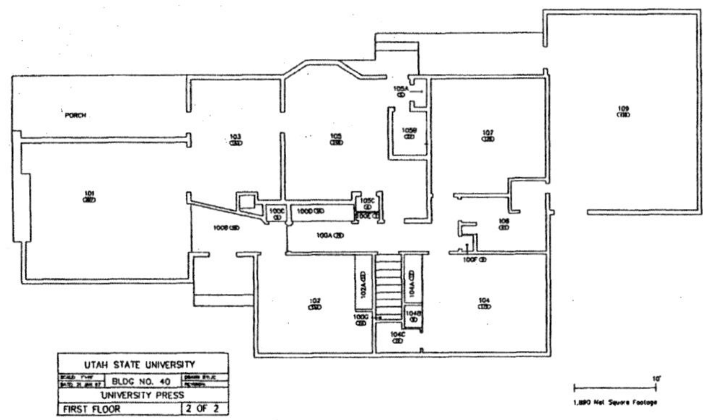

14

From the Inside Out (or the Outside In, Depending)

Christopher Schroeder

> Then when he was taking off his tie, he asked me if I'd written his goddam composition for him. I told him that it was over on his goddam bed. He walked over and read it while he was unbuttoning his shirt. He stood there, reading it, and sort of stroking his bare chest and stomach, with this very stupid expression on his face. He was always stroking his stomach or his chest. He was mad about himself.
>
> All of a sudden, he said, "For Chris*sake*, Holden. This is about a goddam *base*ball glove."
>
> "So what?" I said. Cold as Hell.
>
> "Wuddaya mean *so what*? I told ya it had to be about a goddam *room* or house or something."
>
> "You said it had to be descriptive. What the hell's the difference if it's about a baseball glove?"
>
> "God damn it." He was sore as hell. He was really furious. "You always do everything backasswards." He looked at me. "No wonder you're flunking the hell out of here," he said. "You don't do *one damn thing* the way you're supposed to. I mean it. Not one damn thing."
>
> "All right, give it back to me, then," I said. I went over and pulled it right out of his goddam hand. Then I tore it up.
>
> "What the hellja do *that* for?" he said.
>
> I didn't even answer him. I just threw the pieces in the wastebasket. Then I lay down on my bed, and we both didn't say anything for a long time.

This is not the original piece that I wrote.

The original was a short story in which I had appropriated Holden Caulfield in order to explore literacies, legitimacy, and intellectual work.

As factualized fiction, or fictionalized fact, this story drew upon my educational experiences in order to challenge cultural assumptions about the academy, problematize my original intentions when I proposed this collection to Helen and Pat, and reflect a growing cynicism that I had cultivated while working on this project.

And yet it's not the version you're reading.

I passed around a draft of the original and got dramatically different responses—readers either loved it or hated it. One person said that she started laughing from the opening line. Another said that it offered innovative and engaging challenges to assumptions about the academy. Others argued that I was being self-indulgent or that I was mocking other contributors.

One of the readers who liked the original encouraged me to stick with it, saying that the controversy could be productive and, in many ways, embodied the conflicts that surround alternatives in the academy.

But I couldn't.

I still like the original version better, though. And while I've tried to say the same things, those of us who believe that language and meaning are inseparably intertwined will wonder what's been left out. Something always is.

* * * * *

The cavernous lobby was filled with people schooling against each other. My coeditors and I had been seated at a small table within sight of the registration desk of the hotel. It was 4Cs, and we were having breakfast, talking about our kids, previous conferences, and this collection, when one of them mentioned that *ReInventing the University*, the book I had written on literacies and the academy, had just been released.

"What's the central argument?" said a fourth, who had joined us.

"Well," I said, "that the literacy crisis in the academy is less a crisis of skill and ability and more a crisis of meaning, a crisis of academic culture."

This crisis in meaning, I explained, legislates against engaging intellectual work, and instead of appropriating and being appropriated by conventional literacies, we should assemble literacies from context-specific discursive practices, producing discourses that, resembling Pat Bizzell's hybrid discourses (1999), would lead to more satisfying intellectual work.

"What evidence do you have of this lack of engagement?" this fourth person said.

"That's been tough," I said, reaching for my juice. "I've cited increasing dropout rates and declining test scores, and I've got anecdotal evidence, and my own experiences, but I'm not sure how to justify it academically."

The others at the table began arguing that intellectual work in their institutions was engaging.

That doesn't necessarily mean that there isn't a crisis in meaning, I thought.

I had in mind the arguments that Maureen Hourigan (1994) and Daniel Green (2001) have made about the differences between intellectual work at prestigious institutions and at more mainstream institutions. Hourigan, for example, draws upon statistics and scholarship to argue that the discourse on literacy in the United States often comes from intellectuals who, working in more elite institutions, have different perspectives—Cheryl Armstrong's Harvard basic writer who, despite the BW stereotype, is usually a former AP student in English who has been preparing for prestigious colleges and universities throughout his or her entire educational career—from those who do the bulk of literacy instruction in U.S. colleges and universities (31–39).

Additionally, these differences often extend to the conditions of intellectual work. If, as Stephen North (1991) has argued, his typical semester week—six hours in the classroom, fifteen hours of prepping, and six to eight hours of meetings—requires "careful marshalling" of his resources and leaves him uncomfortable with the commitments embedded in the political language often used to describe liberal and radical perspectives on the academy (131–32), then how much more difficult is it for those intellectuals who must spend twice as many hours in the classroom? (Seventy-seven percent of faculty at private research institutions, for example, teach fewer than eight hours per week while 74 percent of faculty at public comprehensive universities and 75 percent at private liberal arts colleges teach more than eight hours per week [National Center for Education Statistics 2000]. At my first full-time position, I spent fifteen hours in the classroom each week.) At the same time, most of us have social, economic, and institutional resources, including perks like parking or photocopying privileges, that are often denied to adjuncts and graduate students, who perform a significant portion of the intellectual work in U.S. colleges and universities.

These material realities and others, such as promotion and tenure expectations, construct and constrain intellectual work and need to be considered in any conversation that we have about alternative forms of intellectual work. As such, the issues go beyond the specialization and attendant problems of professionalization that Richard Ohmann (1990) criticizes to include problems in an institutional culture in which the realities of intellectual work, at least in the majority of institutions, require academic support groups, replete with their own self-help slogans, such as those Donald Hall offers: "an active, joyous, and multifaceted professional life is possible at a teaching institution"; "careers are always largely local even if they have national implications or aspects"; and a "position at a teaching institution allows: invigorating pedagogical possibilities, less anxiety over publication, and the freedom to set your own goals and define for yourself professional success" (196, 198–99).

Crises come in all shapes and sizes, and functional literacies don't preclude intellectual bankruptcies. They may actually encourage them. Alternative ways of doing intellectual work might provide a way to escape these conditions, or at the least, make them more tolerable.

* * * * *

Though new to the scene, I have experienced differences in the conditions of intellectual work as a graduate student, an adjunct lecturer, and an assistant professor at a range of institutions, including community colleges, private liberal arts colleges, and public and private research institutions in the Midwest, the deep South, the Southeast, and the Northeast. However, one feature that these institutions have in common is their existence, as Bill Readings (1996) describes, as "bureaucratically organized and relatively autonomous consumer-oriented corporations" (11). Such conditions are symptomatic of the mercantilization of meaning that many, from bell hooks to Jean-François Lyotard, have decried.

My experiences in these institutions motivated me to reread what critics call a crisis in literacy as part of larger crises in meaning and education in the United States. Historically, literacy instruction has authorized versions of literacy that have been increasingly separated from the contexts that make these literacies meaningful, a process that, particularly in the United States, has culminated in classrooms designed to teaching nothing but writing and reading.[1] As purportedly context-free literacies, these institutionalized ways of writing and reading authorize a cultural capital that often lacks legitimacy for the communities in which the literacy instruction occurs, a cultural capital that nonetheless is inscribed upon students (and teachers alike) in a paternalism that some have characterized as acts of violence.[2]

As we all know, the primary site of literacy instruction in U.S. colleges and universities has been the English department. Initially at Harvard in the mid-nineteenth century and then spreading to other institutions, English classes were charged with the responsibility of safeguarding the cultural capital of academic institutions.[3] While the presence of the literature classroom, particularly as a source of cultural standards, can still be seen, the composition classroom has, over time, assumed the burden of socializing students into academic culture, a perspective that, John Schilb attests, is shared not only by administrators and faculty in other disciplines but also by many composition specialists themselves (1996, 59).

In my discourse analysis of the best-selling composition and literature textbooks, I confirmed[4] that for the most part, the literacy practices of the academy are largely the practices of essayist literacies: elaborated syntactical and sequential relations; substantial amounts of new information; and truth values instead of rhetorical contexts.[5] As such, these practices give rise to essentialized subject positions of Western rational minds and to versions of the world in which a completely accessible reality is entirely expressible in texts.[6] (Print, to some degree, is responsible for the belief in fixed discourses and essentialized consciousnesses.) As being literate amounts to not only acquiring and/or learning particular discursive practices but also using these to construct acceptable versions of the self, or what socio- and cultural linguists call facework, and to demonstrate membership in particular communities, or solidarity and identification, academic literacy, for example, involves not only producing texts with claims, grounds, and warrants but also selecting acceptable grounds and warrants, as defined by academic communities. Together these practices and awarenesses represent the cultural capital of the academy.

As more of a crisis in legitimacy, the cultural capital represented by institutionalized literacies diverges significantly from the cultures that exist within institutions and society, which is consistent with the fact that historically, literacy crises have been linked to dramatic increases in enrollments.[7] From this perspective, each time literacies and institutions were challenged by the infusion of cultures, critics would declare a crisis in literacy rather than confront increasing discursive and institutional differences. (Tellingly, the rise of the English department coincides with the purported literacy crisis of the 1870s.) Currently, the academy is immersed within another dramatic shift in enrollment. Between 1995 and 2015, the combined undergraduate enrollments at postsecondary institutions in the United States will increase by 19 percent from 13.4 million to 16 million students. More to this issue of legitimacy, over two million of these additional students will be African American, Hispanic, Asian/Pacific Islander, etc., thereby increasing the total number of minority students from 29.4 percent in 1995 to 37.2 percent by 2015 (ETS, 2000). For these, the legitimacy of conventional academic literacies is problematic, as these literacies, and cultures, represent hurdles to overcome or values to resist, often depending, according to Ogbu (1990), upon whether they are immigrant (i.e., voluntary) or involuntary minorities. While negotiating these cultural differences, such as Spanglish, does occur, these highly marked, mixed discourses are routinely dismissed, even by those who control them, as illegitimate forms of intellectual work.[8]

These problems notwithstanding, I am arguing, however, for the crisis in the legitimacy of these practices for minorities and majorities alike. As Jackie Jones Royster and Peter Elbow argue in this collection, conventional academic discourse(s) is no one's mother tongue. Moreover, the legitimacy of this discourse(s) is predicated upon an outdated, and relatively uniform, cultural context. Though there are numerous examples, two of the most obvious are the modes of discourse and static abstractions. While the modes, as discursive manifestations of a universalized human consciousness, and static abstractions, such as unity and coherence, have purportedly fallen from theoretical favor,[9] all of the best-selling textbooks in literature and composition except for Strunk and White's *The Elements of Style* pay homage to the modes as models to imitate at least somewhere in their pages, and all of them invoke unity and coherence.[10]

Though I wonder whether such features ever represented more mainstream communities entirely, I believe that in a postmodern United States, these cannot hope to serve the diverse communities represented in contemporary academic institutions. If legitimacy is not defined in dualist terms—either you have it or you don't—of E. D. Hirsch's cultural literacy, then instruction in academic literacy has always been about acculturation, only though most obviously in periods of increasing enrollments, and classrooms are always already contact zones, or what Mary Louise Pratt (1991) defines as social spaces where cultures come in contact, often in the context of uneven power relations (34). What I am suggesting is that there are more fault lines, to use Richard Miller's (1994) metaphor, than we have been conscious of, more conflicts to be mediated than we often acknowledge or even recognize.

If we are going to do more than declare a literacy crisis, then we will need different ways of doing intellectual work, which is one of the reasons I proposed this collection. If we are in the midst of a crisis in meaning, then such a collection could, I believe, provide legitimacy for alternatives.

* * * * *

All of us have stories to tell.[11] Victor Villanueva (1993) writes of a supervisor who announces a replacement for him while he is on vacation, and Megan Foss (1998) tells of an instructor who insists that her fellow convicts' tattoos are not art while defending the aesthetic value of traditional paintings.

Beyond aesthetic acts, these stories situate Victor, Megan, et al., as intellectuals, within the cultural contexts that inform their meaning-making by highlighting what Daniel Mahala and Jody Swilky (1996) call the politics of location. In making the familiar strange,[12] these stories simultaneously acknowledge the contingency of their understandings and authorize them as credible. In more theoretical terms, these stories enable the tellers to mitigate the loss of foundational authority even as they generate a legitimacy that resists the irrelevance of antifoundationalism.[13]

Nevertheless, the legitimacy of stories as a form of intellectual work often depends upon who does the telling, as the experience of Joel Williamson—Pat Bizzell (this volume) explains—suggests. In her contribution, Pat explains the ways in which Williamson's text, in spite of its author's credibility as a historian, was subject to elaborate rituals in order to be legitimized. In much the same way, I had used stories in *ReInventing* as a way of contextualizing my alienation from conventional literacies although I was conscious of a different set of standards for the stories that I, as a white, middle-class male, was trying to tell. As a result, I had agreed to delete these stories from earlier drafts of the manuscript until Peter Elbow, in responding to a later version, claimed that the tacit stories surrounding the text not only were present but functioned covertly in such a way as to suggest that I lacked the resolution of my conventions, so together with Michael Spooner, my editor, I reinserted them, this time as textboxes, even as I acknowledged the problems that coming from a purported insider, these stories might have for certain readers.[14]

The objection, as I understand them, is that these stories cannot compare to those of other intellectuals, such as those of Richard Rodriguez (1982) or Keith Gilyard (1991) or of the students described by Belinda Kremer or Carmen Kynard (this volume), and to some degree, I can understand these objections—insiders do not encounter the same resistances as outsiders do—which is why I agreed, at one point, to omit these stories. And yet I wonder whether privileging particular stories over others amounts to inverting a cultural binary, which is Haixia Lan's (this volume) assertion, that ignores the ways that status and legitimacy are contingent upon local contexts. In New York City, there is a community of over one hundred thousand people with seven different newspapers at newsstands in which Chinese-Americans never have to use a word of English (Ellis, 1997, 93). In my in-laws' home near St. Louis or with my wife's childhood friends in Chicago, the Tagalog in the air and the *litsón*, or roasted pig, stretched across the table remind me that no matter my status elsewhere, I am always a *banyaga* here, an outsider who, despite the official status of *manugag*, or son-in-law, lacks the legitimacy of an insider. (My perspectives upon alternative discourses are dramatically different as a result of my relationship with a woman of color.) Even more complicated, the legitimacy of Mahal and Mateo, my Filipino American kids, in these communities is contingent upon a host of discursive and cultural variables, as is the case for many who are products of multiracial and multicultural communities, as Laura Long (this volume) also suggests.[15]

Significantly, cultural models delimit the narratives that one can tell, or does tell, and not only the narratives but also the narratives about the narratives, such as what counts as legitimate forms of intellectual work. In part, multiple cultural models are what make discursive acts potentially unique, a position that Sid Dobrin (this volume) also argues, and the intellectual work of academics, even in the most professional of settings, such as an academic conference,[16] evinces substantial discursive differences, as Chris Thaiss and Terry Zawacki's interviews suggest (this volume). To be sure, some appropriations are less dramatic than others, and there are additional politics at play, such as social standing or culturally determined responses, that complicate these situations. Nevertheless, denying the stories of those who have less reconditioning to do in order to acquire the cultural capital of the academy is not only to insist that these stories perpetuate an alienation that is often characteristic of intellectual work in the academy[17] but also to suggest that the stories of purported outsiders, such as Rodriguez or the students in Carmen's classroom, have, or should have, a universal legitimacy for all readers.

If we utilize postmodern theories of print, discourse, and communities, then all stories shift from how one masters monologic discourses and acquires a homogeneous culture, which invoke redemption metanarratives, to how one survives within a mélange of discourses and cultures, or narratives of strategies and tactics[18] that foreground the politics of intellectual work. Such a perspective authorizes all stories, including those of mainstream intellectuals, as revealing of the conditions of intellectual work in the academy. In fact, the narratives of ostensive insiders can call attention to subtle distinctions between and among culturally specific discourses and literacies, distinctions that can be lost when the shift is so dramatic, as is often the case for those who are situated outside of conventional academic communities. Moreover, the stories of insiders can reveal the web of contingency that makes naturalized and legitimized standards for legitimate performance appear natural and legitimate.

So in addition to legitimizing alternatives to functional literacies and to offering an escape from the crisis in legitimacy, another reason I am interested in this collection is that it foregrounds the ways in which legitimacy and intellectual work are contingent upon the discursive practices of local contexts.

* * * * *

My attempts to scrutinize academic culture, both from the inside and from the other side, and to authorize local narratives as responses to the crisis in legitimacy and as alternative, even necessary, forms of intellectual work across the curriculum are efforts to extend the justification for local narratives that exists in (pomo) theory to practice. As James Slevin (2001) has argued, composition classrooms, and I would include WAC programs, offer productive spaces in which to engage in alternative ways of intellectual work that resist the large-scale mercantilization of education, ways that, Slevin claims, range from the conventional, such as producing scholarly publications, directing programs, or serving on promotion and tenure committees, to the more public, such as conducting external reviews of departments and programs, participating in summer orientation programs, or serving on community boards (297, 294 ff).

If those of us who are interested in alternatives are going to achieve the consistency between our politics and our practices that Elbow (1986), North (1991), and others advocate, then we must consider the complicated issues of assessment. (Tellingly, Slevin devotes the bulk of his argument to assessment.) Though I am not as cynical as North, I am as certain as Elbow that there must be a consistency between what we say we're doing and what we authorize through the standards that we use to identify legitimate performance. Obviously, assessing these alternatives is challenging. Although my coeditors and I prepared a session to explore these issues at 4Cs, we speculated whether these issues were too new to say anything substantial about assessment, a perspective that those who attended our session confirmed. As part of the ongoing conversations my coeditors and I have had about this collection, Helen recently speculated that readers' personal preferences seem to play a central role in their assessments of alternative discourses. Pat responded by explaining that the more she reads of a particular alternative author, such as Gilyard, the more she identifies nuances and subtleties that she hadn't recognized previously. And I wondered how many times I have misread acts of intellectual work of students, a condition that as Tom Fox (1999) courageously suggests, happens more often than we realize (40 ff).

So what are we to do? If we merely authorize the standards of marginalized literacies in our classrooms, then we fail, as Xin Liu Gale (1996) points out, in our refusal to acknowledge the ways that these standards are inseparably linked to dominant discourses, as well as in our responsibility to provide experiences of these dominant discourses. Moreover, such a move misrepresents our presence within the academy by not acknowledging the larger discursive and institutional formations that authorize dominant discourses and, in so doing, ensures our tacit participation in institutional tendencies to assimilate even the most radical of challenges and to reproduce itself and our students' exclusion from these dominant discourses and forms of cultural capital.

I believe that though not an answer, *constructed literacies*, which bring together competing and context-specific discursive practices into integrated acts of intellectual work, may offer one way of continuing these conversations about assessment. While there is some sense that such fusion is commonplace,[19] the deliberate act of appropriating competing cultural practices enables intellectuals to practice what John Fiske (1989) calls "the art of being in-between" (36), a space that authorizes, and can be authorized by, local narratives, which serve as a means of exploring discursive and institutional politics. From the perspective of constructed literacies, my function is to learn to listen to, and to encourage, the telling of these stories, especially the narratives of the narratives, whether from my friends in the history department who talk of finding meaningful patterns in seemingly random events or from students in a literature classroom who tell of frustrating efforts to satisfy institutional requirements for intellectual work. From this perspective, it would be inappropriate for me to distinguish between stories that deserve to be heard and those that, some would say, do not. (Stephen North's story (1991) couldn't come from more of an insider.) Now, I am not suggesting that I never experience differences in and among these stories—some of them move me, and others don't—but my job is to listen to, and to authorize and facilitate the telling of, the stories that their authors want to tell.

Within this context, storytelling—not just for aesthetic pleasure but for cultural mediation and existential negotiation—becomes one of the fundamental acts of intellectual work, a means to rereading and rewriting the world no matter how much the narrative aspects are sublimated in the final forms.[20] For example, a student who rewrites what had been previously called flirtatious behavior by a coworker into sexual harassment as a means of securing professional assistance is engaged in intellectual work regardless of whether the final version remains a narrative of her experiences, an argument against relationships in the workplace, or some mixed or hybrid text.[21] In this and other situations, my role is to elicit the stories—as in the contingency of meanings resituated within the contexts in which they were produced—and to juxtapose others' perspectives-as-stories in relation to the ones that are being told. These and other stories require alternatives to conventional academic discourses—how can she tell the full story of her experiences with claims, grounds, and warrants?—that situate intellectuals in the borderlands between and among school, work, home, and other spaces.

And at the same time, I am not naive enough to believe that these stories will automatically be heard in every (academic) community, so I must also encourage translation—Langston Hughes' "Theme for English B," for example, into conventional academic argument or academic summaries into Spanglish—and experiment with and translate my own stuff. As I did to persuade my dissertation committee to sign off on what became *ReInventing*. Or as I have done with this piece.[22]

Notes

1. See Nespor (1991) and Russell (1992, 22–26).
2. See Stuckey (1992).
3. For more, see Douglas (1976) and Miller, S. (1991, 51–53).
4. See, also, Faigley (1995).
5. I have relied upon Scollon and Scollon (1981, 41 ff) in describing essayist literacies.
6. For an extended analysis, see Schroeder (2001, 39 ff).
7. See, for example, Russell (1992, 35) and Hourigan (1994, 3 ff).
8. See, for example, Zentella (1997).
9. See Connors (1981 and 1983).
10. See Kleine (1999, 138 ff) and Schroeder (2001, 45 ff).
11. See, for example, Rodriguez (1982), Rose (1989), Gilyard (1991), Villanueva (1993), Brodkey (1994), and Foss (1998).
12. Soliday (1994) argues that this function is characteristic of all literacy narratives.
13. For an accessible exploration of foundationalism and antifoundationalism, see Bizzell (1990).
14. For more, see Schroeder (2001, 23–27).
15. See also O'Hearn (1998).
16. For an analysis of the discursive differences at a conference, see Johnstone (1996, 59 ff).
17. See, for example, Chiseri-Strater (1991).
18. For more on these practices, see de Certeau (1984, xix ff and 29 ff).
19. See, for example, Duranti and Ochs (1996).
20. Carroll (1997) argues that non-narrative texts are often linked to narratives (927).
21. See Schroeder (2001, 179–80).
22. I would like to thank Pat Bizzell, Ann Dobie, Nicole Carrozzo, Helen Fox, Belinda Kremer, Carmen Kynard, Michael Spooner, John and Stephanie Vanderslice, Victor Villanueva, and Carl Williams, who read or responded to various versions of this text.

Works Cited

Bizzell, Patricia. 1990. "Beyond Anti-Foundationalism to Rhetorical Authority: Problems Defining 'Cultural Literacy.'" *College English* 52 (6):661–75.

———. 1999. "Hybrid Academic Discourses: What, Why, How." *Composition Studies* 27:7–21.

Brodkey, Linda. 1994. "Writing on the Bias." *College English* 56 (5):527–47.

Carroll, Lee Ann. 1997. "Pomo Blues: Stories from First-Year Composition." *College English* 59:916–33.

Chiseri-Strater, Elizabeth. 1991. *Academic Literacies: The Public and Private Discourse of University Students*. Portsmouth, NH: Boynton/Cook, Heinemann.

Connors, Robert. 1981. "The Rise and Fall of the Modes of Discourse." *College Composition and Communication* 32:444–55.

———. 1983. "Static Abstractions and Composition." *Freshman English News* 12:1–4, 9–12.

de Certeau, Michel. 1984. *The Practice of Everyday Life*. Berkeley: Univ. of California Press.

Douglas, Wallace. 1976. "Rhetoric for the Meritocracy: The Creation of Composition at Harvard." In *English in America: A Radical View of the Profession*, edited by Richard Ohmann, 97–132. Hanover, NH: Wesleyan Univ. Press.

Duranti, Alessandro, and Elinor Ochs. 1996. "Syncretic Literacy: Multiculturalism in Samoan American Families." Research Report 16. Santa Cruz, CA: National Center for Research on Cultural Diversity and Second Language Learning, 1–15.

Elbow, Peter. 1986. "The Pedagogy of the Bamboozled." In *Embracing Contraries: Explorations in Learning and Teaching*, New York: Oxford Univ. Press, 87–98.

Ellis, David. 1997. *New York City*. Hawthorn, Australia: Lonely Planet Publications.

ETS. 2000."Soaring Number of Qualified Minority Students Poised to Enter College." [On-line]. Available: <http://www.ets.org/textonly/aboutets/news/00052401.html>. 18 May 2001.

Faigley, Lester. 1995. "Going Electronic: Creating Multiple Sites for Innovation in a Writing Program." In *Resituating Writing: Constructing and Administering Writing Programs*, edited by Joseph Janangelo and Kristine Hansen, Portsmouth, NH: Boynton/Cook, 46–58.

Fiske, John. 1989. *Understanding Popular Culture*. Boston: Unwin Hyman.

Foss, Megan. 1998. "Love Letters." *Creative Nonfiction* 9:13–33.

Fox, Tom. 1999. *Defending Access: A Critique of Standards in Higher Education*. Portsmouth, NH: Boynton/Cook-Heinemann.

Gale, Xin Liu. 1996. *Teachers, Discourses, and Authority in the Postmodern Composition Classroom*. Albany: State Univ. of New York Press.

Gilyard, Keith. 1991. *Voices of the Self: A Study of Language Competence*. Detroit: Wayne State Univ. Press.

Green, Daniel. 2001. "Abandoning the Ruins." *College English* 63 (3):273–87.

Hall, Donald E. 1999. "Professional Life (and Death) under a Four-Four Teaching Load." *Profession 1999*:193–203.

Hourigan, Maureen M. 1994. *Literacy as Social Exchange: Intersections of Class, Gender, and Culture*. Albany: State Univ. of New York Press.

Johnstone, Barbara. 1996. *The Linguistic Individual: Self-Expression in Language and Linguistics*. New York: Oxford Univ. Press.

Kleine, Michael W. 1999. "Teaching from a Single Textbook 'Rhetoric': The Potential Heaviness of the Book." In *(Re)Visioning Composition Textbooks: Conflicts of Culture, Ideology, and Pedagogy*, edited by Xin Liu Gale and Fredric G. Gale, 137–62. Albany: State Univ. of New York Press.

Mahala, Daniel, and Jody Swilky. 1996. "Telling Stories, Speaking Personally: Reconsidering the Place of Lived Experience in Composition." *JAC: A Journal of Composition Theory* 16 (3):363–88.

Miller, Richard. 1994. "Fault Lines in the Contact Zone." *College English* 56 (4):398–408.

Miller, Susan. 1991. *Textual Carnivals: The Politics of Composition.* Carbondale: Southern Illinois Univ Press.

National Center for Education Statistics. 2000. *Digest of Education Statistics, 1999,* [Online]. Available: <http://www.nces.ed.gov/pubs2000/digest99/> . 23 August 2001.

Nespor, Jan. 1991. "The Construction of School Knowledge: A Case Study." In *Rewriting Literacy: Culture and the Discourse of the Other*, edited by Candace Mitchell and Kathleen Weiler, 169–88. Westport, CN: Bergin & Garvey.

North, Stephan. 1991. "Rhetoric, Responsibility, and the 'Language of the Left.' In *Composition and Resistance*, edited by Mark Hurlbert and Michael Blitz, 127–32. Portsmouth, NH: Boynton/Cook, Heinemann.

Ogbu, John U. 1990. "Minority Education in Comparative Perspective." *Journal of Negro Education* 59 (1):45–57.

O'Hearn, Claudine Chiawei. 1998. *Half and Half: Writers on Growing Up Biracial and Bicultural.* New York: Pantheon.

Ohmann, Richard. 1990. "Graduate Students, Professionals, Intellectuals." *College English* 52 (3):247–57.

Pratt, Mary Louise. 1991. "Arts of the Contact Zone." *Profession* 91:33–40.

Readings, Bill. 1996. *The University in Ruins.* Cambridge: Harvard University Press.

Rodriguez, Richard. 1982. *Hunger of Memory: The Education of Richard Rodriguez.* New York: Bantam Books.

Rose, Mike. 1989. *Lives on the Boundary: A Moving Account of the Struggles and Achievements of America's Educationally Underprepared.* New York: Penguin.

Russell, David. 1992. "American Origins of Writing-Across-the-Curriculum Movement." In *Writing, Teaching, and Learning in the Disciplines*, edited by Anne Herrington and Charles Moran, 22–42. New York: Modern Language Association.

Schilb, John. 1996. *Between the Lines: Relating Composition Theory and Literary Theory.* Portsmouth, NH: Boynton/Cook Publishers.

Schroeder, Christopher. 2001. *ReInventing the University: Literacies and Legitimacy in the Postmodern Academy.* Logan: Utah State Univ. Press.

Scollon, Ron, and Suzanne B. K. Scollon. 1981. *Narrative, Literacy, and Face in Interethnic Communication.* Norwood, NJ: Ablex.

Slevin, James F. 2001. "Engaging Intellectual Work: The Faculty's Role in Assessment." *College English* 63 (3):288–305.

Soliday, Mary. 1994. "Literacy Narratives." *College English* 56 (5):511–26.

Stuckey, J. Elspeth. 1992. *The Violence of Literacy*. Portsmouth, NH: Heinemann.

Villanueva, Victor. 1993. *Bootstraps: From an American Academic of Color*. Urbana, IL: National Council of Teachers of English.

Zentella, Ana Celia. 1997. *Growing Up Bilingual: Puerto Rican Children in New York*. Malden, MA: Blackwell.

15

Alternative Discourses
A Synthesis

Paul Kei Matsuda

In November 2000—twenty-six years after the publication of "Students' Right to Their Own Language"—the Conference on College Composition and Communication adopted a position statement entitled "CCCC Statement on Second-Language Writing and Writers" (2001). The adoption of this document by CCCC is an important step for the profession since it acknowledges the growing diversity of the college student population in North America not only in terms of its number but also in terms of its intensity. In essence, the Statement urges teachers and scholars of writing to recognize the regular presence of second-language writers—including international students and permanent residents as well as naturalized and native-born citizens of the United States and Canada—in writing programs across North America, and encourages all writing scholars to include second-language perspectives in developing theories, designing studies, analyzing data, and discussing implications.

In light of this development, I was asked by the editors to respond to this volume from the perspective of a composition specialist whose work transcends the traditional boundaries between first-language and second-language writing, between composition studies and applied linguistics, and between humanities and social sciences. Since contributors to this volume represent a wide variety of perspectives on alternative discourses, each shedding light on a different aspect of the notion, I'd like to begin by synthesizing some of the key insights.

Although the terms *hybrid* (or *mixed*) *discourses* and *alternative discourses* are used almost interchangeably in many of the chapters, I find significant differences between the two. On one hand, the term *hybrid* seems to refer to the characteristics of the discourse itself—the discourse somehow possesses the features that are associated with two or more discourses. *Alternative,* on the other hand, seems to refer to the status of the discourse in relation to mainstream discourses. What we call alternative discourses are, as Royster suggests, alternative assumptions about discourses; the physical texts that exhibit alternative features are discursive manifestations of those assumptions.

As Dobrin points out, all discourses are ultimately hybrid or mixed. Indeed, it is normal—even inevitable—for writers to draw on various other discourse practices in order to develop a socially shared repertoire of discursive options in response to the rhetorical situations they encounter. The key difference between mainstream and alternative discourses is that the hybridity of the former is unmarked in the eyes of the audience whereas that of the latter is marked, thus inviting the labels such as hybrid, mixed, and alternative.

Dobrin also suggests that all discourses are alternative, but this proposition seems to need a qualification: all discourses are alternative *in certain contexts*, and no discourse is essentially or perpetually alternative. That is, discourse practices take on the status of alternative in relation to the dominant or mainstream discourse practices within a particular domain. The alternative status is by no means permanent or innate to those particular discourse practices. As Mao has demonstrated in his discussion of Confucian discourse, what is alternative in one sociohistorical context may become the mainstream discourse in another, thereby rendering the status of alternative to other, coexisting discourse practices. It is appropriate, then, to speak of alternative discourses as marked forms of discourse use within a particular site of discourse practices and in a certain sociohistorical context.

The importance of the context in discussing alternative discourses cannot be emphasized enough. As Dobrin points out, discussing alternative discourses can be dangerous; however, I would contend that it is particularly problematic when it takes place out of context because, in doing so, we risk assigning the status of alternative permanently to those discourses that are less dominant or less privileged. To avoid the essentialization of particular discourses—and of people who are associated with them—it is not enough to examine the consequences of discussing alternative discourses in the abstract; we also need to discuss alternative discourses in situated ways, as many of the contributors to this book have done. Furthermore, all of us need to make explicit what we mean by "alternative" in the particular context of discussion, questioning, as Powell does, what it is alternative to, in what sociohistorical context, and, most importantly, to whom.

In U.S. academic contexts, the answer to the "to whom" question has largely been taken for granted. As Bizzell notes, people who have traditionally dominated the U.S. academy are "male, European American, middle- or upper-class" and, I would add, users of relatively similar, privileged varieties of English. For this reason, assumptions about language, discourse, and ways of thinking that these people brought to the academic discourse situations became the default position, while, as kynard points out, assumptions and practices that seemed to deviate from the "norm" had been treated simply as errors or incoherence, if not signs of carelessness or cognitive deficiencies.

In fact, scholars such as George Braine (2000), A. Suresh Canagarajah (1996), and John Flowerdew (1999) have pointed out that non-native English speakers are having a harder time in getting their manuscripts accepted by English-medium international journals because their texts often embody differing assumptions about discourses. The dismissal of submissions from the linguistic periphery is usually justified in terms of the writers' competency by labeling the discourse "incoherent" or even "bad English"; rarely is it explained in terms of the reader's lack of receptive competence.

Similar situations are found in the classroom. Students who come from other linguistic, cultural, and educational backgrounds sometimes compose texts that seem to lack coherence in the eyes of readers who are accustomed only to dominant varieties of English. As thirty-five years of contrastive rhetoric research has shown, the apparent lack of coherence is not necessarily an indication of the lack of intelligence (Kaplan 1966; Connor 1996); instead, it may come from differing definitions of what constitutes "good writing" (Li 1996). Ann Johns (1991) has also documented the frustration of a second-language writer who excelled in courses in his own disciplines but was not able to pass writing competency exams.

It is important to remember that second-language writers are often highly educated in their own languages; many are even considered good writers in their own languages. Others may not have had the benefit of advanced formal schooling, but that does not necessarily mean they are not intelligent; their seemingly incoherent texts may also reflect rich rhetorical traditions with their own conventions, assumptions about the reader-writer relations, and the use of certain persuasive appeals. This is also true of speakers of other varieties of English or English-based contact languages, such as African American Vernacular Englishes, Caribbean and Hawai`ian Creole Englishes, Tex-Mex, and Singaporean English, just to name a few.

One of the most common responses to the perceived "deficiency" has been to teach students to conform to the existing norm, as Fox points out, or to fail them as academically unprepared. In other words, the goal of writing instruction has been construed as helping students to create texts that are unmarked in the eyes of the native speakers of certain varieties of English. Underlying this attitude to the teaching of writing—and the covert teaching of the dominant variety of English that accompanies it—is the assumption that the context of academic discourse practices is static and unchanging; it is assumed that the presence of the new population of students and scholars in academic discourse communities in no way affects the context of writing. This assumption is at the heart of what I have problematized elsewhere as the static theory of writing (Matsuda 1997, 46–52).

It is important to point out, however, that the static view of writing is becoming increasingly outdated as the makeup of the academic audience is becoming increasingly diverse. Since the English language has become the dominant language of international communication, the audience of scholarly communication is no longer limited to native speakers of dominant varieties of English. Even within the United States, the academic population is changing as a result of institutions actively recruiting students and scholars with various ethnic and socioeconomic backgrounds as well as, by implication, linguistic and cultural backgrounds. In natural and applied sciences, it is not unusual to find graduate programs at U.S.-based institutions where the majority of students are speakers of different varieties of English, if not other languages. The presence of these multilingual and multicultural writers is changing the nature of rhetorical situations in academia because they have brought with them different assumptions about discourses; what used to be alternative is now becoming part of the academy. As Royster and Mao suggest, writing teachers need to recognize how the changing context should give rise to new forms of discourses.

In order to develop discourse practices that are appropriate for the changing rhetorical context, the context of writing needs to be conceived of as dynamic. That is, we need to recognize that, when multilingual and multicultural writers enter the U.S. academy, they are not the only ones who need to learn the conventions and assumptions of U.S. academic discourse practices; everyone in the U.S. academy needs to reassess their assumptions about discourse practices in the academy as they come in contact with unfamiliar discourses. That is, the negotiation of assumptions about discourses has to be a bilateral process. (For a more detailed discussion of the dynamic theory of writing, see Matsuda 1997, 52–56.)

Understanding other rhetorical traditions and discourse practices—through comparative and contrastive studies, as Lan suggests—is important in order for the U.S. academy to benefit from the rich array of discourse assumptions and practices that these multilingual and multicultural scholars and writers bring with them. Such an understanding is especially useful when new rhetorical situations arise. Since rhetorical situations that are new to monolingual English speakers may be similar to the situations that are familiar to users of other languages and discourses, other discourse practices can provide examples of how writers may deal with similar situations in English. In other words, learning from other rhetorical practices can enrich U.S. academic discourse by expanding the socially available repertoire for scholarly communication.

An understanding of other rhetorical traditions can also help U.S. academics develop an appreciation and respect for discourse practices that are different. The recognition of the value of integrating discourse practices of other languages and cultures can also create opportunities for writers from other traditions to contribute their unique perspectives, further enriching the discourse practices within the U.S. academy. Conversely, by not understanding other rhetorical practices, monolingual-English-speaking academics are missing out on the opportunities to learn from knowledge that can only be produced in different parts of the world (Flowerdew 1999, 260).

This does not mean, however, that writers can simply transplant discourse practices from one context to another and expect the audience to accept them without making any adjustments. As Long suggests, "discourses . . . are situated in a time and place," and the alternative discourses must respond to the local conditions. Alternative discourses that do not reflect the awareness of the rhetorical situation risk being dismissed as, to borrow the words of one of Thaiss and Zawacki's informants, "rampant alternative alternativisms."

Although it is possible for the audience to change their expectation in the long run, it does not happen overnight. Furthermore, because of the power relationship that is inherent in the student-teacher relationship, students' attempt to use alternative discourses may not be perceived by the teacher as a legitimate impetus for changing her or his expectations about discourses. To encourage students to construct alternative discourses without providing them with an accurate understanding of the dominant discourse practices would be irresponsible because, as Dobrin points out, students and newcomers to academic discourses are not granted the kind of authority that established scholars have. As teachers, we need to keep in mind that students, not teachers, are the ones who have to face the consequences.

What, then, can we do as writing specialists in order to help linguistically and culturally diverse writers negotiate differences in discourse practices? First, we need to understand more about alternative discourses and how they work by asking questions such as:

- How do scholars and students in various disciplines perceive the existence of alternative discourses and their value?
- How and to what extent are alternative discourses being used in various disciplines, languages, and rhetorical traditions?
- What are the conditions that make certain uses of alternative discourses acceptable or unacceptable to the audience?
- How do writers who have traditionally held less power in the academy (e.g., students, junior scholars, women, writers from less privileged linguistic and cultural backgrounds) negotiate the use of alternative discourses?
- At what point do alternative discourses cease to be alternative and become part of the mainstream? How can the process be facilitated?

Although some of the contibutors to this book—especially Bizzell, Mao, Lan, and Thaiss and Zawacki—have begun to address some of these questions, our understanding of this complex phenomenon is far from complete. We need to continue to investigate these and other related issues.

Somewhat paradoxically, we also need to better understand dominant discourse practices and their boundaries as perceived by the audience in various contexts of writing because alternative discourses are always defined in relation to dominant discourses in a particular context. Without an understanding of the dominant discourse practices, neither students nor teachers would be able to identify or evaluate alternative discourses when they are being employed. Since students who come from diverse linguistic backgrounds may have had relatively little exposure to the dominant discourse practices in U.S. academic contexts, it is important to help them become familiar with those practices along with their complexity and varied nature.

We also need to identify strategies for negotiating differences in discourse practices and teach those strategies. Since students—especially students who come from various linguistic, cultural, and educational backgrounds—already bring with them a wide variety of discursive resources, teaching students to use alternative discourses would mean teaching strategies for negotiating assumptions about discourses with the audience in a specific context of writing.

Finally, we need to always remember that it is not enough for writing teachers to change our assumptions about discourses. If we were to encourage students to use alternative discourses in the writing classroom, we also need to help students understand the risks involved in using alternative discourses. At the same time, writing specialists need to engage in dialogues with faculty across the disciplines to promote the understanding of the complexity of writing and of the changing nature of the academy as well as their implications.

Works Cited

Braine, George. 2000. "Overcoming Barriers to Academic Publication: Hong Kong's Success Story." Paper presented at the symposium on Second Language Writing. September 15, at Purdue University, West Lafayette, IN.

Canagarajah, A. Suresh. 1996. "'Nondiscursive' Requirements in Academic Publishing, Material Resources of Periphery Scholars, and the Politics of Knowledge Production." *Written Communication* 13 (4):435–72.

"CCCC Statement on Second-Language Writing and Writers." 2001. *College Composition and Communication* 52 (4):669–74.

Connor, Ulla. 1996. *Contrastive Rhetoric: Cross-Cultural Aspects of Second-Language Writing*. New York: Cambridge Univ. Press.

Flowerdew, John. 1999. "Problems in Writing for Scholarly Publication in English: The Case of Hong Kong." *Journal of Second Language Writing* 8 (3):243–64.

Johns, Ann. 1991. "Interpreting an English Competency Examination: The Frustrations of an ESL Science Student." *Written Communication* 8 (3):379–401.

Kaplan, Robert B. 1966. "Cultural Thought Patterns in Inter-Cultural Education." *Language Learning* 16:1–20.

Li, Xiao-ming. 1996. *"Good Writing" in Cross-Cultural Context.* Albany: State Univ. of New York Press.

Matsuda, Paul Kei. 1997. "Contrastive Rhetoric in Context: A Dynamic Model of L2 Writing." *Journal of Second Language Writing* 6(1):45–60.